Midnight Marquee's

HORROR MOVIE SCRAPBOOK

1930s

Vol. 2

Upon reflection, several titles listed in Vol. 1 as coming in Vol. 2 have not been included. I felt they were more mystery than horror. Although, you could argue that many of these films may belong in a different genre. Once again the old argument—is it horror, thriller, mystery, sci-fi, etc.—rears it's scary head. But whatever titles left out will hopefully be included in a volume on mysteries, or sci-fi, or fantasy...
—Sue Svehla

Copyright © 2018 Gary J. and Susan Svehla
Interior layout: Susan Svehla
Cover design: A. Susan Svehla

ISBN 13: 9781644300510
Library of Congress Catalog Card Number 2018908712
Manufactured in the United States of America

First Printing by Midnight Marquee Press, Inc., November, 2018

To the lovers of
the true fantastic golden oldies—
the horrors, the mystery-horrors
and the sci-f movies
of 1930-40s

THE BIG ANNOUNCEMENT

UNIVERSAL - PICTURES

VOL. 31 - NO. 20   JUNE 21 - 1930

UNIVERSAL WEEKLY

1930

Just Imagine
The Cat Creeps

Just Imagine

Released U.S. January 23, 1930

Film Flashes.

"JUST IMAGINE

WHAT THE WORLD WILL BE LIKE IN 50 YEARS.—1980.

With the rapid development of the airplane and other modes of transportation and the increasing problem of traffic in our great cities what will New York look like in 1980?

Buddy DeSylva, Lew Brown and Ray Henderson, multi-millionaire authors and song writers, have attempted to answer that question in "Just Imagine", their second Fox Movietone comedy with songs.

Huge modernistic skyscrapers, fleets of airplanes, aerial traffic cops to direct traffic. Great air liners bring all the capitals of the world within a few hours travel of the American Metropolis.

Of the thousand and one novelties which add to the entertainment value of "Just Imagine," this dream city of 1980 probably will stand out as the most effective, when you see it at the Crown Theatre, Wollongong on Monday and Tuesday, April 27, 28, and the King's Theatre, Thirroul on Monday, May 4. Also at the Strand, Corrimal and Royal, Bulli on Friday, May 1.

"JUST IMAGINE" HELD SEASON'S BIG HIT

Just imagine being knocked out by a bolt of lightning . . . and perfectly preserved for fifty years, only to be revived by scientists in 1930!

Just imagine a thick steak, onions, potatoes and bread combined in a single pill!

Just imagine buildings mountain high . . . each a city in itself, with fool-proof planes in greater numbers than flivvers today!

Just imagine El Brendel, Maureen O'Sullivan, John Garrick, Marjorie White and Frank Albertson directed by David Butler!

Just imagine DeSylva, Brown and Henderson writing the story and songs, making a Fox Movietone that's bigger than their "Sunny Side Up"!

Then you'll imagine why "Just Imagine" is the season's biggest sensation!

It is showing at the Elite Theatre next Monday, Tuesday and Wednesday.

Surprises, Fun Abound in Film "Just Imagine"

One can hardly imagine the fun and surprises which abound in "Just Imagine," the El Brendel comedy which opened Friday at the Paramount theater. A spectacular and not at all improbable view of New York City in 1980 is presented, with the popular Swedish comedian the only 1930 note.

The principal entertainment feature of "Just Imagine" is, of course, its comedy. It's just one prolonged laugh from beginning to end, with El Brendel's irresistible clowning keeping the audience shouting with mirth. But the thoughtful fan will realize that deep study and imaginative insight were required to project the story fifty years into the future and still keep it within the realm of possibility.

Television, airplanes so constructed that they can stop in midair, a rocket plane capable of astounding velocity—all might have been incredible a few decades ago, but to the present generation, accustomed to great and amazing changes, they are more than plausible. Unexpected social changes also are in evidence in the 1980 of "Just Imagine," and instead of names, people are known by numbers.

El Brendel, the 1930 golfer, revived fifty years after being killed by a stroke of lightning, finds himself designated as Single O, fed concentrated food and plunged into the most surprising adventures on his trip to Mars. A romance between John Garrick and Maureen O'Sullivan binds the action together, with Marjorie White and Frank Albertson having a slapstick love affair. Hobart Bosworth and Kenneth Thompson also are featured.

De Sylva, Brown and Henderson, who wrote the song hits and produced "Sunny Side Up," have again combined their talents in "Just Imagine." "Camera Trails," an interesting Robert Bruce scenic novelty, and sound news round out the program.

The Martian Twins.

The good-natured Martians are pleased to see visitors from the earth and the First Woman of the planet is quite alluring with a costume that appears to have been influenced by the old god of war. She is a glittering, slender creature, with slanting eyes and long fingers protected by metal tips.

El Brendel figures in the comedy rôle of Single O, who in 1980 is brought back to life after having presumably breathed his last about the present year. In the last scene he encounters his son, Axel, a bearded, aged man. Single O looks forty years his son's junior, but neverthe-

NEW YORK IN 1980

THE New York of the future is a subject that has engaged the attention of artists, scientists, educators and politicians for some years. One man's version, the results would seem to show, is as bad as another's, but the way DeSylva, Brown and Henderson have envisioned Gotham in 1980 in the Fox Movietone production, "Just Imagine," is interesting.

Great modernistic skyscrapers tower 200 and more stories above the street level in some of the scenes of this unusual film, which moves into the Roxy on next Friday. Fleets of airplanes, equipped with helicopters, cruise over the city, and submit with all humility to the red-faced bawlings of a new generation of air traffic policemen.

The aerial traffic cops, from anchored blimps, regulate the ebb and flow of vehicles. Great air liners take off for the far corners of the globe on regular schedule, bringing all world capitals within a few hours of City Hall.

Exclusive of the air lanes, there are nine traffic levels, ranging upward from subways, through surface trams, elevated railways and five different automobile levels, to a novel canal system that permits the ocean liners to traverse the main thoroughfares, discharging freight and passengers as close to your door as the buses of our day.

With these various levels for pedestrian and automobile travel, the surface is left clear for acres and acres of magnificent parklands and playing fields.

The trio of music-makers, abetted by the art directors, Stephen Goosson and Ralph Hammeras, have not stopped there, however. The habits and customs of the day, the new trappings devised by the man of the future to hide his nakedness, the eating and sleeping procedure—these and anything else you can think of have been visaged and mapped out in the studios.

In the course of the film, a trip to Mars in a rocket plane is accomplished and the dead are restored to life by a new and potent elixir.

Just Imagine A Great Hit

Producers of "Sunny Side Up" Make Another Big Musical Smash

DeSylva, Brown and Henderson and David Butler have done it again.

Their new Fox Movietone musical comedy romance, "Just Imagine," at the Strand Theatre, is a worthy successor to their masterpiece of yesteryear, "Sunny Side Up."

"Just Imagine" is novel in theme and treatment, has a brilliant cast headed by the inimitable El Brendel and has a number of songs of the calibre which has made DeSylva, Brown and Henderson the greatest song writing team in the world.

These young men, who also wrote the story and dialog, have projected their picture fifty years into the future. The love interest, which centers about Maureen O'Sullivan and John Garrick, tells of the romance of the "Lindbergh of 1960" in a sprightly and sustained fashion.

Brendel has one of the greatest roles of his career and scores personally. In fact he is here our favorite comedian. Miss O'Sullivan is everything that her enthusiastic friends have said of her, and that is plenty. Garrick reveals a charming singing voice and is handsome and manly in the juvenile male role. His acting is above reproach.

Marjorie White, who all but ran away with the hilarious honors in "Sunny Side Up," does almost the same thing in this picture, although she has much less in the way of role to work with. Her vivacious personality completely dominates every scene in which she appears.

Frank Albertson, in a light comedy role, is a riot in himself. He wishes a perfect team mate for Miss White, and the way they put over their song number, "Never Swat a Fly," is a revelation.

Joyzelle is effective as the Martian queen. Ivan Linow as the Martian slave, and other roles are capably handled by Kenneth Thomson, Herbert Bosworth, Wilfred Lucas and Mischa Auer.—Adv.

It's 1931's Greatest Hit   # "JUST IMAGINE"   It's the Last Word

--1931--

PEACE · PROSPERITY · HAPPINESS

NEW YEAR

BEST WISHES FOR THE SEASON

JUST IMAGINE

DeSYLVA, BROWN and HENDERSON'S
Fox Movietone successor to "Sunny Side Up"

with

EL BRENDEL

MAUREEN O'SULLIVAN · JOHN GARRICK

MARJORIE WHITE

FRANK ALBERTSON

Story, dialog and songs by
DeSYLVA, BROWN and HENDERSON
Dances staged by **SEYMOUR FELIX**

Directed by
DAVID BUTLER

FOX PICTURE

MADE IN U.S.A.

Lee has done a good job in the direction and one of the distinctly funny bits in this story is where Graves throws Rafferty's spying steward overboard, saying as he does so: "Let's see if you can swim."

* * *

9

DeSYLVA, BROWN and HENDERSON'S

FOX MOVIETONE SUCCESSOR TO "SUNNY SIDE UP"

JUST IMAGINE falling asleep in 1930 and waking half a century later. What would you use for money --or thirst? Would you be a back number in loving See what El Brendel did in this merry musical romance. A story that dares to be different!

Story, dialog and songs by DeSylva, Brown and Henderson.
Dances staged by Seymour Felix.

with **EL BRENDEL** • MAUREEN O'SULLIVAN •
JOHN GARRICK • MARJORIE WHITE • FRANK ALBERTSON
Directed by DAVID BUTLER **FOX**

JUST IMAGINE

A CLEVER FILM FANTASY

"Just Imagine" Shows Gotham in 1980— Miss Dressler and Wallace Beery Teamed

By MORDAUNT HALL.

IT is a pity that the clever De Sylva, Brown and Henderson fantasy "Just Imagine" was not presented during the Christmas holidays at the Roxy instead of last week, for it is the very thing that parents would enjoy with their youngsters. It is said that it did not find favor with the generation hovering around the twenties because the believable romance was absent, for which reason it was not held over for a second week.

Be that as it may, it is a beautiful production, and one filled with imaginative ideas. In its episodes there is an impressive conception of Gotham in 1980, a brilliantly conceived trip to Mars, several tuneful songs and finely directed precision drills and dances.

Of the many elaborate settings, possibly the most remarkable is that depicting the producers' idea of New York half a century hence. This clever stage effect may be referred to as a miniature by the film-makers, but if the average individual were privileged to see it he might be pardoned for calling it a monster model. Like the miniature of London for that worthy production "The Sky Hawk," this model was 280 feet long and 80 feet wide. It filled a dirigible hangar. Every tiny detail was attended to with marvelous care, even to electric lights on tiny automobiles and in the 200-story structures.

Crowded Skies.

The results on the screen are wonderful. This city of the future has nine levels, with dirigibles and airplanes in such numbers that it offers an opportunity for a comedy airways traffic policeman. Helicopter airplanes ascend and alight on the roofs of the structures and elsewhere. Virtually everybody owns an airplane, as they do a flivver nowadays.

Bells have gone into the discard with scores of other things. Rings of light serve the purpose of calling persons to the telephone, and there is, of course, television, which is a device at times to be avoided when one is called up. However, it sees only that which is cast into its frame, and so the people of the future still have a measure of privacy left.

One of the ingenious notions in this film is that of having the citizens of the future known by letters and numbers instead of names. The hero is J-21, a celebrated scientist answers to Z-4, the girl in the case is LN-18 and the villain is MT-3. In the rich fund of futuristic touches there is to be considered not only the long voyage to Mars and return, but also the characteristics of the inhabitants of that planet. Here it is set forth that Martians are always born in twins, one being evil and the other good, but both looking as alike as two peas. The visitors from the earth are never sure whether they are talking to a pleasant Martian or the malevolent specimen. And in one of the closing sequences it is illustrated that if one goes at a Martian with a haymaker one falls down, but, on the other hand, if one tweaks the lobe of a husky Martian's ear he is floored.

less he turns to the ancient man and says, "Come, sit on my knee, sonny boy."

There are quite a number of witty lines in this production and one that may interest present-day New Yorkers is that the Gothamite of fifty years hence is still hopefully awaiting light wines and beer.

John Garrick does very nicely as J-21, the valiant young aviator who not only makes the voyage to Mars and wins the girl but also sings of joys and woes. Maureen O'Sullivan, the attractive Irish girl who made her screen début in John McCormack's picture, "Song o' My Heart," is the more than slightly worried but always true LN-18.

It might be mentioned that a drinking song in this offering is particularly well staged. In those far ahead days drinking is done with tiny portions; not a spot but a drop serves the purpose, and food may be taken in capsules. Hence the songsters in this chorus have on the table tiny vials, which, it must be said, are hardly as impressive with the actions and the melody as the good old stein.

*　*　*

The Rival Mates.

tions and the melody as the good old stein.

The Rival Mates.

AN interesting sea story with William Boyd and George Bancroft was at the Paramount. It is called "Derelict," and Messrs. Boyd and Bancroft portray two first mates of freighters who are just about as friendly as Flagg and Quirt were in "What Price Glory," in which play Mr. Boyd impersonated the indomitable Sergeant.

Bill Rafferty (Mr. Bancroft) triumphs over his rival Jed Graves (Mr. Boyd) in the matter of love, for he wins the affection of Helen Lorber, played by the charming Jessie Royce Landis.

So soon as he learns that Graves's ship is in port, Rafferty changes his mind about donning a new white coat and puts on something suitable for a scrap with Graves. Rafferty is not the man to give Graves a chance for peace and when he perceives that Graves is enjoying Helen's society he sends over a steward with a message setting forth that the manager of the line wants to see him. Thus Helen is left free for a flirtation with Rafferty, while Graves himself goes to the office of the manager, who is not there. A subordinate, however, hazards that possibly it is the manager's intention to promote Graves to fill a skipper's vacancy, which the hopeful first mate takes so much for granted than when he encounters Rafferty he tells him that if he (Graves) is made captain of a freighter he is going to ask for Rafferty's services as first mate, as he "knows what a good first mate" Rafferty is. It happens, however, that Rafferty is

the one singled out for promotion and he asks to have Graves appointed to his ship.

Before he learned about the promotion Rafferty had promised to see that Helen was taken aboard his ship to Rio, but as a skipper he realizes that the discovery of a woman aboard his vessel would mean dismissal. So Rafferty discourages Helen from going, not counting on the crafty Graves seeing to it that the girl is not disappointed. Unfortunately for Rafferty, this captain, when his ship is going through a fog, learns that Helen is aboard. There is a collision with another ship while Rafferty is off the bridge and the artful Graves receives credit for the accident not being more serious.

Rafferty, however, after being left at a dismal port, on instructions from headquarters, finally proves his worthiness and is welcomed back to his ship as captain.

Mr. Boyd gives a sterling performance in this film. Mr. Bancroft does quite well, but his team-mate has the better of him, possibly through his New York stage experience. Mr. Bancroft is, however, less extravagant than he has been in his recent pictures and it looks as though this idea of teaming up these two players is an excellent one, next perhaps to having Mr. Boyd appear in a film with Louis Wolheim, with whom he acted on the stage in "What Price Glory."

Much of the success of this yarn of the briny is due to the story contributed by William Slavens McNutt and Grover Jones and the apt dialogue penned by Max Marcin. Rowland V.

Pictures for Week Ending Dec. 6

ROXY—"Lightnin'," with Will Rogers.
CAPITOL—"Min and Bill," with Marie Dressler and Wallace Beery.
PARAMOUNT—"Free and Loose," with Miriam Hopkins.
WARNERS' STRAND—"College Lovers," with Marian Nixon and Jack Whiting.
RIALTO—"The Lottery Bride," with Jeanette MacDonald.
RIVOLI—"Morocco," with Marlene Di[etrich]

PLAZA—Today until Tuesday, "Playboy of Paris"; Wednesday to Friday, "Common Clay."
ASTOR—"War Nurse," with June Walker.
CRITERION AND GAIETY—"Hell's Angels," with Ben Lyon.
GEORGE M. COHAN—"Two Worlds," with Norah Baring, a British production.
MAYFAIR—"Sin Takes a Holiday," with [...]

JUST IMAGINE

FOX PICTURE

"JUST IMAGINE" CONTEST.

If one has a vivid imagination or is somewhat of a prophet he may win a week's guest ticket to the Saenger Theatre. "Just Imagine", starring El Brendel, Maureen O'Sullivan, Marjorie White, and Frank Albertson, which opens at the Saenger Theatre Thanksgiving Day is a smash comedy drama and depicts life on this earth as it will be fifty years from now. In other words the picture is based on the life that the people will lead in 1980. Just imagine the speed we will travel perhaps instead of sitting down to a meal at our dinner table, scientists will have perfected a small pill about the size of an aspirin tablet full of vitamins which we may hurriedly grab and swallow. Just imagine what the fappers of 1930 will be dressed like. Just imagine the effect television will have on our everyday life. Just imagine boys and girls flying to school at 500 miles an hour in aeroplanes???

At any rate here is the idea: Write a story, as short as you wish, and not over two typewritten pages on the way you prophesize the world will be and the way people will live in Biloxi in 1980, and submit it to the contest editor of the Daily Herald. To the first three persons submitting the most unique and interesting manuscript the Daily Herald will give a one week's guest ticket to the Saenger Theatre.

The contest closes Tuesday night at 6 o'clock and all stories must be in the Daily Herald office at that time.

Sensational Hit "Just Imagine" Coming to Fox Theatre

JUST IMAGINE

FOX PICTURE

13

MICKEY MOUSE'S MOVIE COLUMN

Dear Folks:

"Just Imagine" at last you can see this sensational comedy hit, "Just Imagine," at the Fox Theatre starting tonight for three nights with a matinee on Saturday.

"Just Imagine" taking a trip to Mars on a fool-proof rocket.

"Just Imagine" El Brendel in the funniest part he has ever played.

"Just Imagine" "Sunnyside Up" producers giving you something better.

"Just Imagine" how they'll make love and whoopee in 1980.

"Just Imagine" the necking, kissing, petting technic fifty years from now.

"Just Imagine" how New York City will look in 1980.

"Just Imagine" the most refreshing entertainment of the year.

"Just Imagine" the longest, loudest laugh you have had for many months and you will be sure to see "Just Imagine," the great Fox-Movietone special which brings all these to you.

"Just Imagine" plays for ---- days only, starting tonight.

And after you have seen "Just Imagine" the treat in store for you when you thrill to the greatness of the most important motion picture ever made. — Raoul Walsh's "The Big Trail," coming to the Fox Theatre Sunday for three great days, with a continuous show on Sunday, 2 to 11 p. m.

Thoughts while imagining: Neva, the projectionist's little helper, pines that she was just going to squawk about not seeing M. M. collum, just when she seed a few squibs in Monday's paper. Reid Conrad, who with his brother Ray, smashes most of the baggage in the city, can also climb rope single handed. You should have seen him shinning up a rope to the roof of the Fox Theatre the other day. All Centralia wives whose husbands have stenogs will want to see "Office Wife," which opens at the Fox St. Helens Sunday—and all the stenogs, or should we say "office wives," will want to see it also. And if you don't get a chance to see it in Chehalis, "Office Wife" will be shown in Centralia the following week. And, by the way, I always keep the office door open at the Fox Theatre.

Yours.

MICKEY.

The Cat Creeps

Released U.S. November 10, 1930

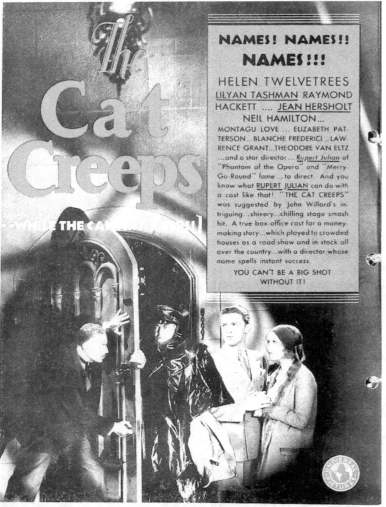

NAMES! NAMES!!
NAMES!!!

HELEN TWELVETREES
LILYAN TASHMAN RAYMOND
HACKETT .... JEAN HERSHOLT
NEIL HAMILTON...
MONTAGU LOVE... ELIZABETH PAT-
TERSON...BLANCHE FREDERICI...LAW-
RENCE GRANT...THEODORE VAN ELTZ
...and a star director... Rupert Julian of
"Phantom of the Opera" and "Merry-
Go-Round" fame...to direct. And you
know what RUPERT JULIAN can do with
a cast like that! "THE CAT CREEPS"
was suggested by John Willard's intriguing...shivery...chilling stage smash
hit. A true box-office cast for a money-
making story...which played to crowded
houses as a road show and in stock all
over the country...with a director whose
name spells instant success.

YOU CAN'T BE A BIG SHOT
WITHOUT IT!

CHILLS, THRILLS IN DIXIE PICTURE

"THE CAT CREEPS," NOW ON, STARS HELEN TWELVE-TREES; BIG CAST.

A breathless quality of suspense pervades "The Cat Creeps," the Universal mystery drama which opens a four-day run today at the Dixie No. 1 Theater. The very atmosphere is heavy with dread, and there are many hair-raising moments when the auditor feels impelled to relieve pent-up emotions with a lusty shriek. This story was adapted from the famous stage "thriller," "The Cat and the Canary," and on the screen it is even more effective than it was on the stage, where it has long been recognized as one of the most spine-tingling plays ever written.

A great cast interprets the screen production, with Helen Twelve-trees bringing her blond beauty and her undoubtedly powerful his-trionic talent to the principal femi-nine role. Appearing opposite her is Raymond Hackett, who con-tributes an altogether pleasing performance as Paul, a young man who is just a little bit afraid of ghosts, in spite of himself. Jean Hersholt and Montagu Love enact their roles with the forceful artistry for which they are well known, and a bright spot is added to the picture by the blase wise-cracking of the irresponsible Lilyan Tashman. Other capable perform-ances are given by Lawrence Grant, Theodore von Eltz, Blanche Frederici and Elizabeth Patterson.

The production has been well directed by Rupert Julian, who has maintained the uncanny atmos-phere of suspense throughout.

The entire story of "The Cat Creeps" is laid within a gloomy mansion which has not been occu-pied for 20 years, but to which a group of relatives have been sum-moned at midnight to listen to the reading of the will of its former eccentric owner. The sinister repu-tation of the house is fully borne out by the terrifying events of the night, culminating in the mys-terious murder of one of the guests, and the mystery is only solved after several hours of terror.

"The Cat Creeps" may be recom-mended as the greatest mystery story to reach the talking screen. Undoubtedly, you will enjoy it.

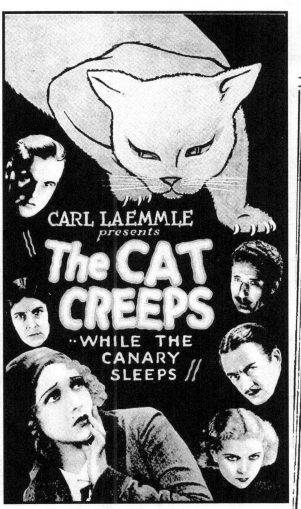

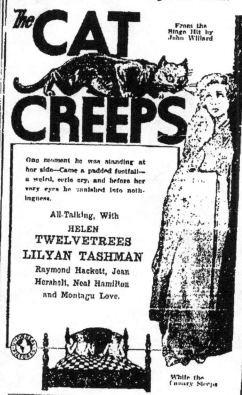

Mystery Film Is Preview Feature

"The Cat Creeps" Continues At Huron Tomorrow; Taken From "Cat And The Canary"

"The Cat Creeps," described as one of the greatest mystery stories in the history of stage or motion pictures, and adapted by Universal for the talking screen from John Willard's famous play, "The Cat and the Canary," forms the next attraction at the Huron theater. It will be shown Sunday with a midnight preview tonight.

This thrilling production presents an all-star cast, headed by Helen Twelvetrees, and including such well known screen artists as Raymond Hackett, Neil Hamilton, Lilyan Tashman, Jean Hersholt, Montagu Love, Lawrence Grant, Theodore Von Eltz, Blanche Frederici and Elizabeth Patterson. The blonde Miss Twelvetrees, a recent recruit to motion pictures, had previously achieved fame on the New York stage. The picture was directed by Rupert Julian, maker of many outstanding successes.

"The Cat Creeps" abounds with mystery and suspense, and its entire action deals with the hair-raising events of a single night in a great mansion which has not been occupied for 20 years. Here a group of relatives gather at midnight to listen to the reading of a will, and thus begins a story which brings to the audience a swift succession of laughs and thrills. Breathless terror grips the characters, and the unexplainable death of one of them adds horror to a mystery which is finally brought to a surprising solution just before daylight.

"The Cat and the Canary" has for years been recognized as one of the greatest mystery "thrillers" of the stage, and "The Cat Creeps," it is said, creates to an even greater degree a "creepy" atmosphere of suspense and terror.

"The CAT CREEPS"
WHILE THE CANARY SLEEPS
A UNIVERSAL PICTURE

FASORNAS NATT

HELEN TWELVETREES
NEIL HAMILTON · LILYAN TASHMAN

ENSAMRÄTT: UNIVERSAL FILM A-B STOCKHOLM

LAST TIMES
TONIGHT
"SCANDAL
SHEET"
Starring
GEO. BANCROFT
KAY FRANCIS
CLIVE BROOK

MIDNIGHT PREVIEW TONIGHT
Also Playing Sunday

The Strangest Mystery Drama Ever Screened!

The ghostly romance of the haunted house of a thousand horrors, but a house that turned into a home of love because of a girl who cared and a boy who was brave!

"THE
CAT CREEPS"

The creepiest, laughiest, shiveriest, funniest mystery play ever screened. From the stage success by Willard.

with

HELEN TWELVETREES   LILYAN TASHMAN
RAYMOND HACKETT   JEAN HERSHOLT
NEIL HAMILTON   MONTAGU LOVE
A Universal Picture

ADDED
Eddie Gribbon in "Dance Hall Marge"
Graham McNamee Newscasting
Tribute to George Washington
Paramount Pictorial

Phone
3473

HURON

Home of
Paramount
Pictures

COMING
MONDAY
OUR THIRD PUBLIX
VAUDEVILLE
UNIT STAGE SHOW

One of the Publix Theatres

Paramount

Prices: Matinee 10-30—Evening 10-50

TODAY-SATURDAY
TWO DAYS ONLY!

"One Must Die by
Morning!"

"I felt an icy breath sweep over me. Out of the darkness a long, clamlike hand reached toward me —it came nearer—nearer! I could not move! It reached for my throat—I screamed—"

The most startling mystery drama of the year!

NEIL HAMILTON
JEAN HERSHOLT
LILYAN TASHMAN
HELEN TWELVETREES
MONTAGUE LOVE

"THE
CAT CREEPS"

Universals All-Talking
Thrill Romance. Adapted from
"The Cat and the Canary."

Added Features
Saturday Matinee Only
RIN TIN TIN in
"THE LONE DEFENDER"

FOUR DAYS ONLY!
SUN. THRU WEDNESDAY DEC. 14-15-16-17
ON THE TALKING SCREEN AT LAST!
AMOS 'n' ANDY
"CHECK AND DOUBLE CHECK"
with
Sue Carol—Irene Rich—Charles Morton

Movies

HELEN TWELVETREES and RAYMOND HACKETT in
"The CAT CREEPS" A UNIVERSAL PICTURE

Most hair-raising situations are shown on the talking screen, in "The Cat Creeps", the mystery drama which comes to the Saenger Theatre on Sunday and Monday. The picture is the screen adaption of the famous stage thriller, "The Cat and the Canary."

The entire action takes place during a veritable night of terror in a great mansion which has not been occupied for 20 years, and when a party of men and women have gathered for the reading of a will. A chain of terrifying events culminates in the mysterious murder of one of the party, and the entire household is reduced to a state of fearful dread. Secret panels in the walls play an important part in bringing about strange events.

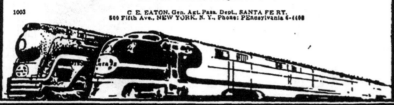
EXCHANGE REPARTEE BY TELEVISION DEVICE

Speakers at Distance Answer Audience's Questions in Schenectady Demonstration.

SCHENECTADY, N. Y., May 21 (*P*)—Characters on a television screen tonight exchanged repartee with an audience in a demonstration arranged by the General Electric Company.

Life-size images of speakers addressing a Rotary Club gathering were projected on a large screen, the speakers making their addresses in the glare of a televisor booth located in a laboratory some distance from the hall.

Sensitive microphones were installed in the hall so the speakers could hear what was being said by the audience. Questions put by members of the audience, speaking in conversational tones, were readily answered.

Spokesmen for the General Electric Company said the demonstration indicated the feasibility of "bringing" a speaker before a massed audience in so far as his picture and voice were concerned to answer open forum questions, although he might be miles away.

1931

Svengali
The Phantom
The Mad Genius

Svengali

Released U.S. May 22, 1931

JOHN BARRYMORE in "SVENGALI" —A Warner Bros. & Vitaphone Production

THERE ARE MORE THINGS ON HEAVEN AND EARTH

. . . . . than you have ever imagined! Strange passions that enslave women! Evil love manufactured by an evil hypnotist! Weird! Unbelievable!

Here is Barrymore at his best. With Marian Marsh, the new screen discovery fans and critics call "sensational!"

J OHN BARRYMORE and his new film, "Svengali," are firmly entrenched at the Hollywood. This picture is based on George du Maurier's novel, "Trilby," and introduces Marian Marsh, a newcomer to the screen, in the leading feminine rôle. "Svengali" is being shown on a continuous program basis. It was directed by Archie Mayo for Warner Brothers, and includes in its cast Carmel Myers, Bramwell Fletcher, Lumsden Hare, Donald Crisp, Luis Alberni and Paul Porcasi.

BARRYMORE AS SVENGALI

The success of George du Maurier's romance of the Latin Quarter is a matter of history. In preparing the scenario of the new version J. Grubb Alexander, the adapter, based his work upon the original novel and not upon the dramatization by Paul M. Potter, which was played all over the English-speaking world during the late '90s and revived in New York in 1915. The fact that du Maurier was an artist as well as an author, and that he not only wrote "Trilby" but illustrated it, has been of great aid to the producers of "Svengali." So far as possible the appearances of the characters and of the scenes have been made to conform to du Maurier's own conception of them, according to advance accounts of the production.

Another Newcomer.

The new Trilby, Svengali's protégée and victim, is Marian Marsh, a newcomer to featured screen rôles. A few months ago she was an extra girl in Hollywood; then, having played the leading feminine rôle in the Los Angeles stage production of "Young Sinners," she was offered a screen test when candidates for the part of Trilby were being considered. Mr. Barrymore is said to have personally selected her from several tests of actresses which were submitted to him. Since the finishing of "Svengali" she has played the heroine of another Barrymore picture, "The Mad Genius."

Readers of the novel, and theatregoers whose memory goes back to yesteryear, will have an opportunity to meet old friends once more when "Svengali" begins its engagement at the Hollywood Theatre next Friday. The Little Billee of 1931 is Bramwell Fletcher. Taffy is portrayed by Lumsden Hare. The Laird is acted by Donald Crisp. Gecko by Luis Alberni, and Honorine by Carmel Myers.

John Barrymore and Marian Marsh in The Mad Genius

John Barrymore

SVENGALI

MARIAN MARSH as TRILBY

A WARNER BROS and VITAPHONE picture

John Barrymore's latest screen venture, "Svengali," is ready for Broadway. The Warners' Hollywood, which has been dark these many weeks, will probably be opened for the occasion and the première will take place within the next week or so. "Svengali" is based on George du Maurier's "Trilby" and was directed by Archie Mayo. Marian Marsh, in the feminine lead, heads a supporting cast which includes Donald Crisp, Carmel Myers, Yola d'Avril, Bramwell Fletcher and Lumsden Hare.

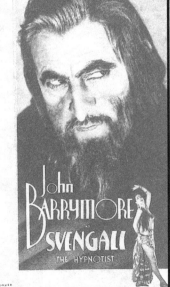

John Barrymore's indisposition has delayed for a few days the completion of his new picture, "Svengali," at the Warner studios. The picture is an adaptation of du Maurier's novel, "Trilby," and includes in its cast Marian Marsh, Lumsden Hare, Carmel Myers, Donald Crisp and Bramwell Fletcher.

BEST PHOTOGRAPHY (Cinematographer's Award)—Edward Cronjager, "Cimarron" (R. K. O.-Radio); Lee Garmes, "Morocco" (Paramount); Charles Lang, "The Right to Love" (Paramount); Chick McGill, "Svengali" (Warners), and Floyd Crosby, "Tabu" (Paramount).

BEST ART DIRECTION—Max Ree, for "Cimarron" (R. K. O.-Radio); Stephen Goosson, "Just Imagine" (Fox); Hans Dreier, "Morocco" (Paramount); Anton Grot, "Svengali" (Warners), and Richard Day, "Whoopee" (Sam Goldwyn-United Artists).

"THE time factor is the most important of all—or nearly the most important—in making a good motion picture," said Archie Mayo, director of "The Doorway to Hell" and "Svengali," who is in New York on vacation.

"I have directed some bad pictures," continued Mr. Mayo, "and also some that were considered pretty good. Now, the interesting thing is that I was hurried and harried on every one of the pictures that flopped, and that I was allowed to take my time on those that succeeded. The moral seems to be that while production schedules are necessary and useful, they ought to be flexible. If it is necessary to devote ten weeks to doing a really good job on a picture that has been allotted only eight on the schedule, it is well worth while to give the director and players the extra fortnight."

He gave examples. "When I was directing 'Svengali' with John Barrymore, we were told that the thing ought to be finished within six weeks. That sounded all right, but we hadn't been at work for a week before I knew that the time allowed would not be long enough. I spoke to Barrymore about it, of course, and he agreed with me. We went together to the big boss, and said, 'Give us eight weeks as a minimum, and we'll try to stay inside it.' We got it and we did finish the job a little short of eight weeks. If we had been held down to the original schedule—well, I can imagine, if you can't, what 'Svengali' might have been.

A WARNER BROS.
and VITAPHONE Picture

WARNER BROS PICTURES Inc.
and The VITAPHONE Corp.
Presents

John
BARRYMORE
in
SVENGALI
with MARIAN MARSH
as TRILBY

BASED ON THE NOVEL "PETER IBBETSON" BY GEORGE LOUIS DUMAURIER
SCREEN PLAY and DIALOGUE by J. GRUBB ALEXANDER

DIRECTED BY
ARCHIE MAYO

The Phantom

Released U.S. November 1, 1931

An enterprising newspaper reporter is the dashing hero of "The Phantom," the weird mystery melodrama at the Imperial today and Monday.

Gwynn "Big Boy" Williams, one of the most romantic figures in Hollywood's screen colony, portrays the role of the inquisitive young journalist who lays the notorious man of mystery by the heels and at the same time, wins himself a beautiful bride, played by Alene Ray.

In this, the most entertaining of Allan James' many absorbing mystery narratives, both the screen hero and heroine are newspaper reporters, the boy an iron-nerved police reporter, and the girl a society writer. Between them, they outwit the police and effect the recapture of the phantom killer and bring him to a delayed justice.

Columbia

FRIDAY ONLY

The Thrill Picture
of the Year

"The Phantom"

Starring
"BIG BOY" WILLIAMS

Starting with a Gala Midnight Show Christmas Eve

"THE PHANTOM" WILL LEAD VIRGINIA BILL

An enterprising newspaper reporter is the dashing hero of "The Phantom," the weird mystery melodrama which comes to the Virginia theater on Wednesday and Thursday.

Gwynn "Big Boy" Williams, one of the most romantic figures in Hollywood's screen colony, portrays the role of the inquisitive young journalist who lays the notorious man of mystery by the heels and at the same time, wins himself a beautiful bride, played by Alene Ray.

In this, the most entertaining of Allan James' many absorbing mystery narratives, both the screen hero and heroine are newspaper reporters, the boy an iron-nerved police reporter, and the girl a society writer. Between them, they outwit the police and effect the recapture of the phantom killer and bring him to a delayed justice.

ISIS—Weird, gripping mystery in "The Phantom," which is a first run film, will hold Isis audiences breathless during the run of this thrilling picture, in which Gwynn (Big Boy) Williams is the iron-nerved newspaper reporter who, with the help of a sister of the press, Allene Ray, lands the elusive "phantom" criminal. Also, there's Genevieve Tobin and Conrad Nagel in "Free Love," a drama of a nagging wife and long-suffering husband who rebels.

Dreamland Film 'The Big Fight' Stars Williams

"Big Boy" Guinn Williams, who appears in the role of the heavyweight battler, Tiger, in James Cruze's "The Big Fight," at the Dreamland theatre, had himself all set for a baseball career. Although Guinn is a well-known all-round athlete, the diamond appeared to him the most satisfying way of achieving fame. Will Rogers, gum-chewing cowboy stage star upset these plans by offering Guinn an opportunity to "get into the movies." This was in 1919. He then appeared in "Black Cyclone" for Pathe, and a series of cowboy pictures for Hal Roach.

The tip-top physical condition in which Guinn keeps himself serves him to excellent advantage in the role of Tiger in "The Big Fight."

The Mad Genius

Released U.S. November 7, 1931

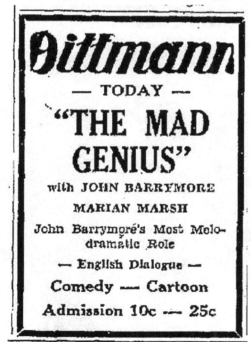

THE MAD GENIUS IS BARRYMORE'S FAVORITE ROLE

Says Such a Piece Comes Once in a Life-Time and He Likes It.

When John Barrymore first read the script of "The Mad Genius," his latest Warner Bros. picture, which opens Wednesday at the Gem Theater next, he said it offered the kind of role that comes but once in a lifetime.

Tsarakoy, the mad genius is indeed such a part—artist voluptuary, master mind and driving force, he dominates men and women by sheer force of will—bends fate to meet his needs and conquers all but the unconquerable human equation which eventually proves his undoing.

The story of "The Mad Genius" moves relentlessly to a tremendous climax built about the powerful personality of the one man, Tsarakov. Few moments in pictures have been so awe-inspiring as the film of "The Mad Genius."

Marian Marsh heads the supporting cast. Others are Charles Butterworth, Donald Cook, Luis Alberni and Carmel Myers. Michael Curtiz directed.

A WARNER BROS AND VITAPHONE PICTURE

JOHN BARRYMORE
THE MAD GENIUS

Spectacular and Brilliant Barrymore

Superb in Title Role of "The Mad Genius"

John Barrymore, who has given so many masterly screen portrayals of characters—tragic, romantic and even comic—offers what many critics consider his finest characterisation in the title role of "The Mad Genius," a picture based in some respects upon the life and work of Serge Diaghileff, world famous master of the Russian Imperial Ballet—now at the Regent.

The star is supported by Marian Marsh, youthful screen discovery of the year who is exquisite as the dancer, Nana. The girl is dominated by the mad genius, Tsarakov, first seen as master of a travelling marionette show, and later as impresario of the Russian Imperial Ballet. Tsarakov, while haunted by

A BURNING DESIRE

to be the world's supreme interpreter of the dance, is prevented by a physical deformity. He is embittered by

this fact and takes an insane delight in pulling the strings to make his grotesque puppets dance, while the yokels applaud.

The picture quickens in action as the plot unfolds, whilst the closing scenes bring out the

SUPERB DRAMATIC TALENTS

of the star.

Seen also in the cast are Charles Butterworth and the Australian, Donald Cook.

'Mad Genius' Acclaimed Barrymore's Best

JOHN BARRYMORE will be seen at the Ohio Theater the next four days in "The Mad Genius," a Warner Bros. production—and the most superb of all his starring vehicles.

Mr. Barrymore again chooses radiant Marian Marsh as his leading lady as he did in his previous picture, "Svengali"—in which she played the role of Trilby, and incidentally won acclaim of critics and public everywhere. Miss Marsh, who is but seventeen, creates a flowerlike and wistfully lovely character in "The Mad Genius," that of Nana the dancer.

Mr. Barrymore is Tsarakov—the mad genius—a man whose club foot has made him as bitterly introspective as King Richard was on account of his deformity. Tsarakov travels from town to town with a marionette wagon show, and one night, Fedor, a peasant's child, rushes into the tent to escape from the lashing of his brutal father.

Tsarakov suddenly has an inspiration. He will kidnap the boy—train him as a dancer—and, through him—enjoy vicariously the applause which he craves, but which the fates have denied him.

The boy Fedor, under Tsarakov's tutelage grows to young manhood and is acclaimed as the greatest dancer of all time. He leads in the ballet of which Tsarakov is impresario—and the ballet master is a drug-crazed fanatic, Bankieff. Among the dancers is Nana, whom Tsarakov discovers is loved by Fedor. Believing that the youth's genius will be cramped by her, he schemes to get rid of the girl.

Believing that she is actually standing in Fedor's way—she goes at the instigation of Tsarakov, to Berlin with a rich man who has admired her. Fedor discovers the perfidy of Tsarakov and leaves him. Hurt to the quick by Fedor's desertion the old man makes it impossible for him to get work at his profession.

Tsarakov finally makes the youth believe that Nana does not love him, and in desperation, Fedor again comes under his evil spell and dances in the ballet.

How Fedor and Nana again meet—how the mad Bankieff kills Tsarakov in the moment of his highest triumph—and many other thrilling dramatic moments make of "The Mad Genius" a picture of tremendous and enthralling power.

Others in the cast are Donald Cook as Fedor—Charles Butterworth as the eccentric secretary of Tsarakov—Luis Alberni as the insane Bankieff—Andre Luget, Boris Karloff, Frankie Darro as the boy Fedor, and Mae

When Boris Karloff was enrolled to play the unctuous religious editor in "Five Star Final" he made the part one of the most disagreeable characterizations of the year. Then he entered the cast of James Whale's "Frankenstein" and interpreted the monster of that nightmarish story in a way that made the picture houses of the land ring with startled screams. His new rôle in "Behind the Mask," a film currently at the Paramount, is in the same tradition. This is all by way of introduction to the interesting fact that Mr. Karloff in private life is an Englishman of excellent education. His birthplace was London and the year was 1857. He took his schooling successively at Uppingham, Merchant Taylor School and Kings College, London University. Arriving in America after appearing on numerous London and European stages, he played in stock for a time and finally attracted the attention of Hollywood with his stage performances in "The Virginian" and "Kongo." Before he blossomed out cinematically in "Five Star Final" he appeared in such films as "The Deadlier Sex," "Criminal Code," "Graft," "Donovan's Kid" and "The Public Defender."

1932

The Monster Walks
Freaks
The Most Dangerous Game
Chandu the Magician
Kongo
The Old Dark House

The Monster Walks

Released U.S. February 7, 1932

HORROR PICTURE WILL BE SHOWN AT GEM TODAY

"The Monster Walks" Will Give You the Creeps for Hour and a Half.

The latest horror picture from the Hollywood studios, "The Monster Walks," will be at the Gem Theater today. This feature production was made by Action Pictures, an independent production company which is making a series of 24 pictures for release during the current year.

According to advance reports, "The Monster Walks," provides the same sort of terrifying thrills that made "Frankenstein" the talk of the movie-goers some time back. The story tells of the efforts of one man to remove all possible heirs to a fortune left by the murderer's cludes the use of a vicious gorilla but, in the end, his plot proves a boomerang and he is murdered by the same means he had chosen to do his dirty work.

Rex Lease, versatile star, heads a splendid cast which includes Vera Reynolds, Mischa Auer, who claims to be the youngest character actor in Hollywood; Sheldon Lewis, who has been doing the villain's job on the screen ever since the days of "The Clutching Hand"; Martha Mattox, a lady who has been causing spine chills from the early days of the motion picture; Sidney Bracy, who is generally teamed up with Miss Mattox and Sleep N' Eat, a darky whose antics always provide considerable amusement.

The direction of the picture was in the capable hands of Frank Strayer, one of the ace megaphone wielders of the cinema capital.

CATCH LINES

Appalling in its horror—gruesome in its details—terrifying in its action—see "The Monster Walks"—another "Frankenstein."

* * *

A sure method of contracting the "jitters"—see "The Monster Walks"—greater than "Frankenstein."

* * *

If your nerves are bad—if your heart is weak—DO NOT see "The Monster Walks"—the most terrifying story ever brought to the screen.

* * *

You trembled at "Frankenstein"—you will gasp with horror when "The Monster Walks."

* * *

Gentle by day—Fiendish at night—souls are terrified when "The Monster Walks."

* * *

An awe inspiring spectacle when "The Monster Walks."

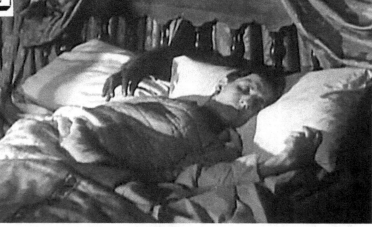

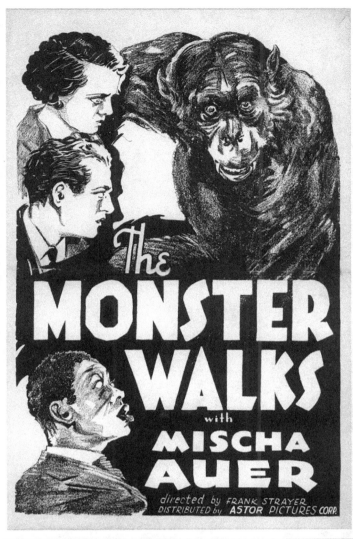

THE
MONSTER WALKS
with
MISCHA AUER

directed by FRANK STRAYER
DISTRIBUTED by ASTOR PICTURES CORP.

"Monster Walks" New Thrill Film

The current attraction at the .... Theatre, is one of the most horrifying stories ever brought to the screen, truly, a second "Frankenstein," though story and action are of an entirely different nature.

The story details the efforts of a rich man's brother to wipe out all possible heirs to the brother's fortune. He uses a vicious ape to carry out his murderous plans, and also the half-witted son of his brother's housekeeper. He manages to eliminate several persons before he is finally tripped up himself.

Action Pictures, Inc., has given the

Auer Youngest Character Actor In Hollywood

Mischa Auer, at 26, is the youngest character man in pictures, playing parts of 45. This means that Auer has to do a very excellent job to withstand the acid test of many comparisons.

This clever young actor is the grandson of Professor Leopold Auer, world-famous violinist. At the age of 14 he ran away from Russia, joining the British Army of Occupation at Constantinople. There his

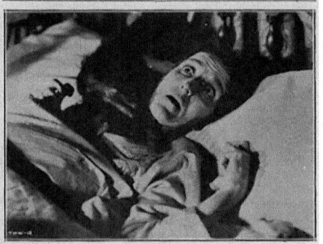

2 Col. Scene Cut or Mat No. 2

picture an unusually strong cast of players, most of them with big reputations as character actors. Rex Lease is starred and he receives wonderful support from Vera Reynolds, who makes a charming heroine, Sheldon Lewis, a noted character actor practically since the inception of pictures; Martha Mattox, Mischa Auer, Sidney Bracy and Sleep N' Eat, the latest colored player to grace the motion picture capital.

"The Monster Walks," drew a tremendous crowd at the opening performance and, judging from the manner in which it was received and the subsequent word-of-mouth advertising, it will remain for a longer period than originally scheduled at the .... Theatre.

You will be amazed at the appearance of this gruesome being, terrifying in all its actions, repugnant to all human beings. This tireless pacing up and down the cage, the inhuman screeches it vomits forth when one of the hated humans approach, and the terrible clutch of its monstrous talons, all these will long linger in your mind after seeing "The Monster Walks."

mother died. Mischa made his way to New York to his grandfather, his only living relative. His first part on the stage was in the role of an extra in "Wild Duck," at the Actor's Theatre, New York. At the close of the run of this play Mischa had been assigned one of the featured parts.

He did plays with Eva LeGallienne and Walter Hampton; also played lead opposite Bertha Kalisch.

On the screen he has made a goodly array of appearances, current releases being "Unholy Garden" (UA), "Mata Hari" (MGM), "Just Imagine," "Yellow Ticket" and "Delicious" (Fox), "Command Performance" (James Cruze), "Inside the Lines" (RKO), and "The Benson Murder Case" (Paramount).

Naturally, Mr. Auer finds the richest entertainment in music. Riding and sailing win first place as to sports.

But he devotes the major portion of his time to studying his roles, putting in many long hours rehearsing lines and business, thus making him one of the most finished performers on the silver screen.

RUTH EARLTON NARROWLY ESCAPES
DEATH BY GRUESOME MONSTER

Freaks

Released U.S. Feb. 20, 1932

DRAKE THEATRE
OIL CITY, PA.
Saturday - Monday - Tuesday
JANUARY 20 - 22 - 23

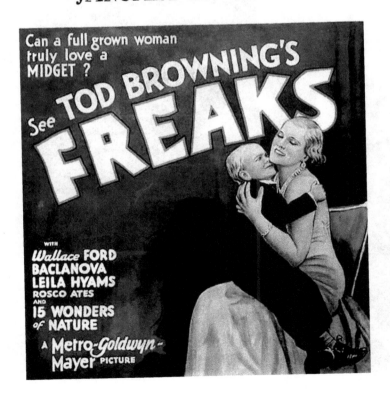

Can a full grown woman truly love a MIDGET?

See TOD BROWNING'S FREAKS

WITH
Wallace FORD
BACLANOVA
LEILA HYAMS
ROSCO ATES
AND
15 WONDERS of NATURE

A Metro-Goldwyn-Mayer PICTURE

A Circus Sideshow.

THE "strange people" of the circus sideshows have long been a subject for wonderment and not a little horror and certainly for interest. Now they have been taken as the theme for a picture which, under the name of "Freaks," is at the Rialto Theatre. The film takes a high place in the history of the pathological drama, even if not so high in that of entertainment.

"Freaks" is a curious affair. It is very good in spots and very bad in others. It has a pronounced anti-climax with which to crown the whole and yet moments of dramatic suspense that are excellent. There is a good deal of horror—in the strict sense of the term—and a good deal of tediousness. The impression at the end is that it is undoubtedly unusual, even though that is not necessarily an unqualified compliment.

The main members of the cast—outside the freaks, around whom the story is built—are Wallace Ford, Leila Hyams, Olga Baclanova, Rosco Ates and Henry Victor. Collectively they perform their parts creditably. But the main part of the picture—in whatever form it takes—is due to the direction of Tod Browning. What there is good is his and all that is bad. It is definitely a picture that is made—or lost, if that point of view is taken—by direction.

The story is about a circus trapeze performer, a strong man and a dwarf. The performer decides to marry the dwarf and then poison him to get his fortune. At the wedding supper the other freaks sing a song that "she is one of us" and, in denouncing them as freaks, she incurs a class hatred. It is discovered that she is attempting to kill the midget and his companions decide on vengeance.

The real end of the picture comes when the woman is changed into a freak herself and her lover, the strong man, is killed by the other "strange people." But, apparently under the belief that the picture as it stood was a little too horrible, the producers have tacked a happy ending on it, marrying the midget off to another dwarf to whom he had earlier been engaged. As the real climax had formed the most powerful part of the picture, the addition is doubly unwelcome.

At all events, "Freaks" is different from the usual run.

* * *

YOU'LL BE AMAZED!

WALLACE FORD IN "FREAKS"

WITH LEILA HYAMS & ROSCOE ATES

IT TAKES A SMOOTH-RUNNING OUTFIT TO CREATE THE BIG, NEW PRODUCTION IDEAS!

FOR INSTANCE! To name just a few coming:

FREAKS—A land-mark in screen daring!
ARSENE LUPIN—John and Lionel Barrymore together!
TARZAN, THE APE MAN—Another "Trader Horn"!
POLLY of the CIRCUS—Marion Davies and Gable together!
PROSPERITY—Dressler-Moran are in again!
LIMPY—Jackie Cooper at the top of his fame!
STRANGE INTERLUDE—A Norma Shearer Triumph!
LETTY LYNTON—Joan Crawford does it again!
—and of course, GRAND HOTEL with Garbo, Beery, Crawford, John and Lionel Barrymore, Lewis Stone.

THE INSIDE STORY OF LOVE-LIFE IN A SIDE SHOW!

CAN A FULL GROWN WOMAN LOVE A MIDGET?

WHAT GRUESOME VENGEANCE DID "The FREAKS" INFLICT ON THIS UNHOLY LOVE?

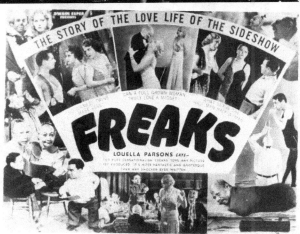

THE STORY OF THE LOVE LIFE OF THE SIDESHOW

FREAKS

LOUELLA PARSONS Says—

"FREAKS"

Well, I have seen that picture "Freaks" and I certainly think that whoever directed it should be ashamed to have put his name to it. I didn't mind its gruesomeness so much, but its cheap vulgarity is something that left a bad taste in my mouth. I cannot understand how anyone in his right mind could have conceived of such a picture. I am not easily shocked and do not hold with rigid censor laws. What amazes me is its frightfully bad taste.

ELIZABETH CONNER, San Diego, Calif.

I had a friend who threatened to sue the theater that showed "Freaks" for bringing such a picture to the place. For me, I thank the theater heartily, for it shows us that there are others who are much worse off than we.

JOAN MASTERS, Nashville, Tenn.

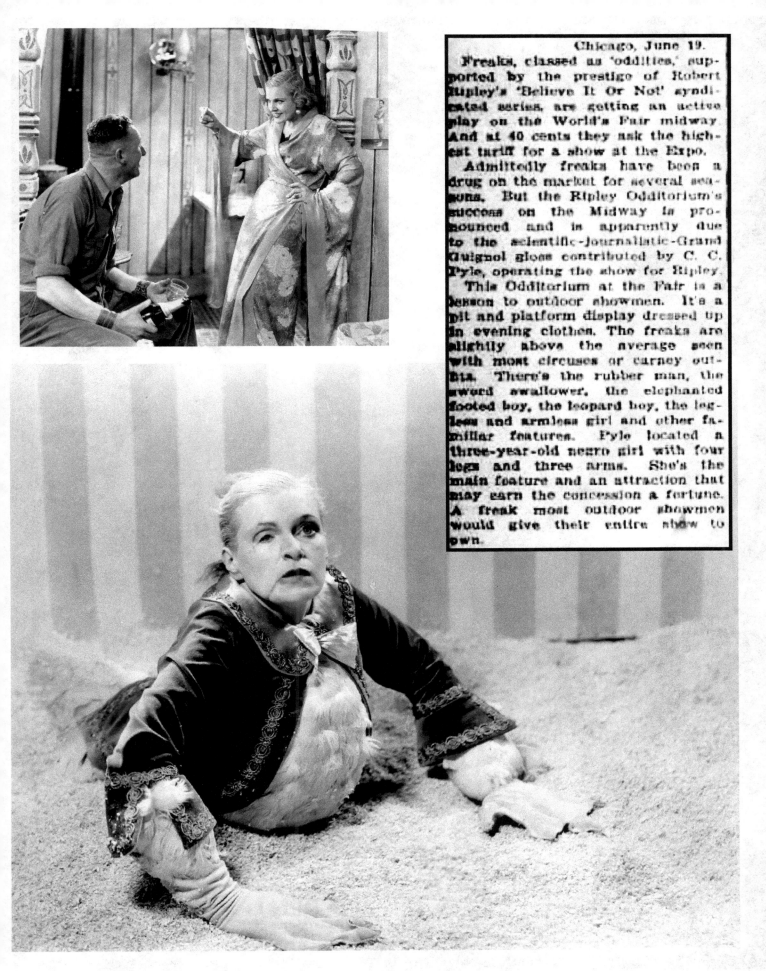

The Most Dangerous Game

Released U.S. September 16, 1932

ONCE IN A BLUE MOON A STARTLING BECAUSE IT IS DIFFERENT!...ENTHRALLING

"THE MOST DANGEROUS GAME"

REUNITING THE TEAM OF

ERNEST B. SCHOEDSACK

AND

MERIAN C. COOPER

An RKO-Radio Production

50

SCREEN NOTES.

"The Most Dangerous Game," with Joel McCrea, Leslie Banks, Fay Wray and Robert Armstrong, opens at the Paramount today. Maurice Chevalier and last week's stage show are being held over.

The MOST DANGEROUS GAME

Then came these two to Zaroff's lonely isle ...to face the fate of others who had gone before them! Fascinating, strange and terrible is their story of adventure on the island of the man who hunted men!..

BARANKA ISLAND
Less than 1000 miles from home!

with
JOEL McCREA
FAY WRAY
LESLIE BANKS
ROBT. ARMSTRONG
BASED ON THE STORY BY
RICHARD CONNELL

An RKO-RADIO PICTURE, of course
DAVID O. SELZNICK
Executive Producer

¡Los más hermosos ejemplares que mate!

"TO A GAME LOSER"

De todas las cabezas que figuraban en su colección la que mas admiraba Zardoff era la de este marino malayo

Zaroff estaba orgulloso de su colección...atraia los barcos a su destrucción para cazar a los supervivientes.

Este muchacho tuvo una muerte rastrera, como se mata a unas gallinas.

Este hombre pudo haber ganado en el juego, pero el miedo lo paraliza

According to the "trailer" concerned with "The Most Dangerous Game" it is THE most exciting picture, which is referred to as a drama about a man who collected heads of men for his trophy room. This is followed by something about this individual's penchant for the hearts of women.

LINKED with Merian Cooper's knowledgeful supervision, the capable direction of Ernest Schoedsack and Irving Pichel, and the highly creditable adaptation of Richard Connell's prize short story by James Ashmore Creelman, there is in the RKO production, "The Most Dangerous Game." Leslie Banks's suave and polished performance. He appears in the leading rôle, that of Baron Zaroff, a mad Russian hunter. It is a case of unusually satisfactory cooperation, which has resulted in this offering being a most intelligent horror tale. For, notwithstanding its fantastic pivotal idea, it is on the whole more plausible than any previous contributions of its stripe.

As it comes to the Paramount screen the outstanding merit is Mr. Banks's portrayal, which in less talented hands might easily have been stereotyped. His poise is impressive and likewise the clarity of his enunciation. He never caricatures the part, always lending rationality to the madness, if one can say so, by keeping both feet on the ground. The dialogue for Zaroff's rôle is particularly well written and the incisive lines are spoken as they should be by Mr. Banks, who is always on the qui vive to make his characterization natural. Zaroff is a distinguished and polite madman.

Mordant Hall: Variety

LA CHASSE DU COMTE ZAROFF
(THE MOST DANGEROUS GAME)

FAY WRAY – JOËL McCREA – LESLIE BANKS – ROBERT ARMSTRONG

Un Film
R.K.O. RADIO

Distribué par la COMPAGNIE UNIVERSELLE CINÉMATOGRAPHIQUE

Chandu the Magician

Released U.S. September 18, 1932

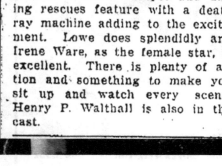

THRILL FILM AT COLONIAL

"Chandu, The Magician" Stars Bela Lugosi In Mystery Film.

Certainly thrill pictures cannot be much more thrilling than "Chandu the Magician," which is now appearing at the Colonial Theatre, starring Edmund Lowe.

Magic, hypnotism and romance provide the interest in an unusual film in which Bela Lugosi, who has gained fame for his thrill roles, is also given a prominent part.

The secrets of the East are used by Lowe to outdo the mystic, Roxor. Narrow escapes and daring rescues feature with a death ray machine adding to the excitement. Lowe does splendidly and Irene Ware, as the female star, is excellent. There is plenty of action and something to make you sit up and watch every scene. Henry P. Walthall is also in the cast.

Eckel Film Is Return to Principles of Early Serials

R. B. BAIN
he Syracuse Herald

As nerve-tingling as a Pearl White serial of our adolescent yesterdays, and speaking candidly, quite as naive, "Chandu, the Magician," radio feature, takes cinematic form on the Eckel's sound-screen this week.

No talkie for the unimaginative, this Fox production, based on the broadcast by Harry A. Earnshaw, Vera M. Oldham and R. R. Morgan, rates as an unalloyed joy for those content to check their thinking caps at the door and to accept its horrific flights of fancy at face value.

Viewed analytically, "Chandu" is the closest approach to the cinema's first principles noted in many a season. All the old reliables of the serial melodrama era are present—maniacal villain, aged inventor, beauty-in-distress and the rest.

But whereas the old-time chapter plays, such as "Perils of Pauline" and "Exploits of Elaine," were wholly unbelievable, the Eckel's offering is endowed with some semblance of plausibility through the use of miniatures and the further medium of trick photography. Hollywood technicians had a field day when "Chandu" was in production.

Even those fans whose fetish is unvarnished realism should find the production values of the weird melodrama intriguing. Max Parker's art direction, the camera effects achieved by James Wong Howe, and the persuasive touches of Marcel Varnel and William C. Menzies commend themselves to the student of cinematics.

For their inspiration, the authors of "Chandu" obviously went back some years to the time when the reported discovery of a "death ray" had the war offices of world powers on edge. Indeed, I recall seeing a filmed demonstration of the machine's martial possibilities at the Strand. It was unpleasantly convincing.

On this occasion, the "death ray" comes from the laboratory of the kindly Robert Regent, is stolen by the maniacal Roxor, and becomes the pawn for which the latter and Chandu contend. The struggle seems to be over when Roxor consigns Chandu to a watery grave in the Nile and holds as captives not only Regent but the latter's wife (Roxor's sister) and two children.

Chandu, a super-Houdini, escapes from his coffin and in good, old serial fashion, turns up in the bromidic nick o' time the save the day. For the how-when-where of it, I respectfully refer you to the Gus Lampe-directed theater.

Edmund Lowe, with "The Spider" to his credit, was the natural choice for Chandu. Bela Lugosi could only be the diabolical Roxor, or vice versa. Irene Ware, wooed and won by Fox from Carroll's Vanities, impresses favorably as Princess Nadji, and June Vlasek, a second newcomer, is another eye-full as Betty Lou. Henry B. Walthall infuses Regena with requisite sympathy, and that sometime Syracusan, Weldon Heyburn, makes Abullah duly villainous.

ECLIPSED!

Greatest Feats in Show History Pale Before This Unparalleled Free Nationwide Radio Tie-up!

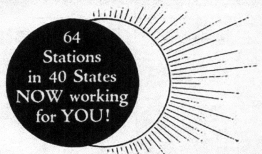

64 Stations in 40 States NOW working for YOU!

FIND THE STATION THAT COVERS YOUR TOWN

23 in the East

Atlanta, Ga.	WSB
Baltimore, Md.	WBAL
Boston, Mass.	WNAC
Buffalo, N. Y.	WBEN
Charlotte, N. C.	WBT
Chicago, Ill.	KYW
Cincinnati, Ohio	WSAI
Cincinnati, Ohio	WLW
Cleveland, Ohio	WHK
Detroit, Mich.	WJR
Hartford, Conn.	WDRC
Milwaukee, Wis.	WTMJ
Nashville, Tenn.	WSM
New York, N. Y.	WOR
Philadelphia, Pa.	WCAU
Pittsburgh, Pa.	WCAE
Portland, Maine	WCSH
Providence, R. I.	WEAN
Richmond, Va.	WRVA
Rochester, N. Y.	WHAM
Schenectady, N. Y.	WGY
Utica, N. Y.	WIBX
Worcester, Mass.	WTAG

41 in the West

Amarillo, Texas	WDAG
Bakersfield, Calif.	KERN
Bellingham, Wash.	KVOS
Boise, Idaho	KIDO
Casper, Wyoming	KDFN
Ciudad Juarez, Mexico	XEJ
Dallas, Texas	KRLD
Denver, Colo.	KLZ
Enid, Okla.	KCRC
Fresno, Calif.	KMJ
Honolulu, H. I.	KGMB
Houston, Texas	KTLC
Joplin, Miss.	WMBH
Kansas City, Miss.	WHB
Klamath Falls, Ore.	KFJI
Las Cruces, New Mexico	KOB
Long Beach, Calif.	KFOX
Los Angeles, Calif.	KNX
Los Angeles, Calif.	KHJ
Medford, Ore.	KMED
Ogden, Utah	KLO
Oklahoma City, Okla.	KFJF
Omaha, Neb.	WOW
Phoenix, Ariz.	KTAR
Pocatello, Idaho	KSEI
Portland, Ore.	KOIN
Pueblo, Texas	KGHF
Sacramento, Calif.	KFBK
Salt Lake City, Utah	KSL
San Francisco, Calif.	KFRC
San Bernardino, Calif.	KFXM
San Diego, Calif.	KGB
Santa Barbara, Calif.	KDB
Seattle, Wash.	KOL
Spokane, Wash.	KHQ
St. Louis, Mo.	KWK
Stockton, Calif.	KWG
Tulsa, Okla.	KVOO
Walla Walla, Wash.	KUJ
Wichita, Kan.	KFH
Yakima, Wash.	KIT

READY-MADE AUDIENCE OF MILLIONS EAGERLY AWAITS "CHANDU" ON YOUR SCREEN

64 powerful stations...broadcasting nightly...for months ..."Chandu" hit of the air. Never before in history such an advance build-up. You cash in...no matter where you are...without lifting a finger. The picture's a pip... crammed to the last frame with weird thrills...a natural even without the advance plug. That's Fox showmanship!

CHANDU
THE MAGICIAN

with

EDMUND LOWE
BELA LUGOSI

IRENE WARE   HENRY B. WALTHALL

From the radio drama by Harry A. Earnshaw, Vera M. Oldham and R. R. Morgan. Directed by Marcel Varnel and William C. Menzies

WATCH FOX THIS YEAR

"Chandu"—"Chandu, the Magician" is at the Grand. The popular radio mystery has as its star Edmund Lowe, an Englishman who studies magic in a Yogi monastery and is sent forth to battle evil in the person of Bele Lugosi.

"Chandu," is fantastic. It reminds one almost of a Sax Rohmer story with its Egyptian princess. But this princess is modernized and would pass for an American debutante any day.

Edmund Lowe is effective as the magician but Bele Lugosi with his personality speaking of strange things and stranger places lends the real effect needed.

"Chandu" should be seen with the same tolerance you would use in reading now some of the fairy stories that enchanted in childhood. It is a modern sort of fairy tale, and should be taken with indulgence.

As entertainment, "Chandu" is satisfying. It isn't so much a mystery except in the magic of Chandu. And since the camera itself with its responding screen is a bit of magic in itself, it shouldn't be impossible to believe in Chandu's magic.

FILM FANS WILL SEE MAGIC WORK IN "CHANDU"

"Chandu The Magician," popular mystery drama of the air, filmed as a feature by Fox, will reach the screen on the Miller Theatre next Thursday with Edmund Lowe portraying the great worker-of-magic in the title role.

60

CHANDU
THE MAGICIAN

with
Edmund LOWE
Bela LUGOSI

FOX PICTURE

EDMUND LOWE AS 'CHANDU' IS AT GRAND-LAKE

Magician of 'The Spider' Gives Portrayal of White Yogi in Mystery Play

EDMUND LOWE, who passed his novitiate as a magician in "The Spider," took a post-graduate course as a yogi at the Grand-Lake over the week-end in "Chandu," and his entertainment diploma was awarded to the hand-clapping of packed houses that found his tricks eminently mystifying.

"Chandu" is a fantastic tale, well beyond the realm of credibility, but expertly acted, intelligently directed and admirably photographed. The result is that those who are not swept away by the melodrama of the piece are captivated by the projection of the tale.

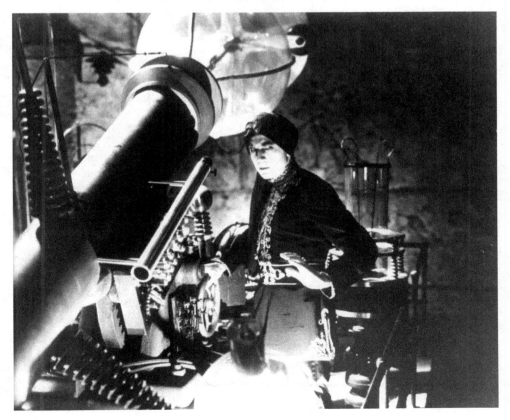

61

Kongo

Released U.S. October 1, 1932

FRIDAY SATURDAY
JAN 27 28

DEEP IN THE HEART OF THE CONGO--*1001 thrills to make you gasp!*

The crack of "Deadlegs" Flint's murderous bull-whip . . . the mysteries of darkest jungle . . . the maddening boom of savage drums heralding the approach of an avalanche of black killers . . . the tumultuous drama of a love tangle that only a terrible doom could solve!

directed by **William Cowen**

with
WALTER HUSTON
LUPE VELEZ
CONRAD NAGEL
VIRGINIA BRUCE

Based on the play by Chester De Vonde and Kilbourn Gordon. Adaptation and added dialogue by Leon Gordon.

1001 THRILLS TO MAKE YOU GASP!

TUES. - WED. - THURS.
"KONGO"
Walter Huston - Lupe Velez
Conrad Nagel - Virginia Bruce

Fri. - Sat. — Buck Jones'
"South of the Rio Grande"

COMING, EDMUND LOWE "CHANDU"

The Woman's Angle

'Air Mail' (U). Heroism of the couriers of the air portrayed by an attractive but box-officeless cast, led by appealingly hard-boiled Pat O'Brien. An action drama whose title, disasters and stoic self-sacrifice are not aimed at the feminine audience.

'Kongo' (MGM). Vengeance wallowing through the mire of the Kongo and a series of revolting, unwholesome sequences. Contains no mitigating feature for the ladies.

'The Conquerors' (RKO-Radio). Cheated of greatness by the hokum flag-waving that motivates its hasty conclusion, an epic of American development stirred by genuine national pride. Fanettes feel deep fondness for the characters whose intimate joys and sorrows reflect larger events in the history of three generations of Americans.

'The Most Dangerous Game' (RKO-Radio). A suspenseful horror film that depends on its ability to validate a psychopathic villain who lusts to stalk and kill his brother men. Though charged with sympathy for its attractive victims, plot is too fantastic and unpleasant to count on strong feminine support.

'The Kid From Spain' (UA). A lavish musical whose uneven production, ineffectual love interest and lack of memorable tunes place a mighty burden on the slight but heroic shoulders of Eddie Cantor. A thin plot, containing no significant lure for the matinee trade, benefits appreciably by the wistful impishness of one of the few gag comedians capable of engaging genuine feminine sympathy.

'Faithless' (MGM). A cold-hearted millionairess, catapulted into declassed splendor, then into hardship and poverty, finds that true love may be bought with self-sacrifice and will thrive on a family budget of $60 a week. An audience-wise theme that invites tender development, has been chilled by superficial treatment, a pleasing but half-hearted performance by Robert Montgomery and Tallulah Bankhead's inability to command sympathetic response.

'Tess of the Storm Country' (Fox). Janet Gaynor and Charles Farrell, adrift in the unrelieved shadows of old fashioned melodrama, unable to translate their box-office charm into solid entertainment. Older fanettes will delight in Miss Gaynor's selfless devotion to the needy and distressed, but the younger element will classify her film as a disappointment—sweet, slow and humorless.

DEEP IN THE HEART OF THE KONGO!

—1001 thrills to make you gasp!

A white man — brutal leader of the world's last stand of the outlaw criminal! A gorgeous half-breed daring unknown terrors impelled by a primitive love for him! A thousand jungle thrills!

SEE—
The Black Avalanche of Savages—
Lovers facing the sacrifice of Devil Worshippers!

KONGO

with

WALTER **HUSTON**

LUPE **VELEZ**

CONRAD **NAGEL**

VIRGINIA **BRUCE**

directed by

William Cowan

Metro Goldwyn Mayer Picture

"KONGO," THRILLING DRAMA OF AFRICA TODAY

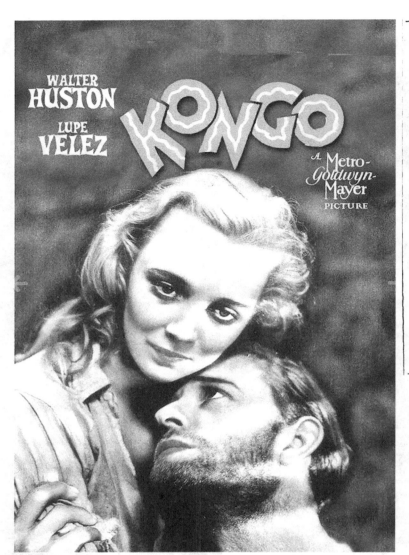

WALTER
HUSTON

LUPE
VELEZ

KONGO

A Metro-Goldwyn-Mayer Picture

EXOTIC WOMEN—CRUEL MEN
TOSSED IN A JUNGLE HELL!

Your spine will tingle—Your
blood will chill—You'll hold
your seats in excitement at
a picture that's greater than
"TARZAN" and "TRADER HORN"!

KONGO

An M-G-M Picture with

WALTER HUSTON
LUPE VELEZ
CONRAD NAGEL
VIRGINA BRUCE
Today—9:30 A.M.

Popular Prices...Continuous Performances

RIALTO

"HOUSE OF HITS" B'WAY AT 42nd

KONGO

A WHITE MADMAN RULING A BLACK EMPIRE FROM A WHEEL CHAIR!

A New Kind of Jungle Love

You Heard the Drums of Doom

He Ruled a Black Empire with a Whip

She was a Mad-Man's Love Slave

1001 THRILLS TO MAKE YOU GASP!
KONGO

WALTER **HUSTON**   LUPE **VELEZ**   CONRAD **NAGEL**   VIRGINIA **BRUCE**

KONGO

A Metro-Goldwyn-Mayer PICTURE

—ON THE SCREEN—
Exotic Women!...
Brutal Men!...

. . . in the world's last terror-shadowed frontier . . .

'KONGO'

a bewitching passion-flower of the jungle . . . Slave of love to a madman . . . A brutal, tyrant leader of the outlaw criminal . . . Savage hate and primitive love!

with
WALTER HUSTON
LUPE VELEZ
CONRAD NAGEL
VIRGINIA BRUCE

———
TALKING CARTOON

"Kongo" At the Graham Theatre Monday-Tuesday

"Kongo," Metro-Goldwyn-Mayer's drama of mystery and thrills in the African jungle, opens Monday at the Graham theatre. As "Dead-legs" Flint, Walter Huston, in the featured role, re-enacts the part he first created in scoring one of his biggest New York stage successes.

Black magic a terrifying plot for revenge, the resentment of the war-like Congo blacks against the cruel domination of a white master, and the fight of the white race against the jungle lure, form the admixture from which this strange melodrama was evolved.

As "Deadlegs" Walter Huston enacts his powerful role from a wheelchair, bullwhip in hand, driving whites and blacks before the crack of his lash. He wields the tricks of magic which keep the superstitious blacks under his spell and concocts the scheme which is to trap his rival and send a white girl out to be hurled into the swamps by the natives—a diabolical scheme of vengeance.

Virginia Bruce, who recently became the wife of John Gilbert, is the white girl to be sacrificed. Conrad Nagle is the derelict Englishman, a doctor who seeks to save her. Between these two falls the romance that contrasts with the powerful melodrama of Huston's rule. Lupe Velez, as the Portuguese girl who is the slave of the paralyzed white "witch doctor's" whims, has the type of role at which she excels. C. Henry Gordon, who was so forceful in trapping Greta Garbo in "Mata Hari," has a robust dramatic role in "Kongo." William Cowen directed the production from Leon Gordon's adaptation of the play which Chester DeVonde and Kilbourn Gordon wrote for the stage.

All the action of 'Kongo' takes place in the swamp and fever infested jungles of interior Africa. A large expanse of jungle, with trading post, and stockade, and a river winding through, was built for the production. Hundreds of blacks in the grotesque paint and traditional adornments of the superstitious African natives, take part. The cunning of the whites in holding them in subjection through their fear of 'ju-ju' or voodoo magic is vividly shown.

Harold Lloyd lets the "rabbit out of the dish" in a scene from his comedy, "Movie Crazy," coming Monday to the Paramount theatre. [...] is the new Lloyd leading lady in "Movie Crazy."

LIVELY PROGRAM OF VAUDEVILLE AT THE MILLER

Chant of Jungle and Merrier Music of Tennessee Mountaineers at Sunday Show

The chant of the jungle with its black magic is heard in "Kongo", a drama of mystery and thrills which is to be shown here today at the Dubinsky Miller Theatre. Walter Huston is featured in the film version in the role which scored for him one of his greatest successes on the New York stage.

The setting of "Kongo" is one of the photographic marvels of the present day motion picture studios. A quarter mile of the African Jungle was duplicated for its filming. Through this jungle, with its tangle of trees and dense underbrush, roam savage blacks, beating their war drums, lashing themselves to frenzy in preparation for an attack on the white trading post where Huston(Lupe Velez, Conrad Nagel, Virginia Bruce and other white members of the cast act out the principal scenes of this weird melodrama.

"Kongo" is a grim drama, with Walter Huston in the role of the sinister "Deadlegs" Flint, a tyrant of a man who has become confined to a wheelchair through a fight with an enemy. By means of his conversance with black magic, he becomes the white witch-doctor of the natives, and uses his power in this plot for vengeance on the man who has crippled him.

The Old Dark House

Released U.S. Oct. 20, 1932

Two Boris Karloff productions went into the hands of the adapters last week at the Universal plant. Benn W. Levy, author of "The Devil Passes" and "Mrs. Moonlight," is in charge of "The Old Dark House," a novel by J. B. Priestley. With this assignment "The Old Dark House" takes on a more or less British hue. Mr. Levy is an Englishman, and so is Mr. Priestley, and so is James Whale, who will direct the film. Mr. Karloff also hails from the other side of the pond.

The second of Mr. Karloff's productions is "The Invisible Man," one of H. G. Wells's stories. Garrett Fort is handling the work of adaptation. Mr. Fort, by the way, adapted "Frankenstein" and "Dracula." Robert Florey, having completed "Murders in the Rue Morgue," will direct "The Invisible Man," which is about a scientist whose ability to disappear into thin air causes some unusual complications.

The Rialto will revive the Universal productions, "The Old Dark House," with Charles Laughton and Raymond Massey, and "The Black Cat," with Boris Karloff and Bela Lugosi, beginning tomorrow. . . .

"THE OLD DARK HOUSE"

CARL LAEMMLE *presents*

"THE OLD DARK HOUSE"

from the novel by J. B. PRIESTLY

with KARLOFF, MELVYN DOUGLAS

GLORIA STUART, CHARLES LAUGHTON, LILIAN BOND

Ernest Thesiger, Eva Moore, Raymond Massey, Brember Wills, John Dudgeon

GOOSE PIMPLES! O-O-o-o-o!

What mystery! What eerie suspense; They lived a lifetime in a night! Trapped by a terrific storm, they were forced to find shelter in a forbidden house—two beautiful girls with three men to defend them from the fearful things that soon happened! Gasping surprises! Trembling thrills — thrills — thrills!

Directed by JAMES WHALE
who gave you "FRANKENSTEIN"   A UNIVERSAL PICTURE   *Produced by* CARL LAEMMLE, JR.

MISS STUART'S GOOD FORTUNE

THE life of a newly created film favorite was revealed at the St. Moritz on a rainy afternoon recently. Gloria Stuart had enjoyed her first look at the celebrated New York night life and was ready to call it a day, or a couple of days. But there were photographers. For Miss Stuart was on Broadway simultaneously in two pictures—"The Old Dark House," at the Rialto, and "Air Mail," at the Mayfair—and her public had to be appeased.

Holding a weary hand to a blonde and weary head, Miss Stuart was willing to pose if it killed her, which she thought it probably would. But the photographer wanted a dog, and all the room offered was a vase of white chrysanthemums and a hazy view of Central Park. Silence, while the photographer wracked his brain. Then somebody remembered that a Miss Somebody on the floor below had been seen in the elevator with a beautiful black chow. Two minutes later the chow was in the room and Miss Stuart was posing.

Betimes she explained how she had gotten where she was and how generally she was bewildered by it all. For Miss Stuart, who is a California girl, never really harbored any serious designs on the cinema. She acted for various little theatre groups and happened to be in Los Angeles when somebody suggested that she might as well take a test. She went to Universal, where they were seeking a leading lady for "Back Street—that was last Spring—and then went to Paramount. Universal heard that Paramount was interested in her, and Paramount heard that Universal was interested in her, and the result was a feud in which Universal got her name down on a contract.

Before her marriage she had been Gloria Stewart and now she became Gloria Stuart, which was practically the same thing. They gave Irene Dunne the rôle in "Back Street," and when Marian Marsh over at the Warner Brothers balked at the idea of playing a subsidiary rôle in "Street of Women," Miss Stuart was sent over to play the part. It was her first. The girl who had never, as she phrased it, made a nickel out of acting, now found herself getting a good deal more than she expected. She appeared in "The Old Dark House" and in "Air Mail" and finally in "The All American," which was released first. Now she has had to hurry back to California to make some retakes for "Laughter in Hell," which will be her next. After that she will have to do a lot of screaming opposite Boris Karloff in "The Invisible Man."

Pictures for Week Ending Nov. 12

CAPITOL—"Red Dust," with Jean Harlow and Clark Gable.

PARAMOUNT—"Hot Saturday," with Nancy Carroll.

ROXY—"Rackety Rax," with Victor McLaglen and Greta Nissen.

WARNERS' STRAND—"Three On a Match," with Warren William.

RIALTO—"The Old Dark House," with Boris Karloff.

RIVOLI—"Magic Night," with Jack Buchanan.

CAMEO—"Goona Goona," Andre Roosevelt's film of Bali.

CRITERION—"Maedchen in Uniform," a German language picture.

EUROPA—"Luise, Koenigin von Preussen," closes tomorrow evening; "Kameradschaft," opens Tuesday.

LITTLE CARNEGIE PLAYHOUSE—"Mensch Ohne Namen," a German dialogue film.

LITTLE PICTURE HOUSE—Today, "The Sign of the Four"; tomorrow, "The Dark House"; Tuesday and Wednesday, "The Devil and the Deep."

FIFTH AVENUE PLAYHOUSE—"Coiffeur pour Dames," closes today; "Rasputin, Sinner or Saint" opens tomorrow.

HINDENBURG—"Barberina, die Taenzerin von Sanssouci," a German language picture.

ASTOR—"Strange Interlude," with Norma Shearer and Clark Gable.

MAYFAIR—"Air Mail," with Pat O'Brien and Ralph Bellamy.

PALACE—"The All American," with Richard Arlen.

BEACON—"Grand Hotel," through Monday; "Pack Up Your Troubles," Tuesday to Thursday.

WINTER GARDEN—"Scarlet Dawn," with Douglas Fairbanks Jr.

SEVENTY-SECOND STREET — "Wenn die Soldaten," a German dialogue film.

SEVENTY-NINTH STREET — "Purpur und Washblau."

TOBIS—"Gloria," a German language picture.

ACME—"Anush," a Russian silent film.

LOEW'S PARADISE, STATE AND VALENCIA—"Movie Crazy."

LOEW'S METROPOLITAN—"Red Dust."

LOEW'S LEXINGTON AND SEVENTY-SECOND STREET — Today, "Movie Crazy"; tomorrow and Tuesday, "Payment Deferred."

LOEW'S SHERIDAN — Today, "Tiger Shark"; tomorrow and Tuesday, "A Successful Calamity."

FOX (BROOKLYN)—"Once in a Lifetime," with Jack Oakie.

PARAMOUNT (BROOKLYN)—"Hot Saturday."

ALBEE (BROOKLYN)—"The All American."

WARNERS' STRAND (BROOKLYN)—"They Call It Sin," with Loretta Young.

"The Old Dark House."

ANOTHER film for which Mr. Laemmle is responsible is "The Old Dark House," a pictorial translation of J. B. Priestley's novel of the same name. This production, which is now at the Rialto, is chiefly remarkable for the performances of the players, for the tale is disappointing and incomplete. For one of the rôles, that of a madman, James Whale, the director, brought Brember Wills from London. Others in the cast include Melvyn Douglas, Charles Laughton, whose work in "Devil and the Deep" on the screen, and in "Payment Deferred" on the stage, won glowing praise; Raymond Massey, one of Britain's top-notch players; Ernest Thesiger, an accomplished character actor; Boris Karloff, who appeared as the Monster in "Frankenstein"; Lillian Pond, Eva Moore and Gloria Stuart, a charming and competent actress.

With these players most of the hysteria in this fable is compelling. Added to this there are impressive settings of the old dark house, which happens to be somewhere in the Welsh mountain region. Mr. Karloff, who is an adept at hideous make-up, appears here as Morgan, the servant for Horace Femm and his sister Rebecca, who live in the dark house.

THE CAST

	played by	
Morgan		Karloff
Roger Penderel		Melvyn Douglas
Margaret Waverton		Gloria Stuart
Sir Wm. Porterhouse		Charles Laughton
Gladys Du Cane		Lillian Bond
Horace Femm		Ernest Thesiger
Rebecca Femm		Eva Moore
Philip Waverton		Raymond Massey
Saul Femm		Brember Wills
Sir Roderick		John Dudgeon

Commencing Sat. 6th Jan. 1934.

TO-NIGHT.   THIS WEEK.

THE MONSTER
OF
"FRANKENSTEIN"
BORISS KARLOFF
IN
THE OLD DARK HUOSE
WITH
CHARLES LAUGTON.

Daily 6, 8 & 10 p. m.
Sat. Sun. & Thurs. 4 p. m.

"THE OLD DARK HOUSE"

PRINTED IN U.S.A.   MAJESTIC PRINTING PRESS, BOMBAY 7.

D. L. SELLERS
GROCERY and MEAT MARKET

WE DELIVER — — — — — — — — — — PHONE 498

BANANAS, APPLES, ORANGES, each	1c
POTATOES, California, 10 Lbs.	32c
CORN FLAKES, Miller's, 2 Pkgs.	19c
BAKING POWDER, Health Club, 2-Lb. Can and 1 5c can Free	23c
FLOUR, Peerless, 48-Lb. Sack, $1.50; 24 Lbs.	80c
SUGAR, 10 Lbs.	50c
QUAKER CRACKLES, 2 Pkgs.	15c
SALT, 3 5c Pkgs.	10c

FREE $30,000 CASH · 15,000 PAIRS SILK STOCKINGS
with IVORY FLAKES Small Size .. 9c   Large Size 24c

MINERAL CRYSTALS, ½-Lb. Pkg.	30c
MACARONI or SPAGHETTI, 3 Pkgs.	9c
HOMINY, PEAS, SPINACH, SOUP, SPAGHETTI	5c
VANILLA WAFERS, 1-Lb. Pkg.	15c
PRUNES, 2-Lb. Pkg.	15c
COFFEE BRIGHT & EARLY, 1-Lb. Pkg.	22c
ADMIRATION, 1-Lb. Pkg.	26c

CAMAY The Soap of Beautiful Women   3 Bars, 1 Bottle Perfume **19c**

SUNBRITE CLEANSER, 2 Cans	9c

FREE A Big 1-Lb. Can of Folger's Coffee has been set aside as a FREE GIFT for Will Morris, Rt. 3, if he will whack this ad out and bring to us Friday or Saturday.

—Market Specials—

Cream CHEESE, Pound	20c	LETTUCE, 2 Heads	9c
STEAK, 7 Style or Chuck, Lb.	18c	TOMATOES, Fresh, Pound	5c
Picnic HAM, Boneless, Lb.	29c	CUCUMBERS, Each	1c
LUNCH MEAT, Mixed, Lb.	25c	CARROTS, 2 Bunches	6c
Tenderloin STEAK, Pound	25c	GREEN BEANS, 2 Pounds	9c
		PEAS, Fresh Black-eye, Pound	5c

1933

**The Monkey's Paw
Murders in the Zoo
Supernatural
Night of Terror
It's a Great Feeling
The Ghoul**

The Monkey's Paw

Released U.S. January 13, 1933

"THE MONKEY'S PAW."

Though it is presented by an American company, and has been directed by an American director, the cast of "The Monkey's Paw" is almost entirely English, and the film is decisively English in feeling. It is an elaboration of a famous short story of the same name by W. W. Jacobs. A soldier who has served in India brings home a magical monkey's paw, the holder of which has the power of having three wishes granted. The paw comes into the possession of a simple old couple in a small English town. From this stage onwards the camera seldom moves outside the walls of the old couple's cottage. When it does, it goes no farther than the snow-covered street outside and an electric power station near by. In its modest way this picture shows how much is to be gained by concentrating the action in this manner. The requisite atmosphere of eeriness is created with marked success, and the contrast between the happy domesticity of the two old people (played by Ivan Simpson and Louise Carter) and the strange events brought about, as one of them believes, by the magical paw, is most effective. It is doubtful, however, whether any added value has been given to the film by twisting the eerie tale so as to provide it with a more cheerful ending. "The Monkey's Paw" is released by R.K.O., and is at the Empire Theatre.

HERE'S A PANCAKE CONTEST!

HIS idea should be good for the Woman's Page of a newspaper tying up with your engagement of "THE MONKEY'S PAW." Run the cut and offer prizes for the best pancake recipe sent in by readers.

She Wants A Recipe!!!

Betty Lawford, pretty English screen actress, is shown in her latest RKO-Radio photoplay tossing off a few pancakes at the griddle. They were made from a chance studio recipe, but Betty is not satisfied with it. Some reader probably has a better recipe. SO SEND IT IN. It may be just a plain home spun pancake, or it may be a French or German style pancake. The judges will decide which recipe seems to be the most appetizing or the most practical. Awards of guest tickets to "THE MONKEY'S PAW" in which Betty is the heroine at the _____ Theatre next week, will be made for the ten best recipes.

Betty Lawford as the sweetheart whose romance is tied up with the magic talisman in "THE MONKEY'S PAW," RKO-Radio picture coming to the _____ Theatre next week. Bramwell Fletcher plays opposite her in this mystery story.

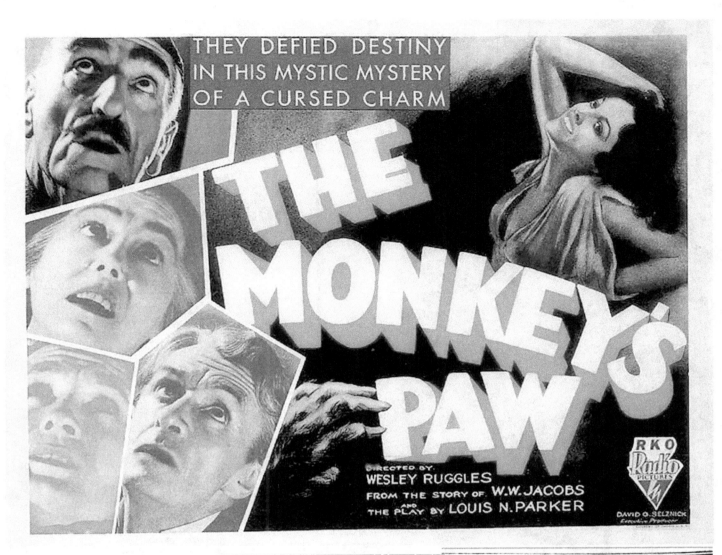

THEY DEFIED DESTINY IN THIS MYSTIC MYSTERY OF A CURSED CHARM

THE MONKEY'S PAW

DIRECTED BY
WESLEY RUGGLES
FROM THE STORY OF W. W. JACOBS
AND THE PLAY BY LOUIS N. PARKER

RKO Radio Pictures

DAVID O. SELZNICK
Executive Producer

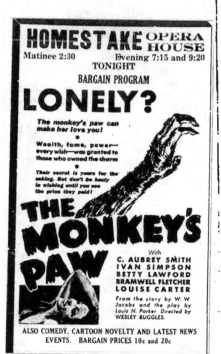

HOMESTAKE OPERA HOUSE

Matinee 2:30 Evening 7:15 and 9:20
TONIGHT
BARGAIN PROGRAM

LONELY?

The monkey's paw can make her love you!

Wealth, fame, power—every wish—was granted to those who owned the charm

Their secret is yours for the asking. But don't be hasty in wishing until you see the price they paid!

THE MONKEY'S PAW

With
C. AUBREY SMITH
IVAN SIMPSON
BETTY LAWFORD
BRAMWELL FLETCHER
LOUISE CARTER

From the story by W. W. Jacobs and the play by Louis N. Parker. Directed by WESLEY RUGGLES

ALSO COMEDY, CARTOON NOVELTY AND LATEST NEWS EVENTS. BARGAIN PRICES 10c and 20c

---

At The Theaters

RIALTO

"The Monkey's Paw"

Many properties used in "The Monkey's Paw," the thrilling action drama now on the Rialto screen, were imported directly from England by the RKO-Radio Pictures' studio.

"The Monkey's Paw" is an authentic picture of English home life; its characters are men and women caught under the spell of a mystic Hindu charm credited with supernatural powers. How these victims of their own imagination build up a tragedy to a smashing climax of high melodrama, offers one of the most absorbing pictures of the year, critics state.

C. Aubrey Smith, Ivan Simpson, Betty Lawford, Louise Carter, and Bramwell Fletcher, are featured in the cast, which was directed by Wesley Ruggles.

STATE

IN PERSON — TODAY
5 GREAT VAUDEVILLE ACTS

ON THE STAGE
TIM GANG
MOORE and JINES
Comedy Stars of Leslie's "Blackbirds"
Radio and Recording Stars

RADIO ROMEO'S
Favorites of Station WOR
In a Popular Song Revue

EDDIE HALL & CO.
Sensational Musical Comedy Stars

| PEGGY WARD | AL. HUNTER'S STAGE BAND |
| HOT-CHA DANCER! | Music as Hot as Old Radea Itself |

We've Had Many Big Shows But Never One Like This!

ON THE SCREEN

"The Monkey's Paw"

If You Owned It Would You Dare Use It?

Wealth, Fame, Life, Love! Every wish was granted to those who held this curious charm!

with
BETTY LAWFORD
C. AUBREY SMITH
IVAN SIMPSON
LOUISE CARTER
BRAMWELL FLETCHER

Murders in the Zoo

Released U.S. March 31, 1933

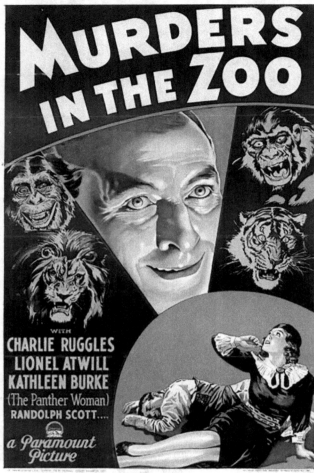

"MURDERS IN THE ZOO"

MURDER Committed by a MADMAN... More Deadly Than The Jungle BEASTS!

NOW

He Killed for Love!

Murders in the Zoo
with
CHARLIE RUGGLES
LIONEL ATWILL
Kathleen BURKE
The PANTHER WOMAN
RANDOLPH SCOTT

FRANK ALBERTSON Comedy
SOUVENIRS
NEWS

TIL 1 P.M. 20c AZTEC

WEEK VAN 8 JUNI
DIXI - De Buitengewoon Aangrijpende Film
KINDEREN NIET TOEGELATEN

Paramount présente
Le serpent mamba

CHARLIE RUGGLES · Lionel ATWILL
KATHLEEN BURKE La femme Panthère · Randolph SCOTT
SUTHERLAND L'est un Film Paramount

Mystery Film at Granada

"Murders in the Zoo," mystery meodrama featuring Charlie Ruggles, Lionel Atwill, Kathleen Burke, (the Panther Woman), Randolph Scott, John Lodge and Gail Patrick, has been booked for the Granada theater, where it will open Friday.

"Murders in the Zoo' 'centers around a sadistic madman insanely jealous of his wife. On a trip to India to collect new specimens for a zoo in which he is interested, he sews up the lips of a man who, while drunk, had kissed his wife, and then leaves him to the mercy of jungle tigers.

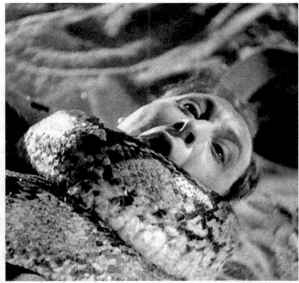

Aztec

The wild beasts of the zoo—
snarling behind the bars of their
cages in the Carnivora House—are
the witnesses of the screen's newest and most ingenious death method in Paramount's "Murders in the
Zoo," which is showing currently
at the Aztec, featuring Charlie
Ruggles, Lionel Atwill, Kathleen
Burke (the Panther Woman),

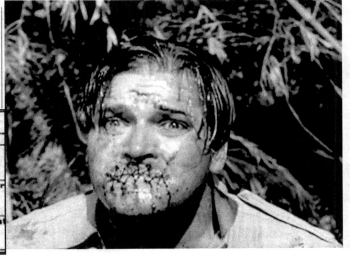

MINNEAPOLIS

	April 27	May 4	May 11	May 18
STATE (2,200; 55) High. $28,000 Low 3,800	Bedtime Story $7,800	Cavalcade $7,000	White Sister $6,300	Central Airport $4,400
ORPHEUM (2,600; 40) High. $25,000 Low 2,500	King Kong $32,000 Stage Show	Vampire Bat $14,500 (White's Scandals)	Sweepings $3,500	Christopher $4,000 (6 days)
LYRIC (1,300; 35) High. $17,000 Low 1,200	Clear Wires $2,800	Hello Sister $1,900 (6 days)	Murder Zoo $1,700	Elmer Great $3,800

Supernatural

Released U.S. April 21, 1933

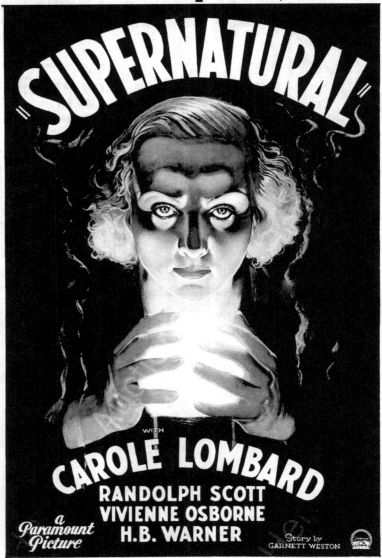

Supernatural"
Carole Lombard is featured in this picture by the producers of "White Zombie." She is supported by Randolph Scott and H. B. Warner. The cast also includes Allan Dinehart, William Farnum and Beryl Mercer.

WEDNESDAY, JULY 19, 1933

MAYNARD
THEATRE

WED.—THURS.

"THE BIG CAGE"
Anita Page — Clyde Beatty

FRI.—SAT.

"SUPERNATURAL"
Carole Lombard — Randolf Scott

SUN.—MON.—TUES.

"THE GIRL IN 419"
James Dunn — Gloria Stuart

It'll Still Burn

Halperin Brothers, producing 'Supernatural' for Paramount, will photograph a woman being electrocuted for murder.

Producing brothers, however, will give the scene a new touch; woman will wear an evening gown in the chair.

Night of Terror

Released U.S. April 24, 1933

BELA LUGOSI HEADS CAST OF MYSTERY DRAMA

"Night of Terror," Gem Feature Today, Has Weird Characters

Those who enjoy the game of attempting to identify the murderer in cinema mystery dramas will experience a particularly difficult task in naming the guilty one in "Night of Terror," which is the feature at the Gem Theatre today.

Bela Lugosi in "Night of Terror" adds his own weird personality to this spooky picture.

Suspicion points to any of eight individuals who might be the perpetrator of the series of ghastly murders that are committed in the strange home of Professor Rinehart. There is a maniac at large, a young scientist who is buried alive, a sinister Hindu servant and his forbidding wife, a perpetually present newspaper reporter, and two individuals who jealously covet the estate of the aged professor.

Each person's motive are cloaked with shadows as one death after another strikes terror into the hearts of the occupants of the fantastic home, while the police can do nothing but register bewilderment.

Bela Lugosi, who created the title role in the famous play, "Dracula" is cast as a sinister figure in this sensational mystery. Other important characters are played by Sally

THE WEIRDEST MYSTERY EVER FILMED!
BELLA "Dracula" LUGOSI
IN

NIGHT of TERROR

With
SALLY BLANE
WALLACE FORD
TULLY MARSHALL
Added
JUNIOR FEATURES—NEWS

Mat. 15c **STATE** All
Nite 25c Week

maybe $1,500.
State (Monroe) (500; 10-15-25)
'Be Mine Tonight' (U). Held over
for three days; $1,500 in all. 'Be
Mine' built all the way after a
dawdling start. 'Night of Terror'
(Col) comes in next.

PRINCESS THEATRE

Sat. Oct 28: Hand painted china
gift night. Salad plate first prize, and
a set of cups and saucers second
prize. Also additional chances on the
Chevrolet which will be given away
at the Princess November 16. See rules
on back of November calendars.

"Night of Terror" is not recom-
mended for people with heart trouble
but if there's nothing wrong with
your heart don't miss it. Bella Lugosi
is even better in "Night of Terror"
than he was in "Dracula." Terror
looked in at the window, murder
prowled in the garden, dread stalked
the hall and sinister shadows climbed
the stairs. Shrieks! Chills! Shudders!
And you'll sit on the edge of your
seat and forget that it's only a movie
after all, as this weird story unfolds
on the screen. Also, "Paramount Pictorial," a cartoon and "The Last Frontier."

A TALE OF HORRORS in a HOUSE OF MYSTERY

'NIGHT of TERROR'

FOX GRAND

Tonite
Starts
11 P. M.

On the Stage

All
Seats 25c

GHOSTS

GHOSTS. (the ghost
sometimes becomes
angered. leaves the
stage, comes into the
audience and "sits"
with you.

Be Prepared to Be
Scared

Special Midnight
SPOOK PARTY
ALI-DIN
Presenting
Spirit Slate Writing
Spirit Table Raising
Talking Skulls
GHOSTS!

ON THE SCREEN
Bela Lugosi
in
"A Night of Terror"

TICKETS ON SALE 10 P. M.
You can buy your ticket for the Spook Party at 10
P. M. and see the remainder of our first show and
the Spook Party. Spook Party starts 11 P. M.
All seats 25c.

NIGHT OF TERROR' AT PARAMOUNT TODAY AND TOMORROW

The much chilled spines of cinema fans will be subjected to more cold waves, it is predicted, with the showing of "Night of Terror," the Columbia murder-mystery which opens at the Paramount theater today.

Willard Mack, famous stage impressario, in framing the original

Bela Lugosi and Mary Frey in "Night of Terror"

plot for the picture left nothing to be desired in the way of thrills and excitement. There are several murders, a maniac at large, a gruesome face whose dreaded appearance means certain death, a sinister Hindu servant, and a man buried alive, all of whom are involved in a drama that is said to set a new peak for cinema shocks.

Bela Lugosi, whose name is synonymous with his famous characterization of the internationally known "Dracula," a role he created on the stage and screen, appears as the Hindu servant, a part that permits him to exhibit all the menacing and mysterious qualities at his command.

Sally Blane furnishes not only her blonde loveliness but a delightful romance with Walace Ford who is cast as a breezy young reporter.

An excellent supporting cast includes Tully Marshall, famous veteran of the screen, Gertrude Michael who is prominently cast in Chevalier's "A Bedtime Story," and Bryant Washburn, well-known leading man of Hollywood's silent era, who makes a successful return to the screen in this mystery drama.

"NIGHT OF TERROR" WEIRD MYSTERY THRILLER AT THE PARAMOUNT THURSDAY AND FRIDAY

George Meeker, Sally Blane, Bela Lugosi and Tully Marshall ʼ "Night of Terror"—A Columbia Picture

The much chilled spines of cinema fans will be subjected to more cold waves, it is predicted, with the showing of "Night of Terror" the Columbia murder mystery which opens at the Paramount theater Thursday

Willard Mack famous stage impressario in framing the original plot for the picture left nothing to be desired in the way of thrills and excitement. There are several murders, a maniac at large a gruesome face whose dreaded appearance means certain death a sinister Hindu servant and a man buried alive all of whom are involved in a drama that is said to set a new peak for cinema shocks

Bela Lugosi, whose name is synonymous with his famous characterization of the internationally known Dracula a role he created on the stage and screen, appears as the Hindu servant a part that permits him to exhibit all the menacing and mysterious qualities at his command

Sally Blane furnishes not only her blonde loveliness but a delightful romance with Wallace Ford who is cast as a breezy young reporter

An excellent supporting cast includes Tully Marshall, famous veteran of the screen Gertrude Michael who is prominently cast in Chevalier's A Bedtime Story and Bryant Washburn well known leading man of Hollywood's silent era, who makes a successful return to the screen in this mystery drama

Maurice Chevalier in 'A Bedtime Story' will be shown at the Paramount for the last times tonight

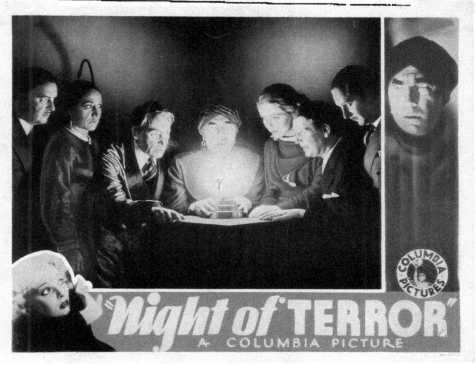

Night of TERROR A COLUMBIA PICTURE

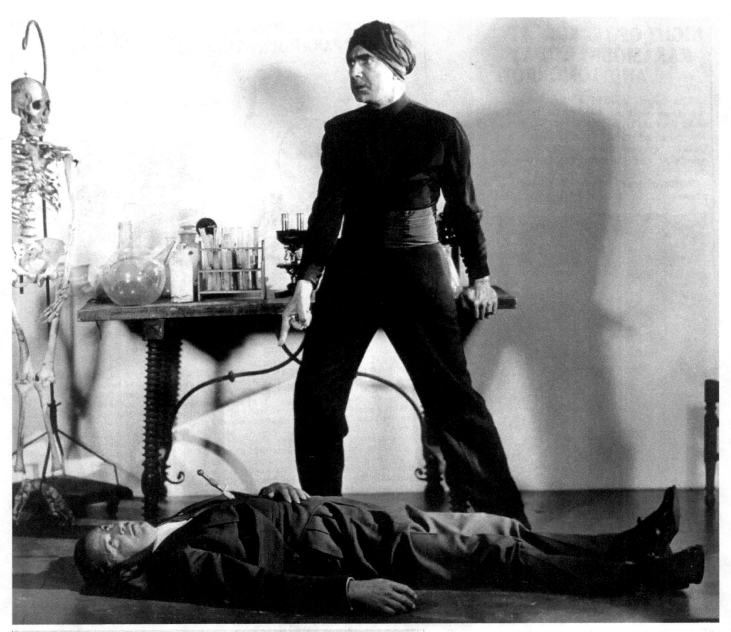

"Night of TERROR"
A COLUMBIA PICTURE

Horror in a House of Mystery

Night of TERROR

With

BELA "Dracula" LUGOSI
SALLY BLANE
WALLACE FORD
TULLY MARSHALL

COLUMBIA PICTURES

Story by WILLARD MACK
Directed by BENJAMIN STOLOFF
A COLUMBIA PICTURE

a mad murdering midnight menace!

"Night of TERROR"

with

BELA "Dracula" LUGOSI
SALLY BLANE
WALLACE FORD
TULLY MARSHALL

Story by WILLARD MACK

Directed by BENJAMIN STOLOFF

A COLUMBIA PICTURE

Copyrighted by Columbia Pictures Corp., New York, N. Y. 1933

It's a Great Feeling

Released U.S. July 8, 1933

A-MUSE-U

Direction of
C. J. Jamison

A HOME ENTERPRISE FOR HOME PEOPLE

A Home Enterprise

Sunday and Monday

WHAT WOULD YOU DO

If you were the

LAST MAN ON EARTH?

Let your imagination run wild and you'll get an idea of the gayety, the spiciness, the tunes and the laughs you'll find in

Fox Film's

IT'S GREAT TO BE ALIVE

with

Raul ROULIEN   Gloria STUART
Edna May OLIVER   Herbert MUNDIN
Joan MARSH

Directed by Alfred Werker
From a story by John D. Swain
Music and lyrics by William Kernell

Comedy—Pitts and Todd in "ONE TRACK MINDS"
Cartoon—Flip, the Frog, Pathe News

Matinees 10c

Evenings 15c

At Strand Tomorrow

"It's Great to Be Alive" the new Fox musical comedy which will show at the Strand tomorrow and Monday is a real treat. With dances staged by Sammy Lee, new tantalizing dance tunes and an unusual plot, it is on the preferred list.

Telling the story of a man who finds himself literally the last man on earth, the film depicts a world populated entirely by women, each of whom has one end in view—to get that solitary mate. It is a dread disease that wipes the globe clean of the masculine sex. The women are unprepared for such a contingency, and what goes on toward a solution of this emergency forms the extremely funny basis for the picture.

Raul Roulien, the South American star, plays the highly enviable role of being the last man. The fact that he is a castaway on a desert island when the scourge of men occurs, merely adds to his own amazement when he finds in himself a complete sex. In the story he is an aviator, popular with the women even in a world of men, but devastating as the only man in the world. Roulien's performance is excellent. He is a finished actor,

---

A scene from the Fox Film production, "IT'S GREAT TO BE ALIVE," with Raul Roulien, Gloria Stuart, Edna May Oliver and Herbert Mundin

American stardom, he is wholly successful.

With the comedy in the expert hands of Edna May Oliver and Herbert Mundin, "It's Great to Be Alive" has a generous supply of scintillant moments. Gloria Stuart is lovely in the leading feminine role, and the actors, in support of the principals, are each splendid in the individual portrayals. Among these are Joan Marsh, Dorothy Burgess, Emma Dunn, Edward Van Sloan and Robert Greig.

The Ghoul

Released U.S. Nov. 25, 1933

"THE GHOUL"

UN FILM GAUMONT BRITISH
DIRIGIDO POR T HAYES HUNTER
INTERPRETES DOROTHY HYSON
ERNEST THESIGER HAROLD HUTH
Y EL INIMITABLE

BORIS KARLOFF
EL RESUCITADO
(THE GHOUL)

GAUMONT BRITISH PICTURES

Un film 100 por 100 Boris Karloff

95

96

WHO'S WHO IN PICTURES

Boris Karloff's Career as a Monster in the Films—Irene Hervey and Others

BORIS KARLOFF, who has succeeded the late Lon Chaney as the apostle of fright, continues his régime of terror in "The Ghoul" at the Rialto. Personally conservative, and even shy, Mr. Karloff has portrayed half-men, mummies, revivified corpses, synthetic demons and crazed scientists with such hearty gusto that his employers are reluctant to waste his macabre talents on ordinary rôles. His name originally was Charles Edward Pratt and he is an Englishman of excellent education. Born in London in 1887, he grappled with his textbooks successively at Uppingham, Merchant Taylor School and King's College, London University. He prepared for the consular service and went on the British stage instead. It was as long ago as 1909 that Mr. Karloff crossed the sea to Canada and put in a season of stock at Kamloops, B. C. Finally he attracted the attention of Hollywood with his stage performances in "The Virginian" and "Kongo." Mr. Karloff did not immediately go to work with fang and knife; he played average every-day parts, gangsters and things. When Universal, with the aid of the most grisly make-up seen in the films in many a day, presented him as Dr. Frankenstein's monster, his fortune was made. Since that time he has slunk, crawled, growled, pillaged and murdered in such exhibits of the nightmare school as "Behind the Mask," "The Mummy," "The Mask of Fu Manchu" and "The Old Dark House." "The Ghoul" is British-produced. At Universal City they are plotting several new horrors for him—Poe's "The Black Cat," "The Return of Frankenstein" and "A Trip to Mars." Mr. Karloff, appropriately, occupies the dressing room formerly used by Lon Chaney. For diversion he does not eat babies; he plays golf and cricket and fancies a pot of tea in the afternoon.

always adds that he is not an expert at either sport.

Warner Baxter, Rachel Crothers's specimen male in "As Husbands Go," at the Radio City Music Hall, was a reasonably inglorious salesman for farm implements when a capricious fate tossed him on the stage. Dorothy Shoemaker was to open at Louisville on a Monday afternoon, and her partner took sick in Columbus on the preceding Saturday night. The youthful Mr. Baxter, who had a local reputation as a dramatic actor in high school opera, was hastily summoned. He spent Sunday and the early hours of Monday learning two songs and the "business," and opened Monday afternoon. He remained in the act four months and finally, capitulating to his mother's insistent reproaches, returned to Columbus and became an insurance agent. He saved his money, bought a half interest in a garage in Tulsa, Okla., lost every cent, and joined a stock company in Dallas as leading man at $30 a week. Accumulating another modest bankroll, he went to

KARLOFF THRILLER COMES TO OLYMPIC

Boris Karloff, creator of the screen roles of Frankenstein and the Mummy, dispenses even more chilling and thrilling excitement in "The Ghoul," which comes to the Olympic theatre Saturday for a week's engagement. The story, by Frank King and Leonard Hines, concerns the stealing of a remarkable jewey from a famous Egyptian tomb and the strange manner of its recovery.

In the capable hands of T. Hayes Hunter, the story has been cleverly directed and the picture is said to provide an abundance of thrills, many of a spine chilling nature.

The atmosphere of sinister mystery is created by masterly lighting effects and enhanced by the brilliant clever photography of G. Krampf. Karloff's make-up is onsidered the last word in monstrous appearance, particularly when he arises from the "tomb.' ' This is a hair-raising scene if ever there was one.

The acting of Karloff's supporting cast is uniformly excellent, with outstanding performances given by Ernest Thesiger, Cedric Hardwicke, Harold Huth, Clarke Smith, Dorothy Hyson and Anthony Bushell.

"THE GHOUL"

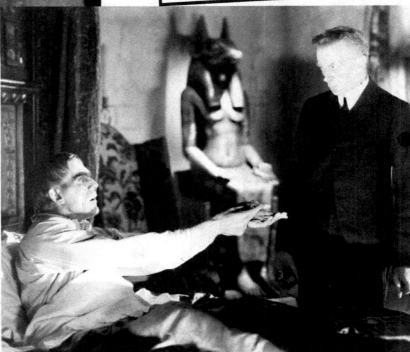

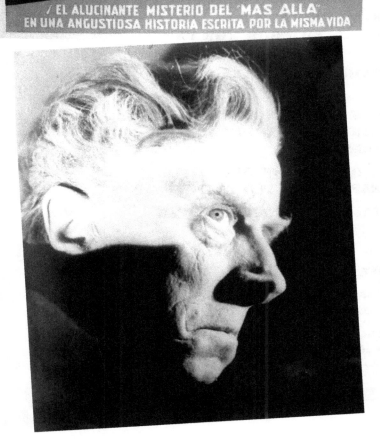

WHEN DO CENSORS SAY "NO!" AND WHY?

Movie Secrets Revealed!

Pictures from Hollywood actors and directors which movie stars would pay thousands of dollars to keep out of circulation

Starting Sunday, August 19th and continuing each Sunday thereafter for approximately three months, the Journal-Post, altogether, will print approximately four hundred pictures from Hollywood.

It has taken weeks and weeks to gather these pictures at a great expense. They will appear each Sunday in the Kansas City Journal-Post in a roto-gravure section. You will want them by all means.

THESE AND MANY MORE QUESTIONS WILL BE ANSWERED IN PICTURES:

WHAT WAS THE WORST SCANDAL IN MOVIE HISTORY?

WHICH POPULAR ACTRESS HAS A DOUBLE CHIN WHICH HAS TO BE CONCEALED FROM THE CAMERA?

WHAT IS THE MOST FAMOUS BED IN HOLLYWOOD?

THAT THEY FREQUENTLY MAKE THE SAME MOVIE TWICE—A DARING VERSION FOR FRANCE, A TAME VERSION FOR YOU TO SEE?

WHICH ACTOR WAS DENIED STARDOM FOR YEARS BECAUSE HIS EARS WERE TOO BIG?

WHICH MOVIE STAR HAS BEEN MARRIED THE MOST TIMES?

These and hundreds of other startling questions will be answered in pictures every Sunday

"Hollywood Unmasked" starts in the Kansas City Journal-Post Sunday, August 19th. Read it each Sunday.

Order the Kansas City Journal-Post today from your agent or buy a copy from your druggist or newsdealer each week

1934

Gold
Death Takes a Holiday
House of Mystery
Chloe
Alraune
Black Moon
Vampyr
Maniac
The Man Who
Reclaimed His Head

Gold

Released Germany, 1934

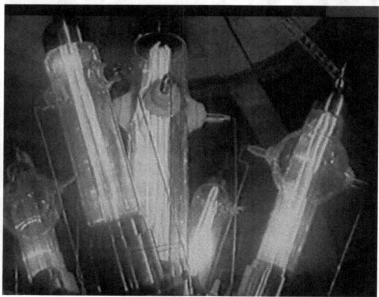

Ocean Travelers

Prominent passengers arriving today on the French liner Normandie include Max Reinhardt, producer; Brigitte Helm, German actress; Gilbert Miller, producer; Frederick H. Ecker, president of the Metropolitan Life Insurance Company, with Mrs. Ecker; Judge Julian W. Mack of the United States Circuit Court, with his family; Charles S. Dewey, former financial adviser to the Polish Government, with Mrs. Dewey; Senator Daniel O. Hastings of Delaware, James Byron Drew, justice of the Supreme Court of Pennsylvania. Others on the ship are Dwight Deere Wiman, Nancy Deere Wiman, W. Francklyn Paris, Beatrice Mathieu, Miss Carola Kip, Marcel Aubert, M. Chaulmeau, Pierre de Malglaive, Mrs. Daniel Sickles, Mrs. Roswell Eldredge, Mr. and Mrs. Commins Catherwood.

Michael Bohnen und Brigitte Helm

Vor kurzem schlendere ich durch die um die Mittagszeit scheinbar wie ausgestorben daliegenden Ateliers der Ufa. Plötzlich höre ich von weitem Musik. Durch Gänge und Winkel, über Treppen und Treppchen gehe ich den Tönen nach. Wo lande ich? In einem kleinen Eckchen der großen Tonfilmhalle, abgedeckt durch zufällig dort stehende Kulissen. Was sehe ich? Einen riesenhohen Gobelinsessel und darin eine blonde, schlanke Frau: Brigitte Helm. Sie hält die Augen geschlossen und den Kopf aufgestützt, leise wippt sie mit dem Fuß den Takt zum Tango. Vor ihr auf einer niedrigen Holzkiste steht ein Grammophon, ein Koffergrammophon ein Koffergrammophon. Sorgsam, um die Künstlerin nicht zu stören, legt ein junger Bühnenarbeiter immer wieder eine neue Platte auf, und so hält Frau Brigitte ihre Mittagsruhe.

Ich kuschle mich ganz leise auf eine andere Kiste, mache auch die Augen zu und döse.
— Frau Helm hat mich bemerkt und fängt an zu lachen. „Das nennt man aber nanauern! Das ist meine Musik. Was wollen Sie hier? Wenn Sie mich etwa interviewen wollen — damit haben Sie jetzt kein' Glück!"

„Aber, gnädige Frau, solche Gefühlsroheit trauen Sie mir doch hoffentlich nicht zu! Wie käme ich darauf?"

Brigitte Helm, Hans Albers und der „Gold"-Regisseur Karl Hartl   fot. Ufa

(Ich dachte an die Worte: Nutze den Tag!)" Aber es würde mich interessieren, mal so ganz privat ein bißchen über Ihre Rolle in diesem Film zu hören."

Ein leises Lächeln kann Frau Helm nicht unterdrücken und im Inneren denkt sie todsicher — na, mir ist es egal, was sie denkt. Die Hauptsache ist, sie antwortet.

„Ja, wissen Sie, diese Rolle, die ich da in ,Gold' spiele, ist für mich etwas ganz Neuartiges. Ich bin also, kurz gesagt, die sehr selbständige Tochter eines übermenschlich reichen Vaters. Ich bin von früher Jugend auf daran gewöhnt, mir mein Leben so einzurichten, wie es mir gefällt. Ich treibe meine Studien, huldige dem Sport in jeder Art, mache meine Reisen, wie es mir beliebt, und kümmere mich sonst um nichts in der Welt. Jetzt bin ich gerade von einer Weltreise zurückgekommen und finde im Hause meines Vaters Logierbesuch vor. Die Gäste meines Vaters interessieren mich sonst herzlich wenig, und ich gehe diesen Eindringlingen meistens aus dem Wege. Durch einen Zufall aber werde ich Ohrenzeuge eines Gesprächs, das mein Vater mit einem andern Herrn führt. Ich habe Veranlassung anzunehmen,

Hans ALBERS in

Gold

Regie: Karl Hartl   ASTOR FILM

The protean Sacha Guitry as author-director and (above) as four characters in "The Story of a Cheat," opening tomorrow night at the Fifth Avenue Playhouse.

ARTISTS IN EXILE

By PHILIP STERLING

WHEN Peter Lorre, cherubic little badman of the movies, heard that the Nazis had seized power, he exclaimed, "There is no room in Germany for two such villains as Adolf Hitler and me." Lorre's bitter jest was an epitaph for the international importance of the German film industry, whose impact had shocked even the self-satisfied Hollywood of the Nineteen Twenties into a new artistic alertness.

From 1922, when "The Cabinet of Dr. Caligari" zoomed impressionistically across the chaotic movie firmament, to 1930, when "Zwei Herzen im ¾ Takt" started a two-year run in New York, the German film was an artistic and commercial power which rivaled Hollywood. Today American importation of German celluloid is confined largely to neighborhood theatres subsisting on hyphenated patronage. Friends and foes of the Third Reich may be at violent variance in their explanations of the German film's decline, but one major cause is uncontroversial. Nazi "coordination" systematically has driven beyond its borders thousands of film workers in whose persons reside the talents which produced "Variety," "The Last Laugh," "The Beggars Opera," "The Blue Angel" and hundreds of other works which added power and substance to the body of film

Unity Pictures in London. Erik Charrell, director of the pre-Nazi "Congress Dances," now banned in Germany, directed "Caravan" for Twentieth Century-Fox in 1934 and the legitimate production, "White Horse Inn" in 1936. Henry Koster, taking refuge in Hollywood in 1936, discovered Deanna Durbin and turned her into an important financial asset for Universal, directing her in "Three Smart Girls" and "100 Men and a Girl."

* * *

Fritz Lang is one of Hollywood's name directors, but his reputation was international long before the German film acquired its present deep-sepia tint. Now on the Paramount payroll, Lang has directed "Fury," "You Only Live Once" and "You and Me." He has applied for American citizenship.

G. W. Pabst, Aryan, who directed Greta Garbo in her first important film, "Joyless Street," in 1925, is the creator of a long series of powerful German films, but he has not

was roundly reviled by the Nazi press when her American naturalization was announced. Cameraman Karl Freund, now an American, and Directors William Dieterle, Wilhelm Thiele and E. A. Dupont are regarded as exiles by their countrymen.

* * *

The UFA company, under whose auspices the heroic days of the German film were ushered in, not only established a brisk export trade to the United States but succeeded, for the first time since the war, in establishing the popularity of foreign stars on the American screen. When Emil Jannings burst like a beefy bombshell on American audiences in E. A. Dupont's "Variety" and repeated his triumph in "The Last Laugh," he set off a tidal wave of German stars which receded only with the advent of sound. Jannings, Pola Negri, Lillian Harvey and others, finding themselves unable to learn English, have been forced to content themselves with the limited audiences offered by the coordinated cameras of the Third Reich. Others, with more enduring qualities, have survived both sound and Hitler.

Elisabeth Bergner is now in London working with her husband and director, Paul Czinner. Since her proscription she has made "Catherine the Great," "As You Like It" and "Escape Me Never" in British studios. Mady Christians, Aryan, who added wistful charm to "The Waltz Dream," has worked since her expatriation in "Wicked Woman" (MGM), "Come and Get It" (United Artists) and "Seventh Heaven" (Twentieth Century-Fox). She has applied for American citizenship.

From 1922, when "The Cabinet of Dr. Caligari" zoomed impressionistically across the chaotic movie firmament, to 1930, when "Zwei Herzen im ¾ Takt" started a two-year run in New York, the German film was an artistic and commercial power which rivaled Hollywood. Today American importation of German celluloid is confined largely to neighborhood theatres subsisting on hyphenated patronage. Friends and foes of the Third Reich may be at violent variance in their explanations of the German film's decline, but one major cause is uncontroversial. Nazi "coordination" systematically has driven beyond its borders thousands of film workers in whose persons reside the talents which produced "Variety," "The Last Laugh," "The Beggars Opera," "The Blue Angel" and hundreds of other works which added power and substance to the body of film art.

* * *

Immediately after Jan. 30, 1933, thousands of film workers suddenly stigmatized as non-Aryan, or anti-Nazi, fled from Germany. Today the process is complete, and every important film center in the world has its colony of Germans, many of whom have achieved new successes, while others subsist in frugal obscurity, unable to adapt themselves to alien environments.

The list of film crafts represented by the exiles ranges from "grips" to producers, but the Third Reich never cut off its nose to spite its face so ruthlessly as in the case of its directors. The importance of the Hollywood director is his ability to follow and build upon an accepted pattern. The directors of Germany's Golden Age achieved greatness by their almost uniform gift for successful extension of cinematic idiom: Robert Wiene for the impressionism of "Dr. Caligari," G. W. Pabst for the development of the psychological film, Richard Oswald and Wilhelm Thiele for the advancement of the musical film before and after sound, Fritz Lang for his unique ability to suggest the weight of society on the individual and for his development of visual counterpoint and symbolism.

Kurt Bernhard, non-Aryan director whose "Rebel" and "The Last Company" were cited by Minister Joseph Goebbels as models for Nazi film makers, is now a managing director and producer for British

Germany, directed "Caravan" for Twentieth Century-Fox in 1934 and the legitimate production, "White Horse Inn" in 1936. Henry Koster, taking refuge in Hollywood in 1936, discovered Deanna Durbin and turned her into an important financial asset for Universal, directing her in "Three Smart Girls" and "100 Men and a Girl."

* * *

Fritz Lang is one of Hollywood's name directors, but his reputation was international long before the German film acquired its present deep-sepia tint. Now on the Paramount payroll, Lang has directed "Fury," "You Only Live Once" and "You and Me." He has applied for American citizenship.

G. W. Pabst, Aryan, who directed Greta Garbo in her first important film, "Joyless Street," in 1925, is the creator of a long series of powerful German films, but he has not flourished in the alien environments to which he was driven by Hitlerian coordination. The director of "Jeanne Ney," "The Beggars Opera," "Kameradschaft" and "Don Quixote" found no nutriment in Hollywood soil for his genius and after making "A Modern Hero" for Warner Brothers in 1934, he went to Paris, where he is now directing "Drame de Shanghai."

Joe May has become a Warner Brothers director. Max Ophuels who directed "Liebelei" and "The Bartered Bride," sought refuge first in the studios of Holland, then in Italy, where he directed Isa Miranda in "La Signora di Tutti." In Paris, he has just completed "Yoshivara" for Pathé. Léontine Sagan, the capable woman director who made "Maedchen in Uniform" is also in Paris. Hans Schwarz, director of "The Lie of Nina Petrovna" is freelancing somewhat precariously in Hollywood after several years in English films. Berthold Viertel is in London, as is Robert Wiene, director of "The Cabinet of Dr. Caligari." Richard Oswald is in Paris.

* * *

Also absent from Nazi screens are actors and directors who left the country before Hitler came to power, but who have abandoned all hope of returning to their native land while the regime lasts. Ernst Lubitsch applied for American citizenship after he was exiled by decree in 1933 because his parents were Polish Jews. Marlene Dietrich

ceded only with the advent of sound. Jannings, Pola Negri, Lillian Harvey and others, finding themselves unable to learn English, have been forced to content themselves with the limited audiences offered by the coordinated cameras of the Third Reich. Others, with more enduring qualities, have survived both sound and Hitler.

Elisabeth Bergner is now in London working with her husband and director, Paul Czinner. Since her proscription she has made "Catherine the Great," "As You Like It" and "Escape Me Never" in British studios. Mady Christians, Aryan, who added wistful charm to "The Waltz Dream," has worked since her expatriation in "Wicked Woman" (MGM), "Come and Get It" (United Artists) and "Seventh Heaven" (Twentieth Century-Fox). She has applied for American citizenship.

Brigitte Helm, the siren princess of "Metropolis" and the star of "The Lie of Nina Petrovna," has disappeared from the German screen. Guilty of "race defilement" because she married a Jew after the establishment of the Nazi regime, she has been working in Paris, where she made "Adieux les Beaux Jours" in 1934.

Fritz Kortner, veteran of the pre-Nazi stage and screen and best known for his role in the German film version of 'The Brothers Karamazov," shuttles currently between New York and Hollywood. In addition to writing a play with Dorothy Thompson, he has sold movie scripts on the West Coast and will appear in a Broadway role this season.

* * *

Unique is the case of Leo Reuss who went to Vienna, dyed his hair and beard and achieved such popularity that Nazi supporters held him up as a shining example of Nordic manhood. At that point he revealed his subterfuge, announced publicly that he was a Jew and sailed for the United States and a contract with MGM.

As with actors and directors, so with camera men, musicians, set designers, writers, producers. Sepp Allgeier, Hans Schneeberger and Gunther Krampf, all crack camera men, are in exile. Hans Eisler, Friedrich Hollander, Kurt Weill, Franz Waxman, Karol Rathaus and Mischa Spoliansky, ranking film musicians, are either in Hollywood or London.

Death Takes a Holiday

Released U.S. March 30, 1934

Never before in the history of the American photoplay has a picture been so excellently cast as is Paramount's superb "Death Takes a Holiday" which will open Wednesday at the Tivoli Theatre.

Fredric March in the starring role makes another bid for the best acting award of the Academy of Motion Picture Arts and Sciences which he won for his role in "Dr. Jekyll and Mr. Hyde" in 1932.

Evelyn Venable, formerly leading lady to Walter Hampden, is serenely beautiful in the featured feminine role.

Cast Is Superb

Sir Guy Standing, Kent Taylor, Katherine Alexander, Henry Travers, and G. P. Huntley, Jr., complete the cast of superb actors each of whom gives an outstanding performance in a play that demands was direct by Mitchell Leisen, youngest in experience of all Paramount directors. Yet it is a real achievement, ranking head and shoulders above the best in entertainment that the pictures have given us thus far. Leisen's only previous effort was on the beautiful "Cradle Song" which introduced Dorothea Wieck to American audiences. "Death Takes a Holiday," is based upon the play by Alberto Casella, adapted into English by Walter Ferris. The screen play was written by Maxwell Anderson and Gladys Lehman. It was photographed by Charles Lang.

Provocative Theme

Its frankly provocative theme concerns the problem of Death taking a three-day holiday that he may study life, learn why men love living and fear the eternal parting.

He comes to earth as a gay, dashing, romantic lover, enthusiastically taking part in all of life's pastimes and games. But nothing intrigues him.

Saves Love Till Last

He saves love till the last, until almost the end of his holiday. He finds no difficulty in meeting women who offer him love, but finds no love that is unselfish, eternal, until his holiday is almost over. Then, in a series of dramatic circumstances, he finds an enduring love, and, in the arms of a beautiful girl, learns all that is beautiful in life. But he, like any mortal man, must depart—and dreads the thought of leaving behind the life he found so rapturous.

"Death Takes a Holiday" is a picture you can't afford to miss. It is one of the great productions of the screen, rich in beauty and drama.

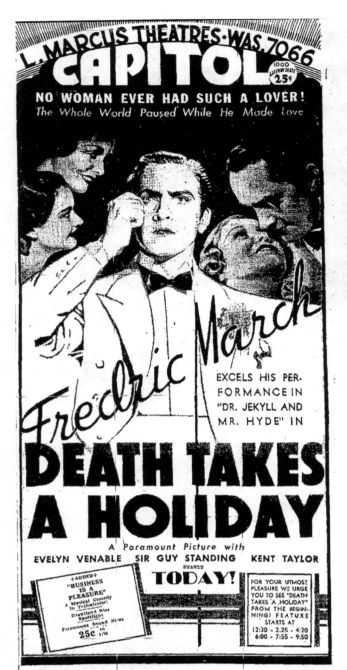

L. MARCUS THEATRES · WAS. 7066

CAPITOL
1000 BALCONY SEATS 25¢

NO WOMAN EVER HAD SUCH A LOVER!
The Whole World Paused While He Made Love

Fredric March

EXCELS HIS PER-
FORMANCE IN
"DR. JEKYLL AND
MR. HYDE" IN

DEATH TAKES A HOLIDAY

A Paramount Picture with
EVELYN VENABLE · **SIR GUY STANDING** · **KENT TAYLOR**

STARTS **TODAY!**

+ADDED+
"BUSINESS
IS A
PLEASURE"
A Musical Comedy
In Technicolor!
Grantland Rice
Spotlight
Paramount Sound News
25¢ to 1:14

FOR YOUR UTMOST
PLEASURE WE URGE
YOU TO SEE "DEATH
TAKES A HOLIDAY"
FROM THE BEGIN-
NING! FEATURE
STARTS AT
12:30 - 2:25 - 4:20
6:00 - 7:55 - 9:50

Fredric MARCH in **"DEATH TAKES A HOLIDAY"** — EVELYN VENABLE, SIR GUY STANDING and KENT TAYLOR. *A Paramount Picture*

DEATH TAKES A HOLIDAY

Frederic March makes his sec-
ond bid for the Academy of
Motion Picture Arts and Sciences
acting award with his role in
"Death Takes a Holiday," coming
Wednesday to the Tivoli Theatre.

"DEATH TAKES A HOLIDAY" OPENS TONIGHT AT THE INDIANA AND HOOSIER FOR TWO DAYS

DEATH TAKES A HOLIDAY

The well-mounted Paramount
production of "Death Takes a Holiday," opens today at the Indiana
and Hoosier theaters to an appre-
ciative audience that obviously ap-
plauded one of the finest pictures
ever produced in America.

Admirably cast with Frederic
March and Evelyn Venable in leading roles, expertly directed by Director Mitchell Leisen, and utiliz-
ing superb presentation by such capable craftsmen as Rodwell Anderson, Felmar Ellis Street, and Gloria Lehman. "Death Takes a Holiday" easily all of the praise thus
far centered upon it.

The picture is based upon the fa-
mous drama of similar Italian by
Alberto Casella, adapted to English by
Walter Ferris. The screen play relates

all of the charm and beauty of the
stage production, and one can detect
the matchless writing of Maxwell Anderson in several well-celebrated beautiful love scenes.

It was on a battlefield that Alberto Casella first conceived just what
would happen if Death should take
a holiday from his eternal task, and
come to the world for a social holiday. The translation of that conception idea into the photoplay was an
ambitious task, but one which Paramount has proudly accomplished.

The picture tells how this mysterious form, becomes, for a three-day
holiday, a gay, dashing romantic lover.
He comes to a house party, conceal-
ing his identity from every one, but
the host, who introduces him as a
friend.

110

Fredric March in "DEATH TAKES A HOLIDAY" with Evelyn Venable, Sir Guy Standing and Kent Taylor
A Paramount Picture

FREDRIC MARCH

döden tar semester

EVELYN VENABLE
SIR GUY STANDING
KENT TAYLOR

["DEATH TAKES A HOLIDAY"]
REGI: MITCHELL LEISEN

EN PARAMOUNTFILM

Friday and Saturday

Fredric March

equals his performance of
'Dr. Jekyll & Mr. Hyde' in

"Death Takes A Holiday"

A Paramount Picture with
EVELYN VENABLE

ALL THE CRITICES RAVED ABOUT IT—AND YOU WILL TOO. FOR THREE DAYS ONLY!

Dangerous! . . . Fascinating! A lover tasting the joys of mortal emotion for the first time . . . while the world stood still and waited for it to be over!

FREDRIC MARCH

Equals his performance of 'DR. JEKYLL AND MR. HYDE' . . . in

"DEATH TAKES A HOLIDAY"

111

House of Mystery

Released U.S. March 30, 1934

An unseen and mysterious monster
that strikes in the dark—a weird
Hindu curse that descends upon all
who touch the jewels of Kali—murder
after murder—these are just a few of
the ingredients of "The House of
Mystery," the thrilling murder mystery.

With a cast headed by Ed Lowry,
nationally famous master of ceremonies, Verna Hillie, national beauty
contest winner, and Brandon Hurst,
John Sheehan and Joyzelle, famous
stage and screen dancer, "The House
of Mystery" is an intriguing combination of mystery and comedy with refreshing moments of romance.

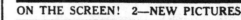

"HOUSE OF MYSTERY"

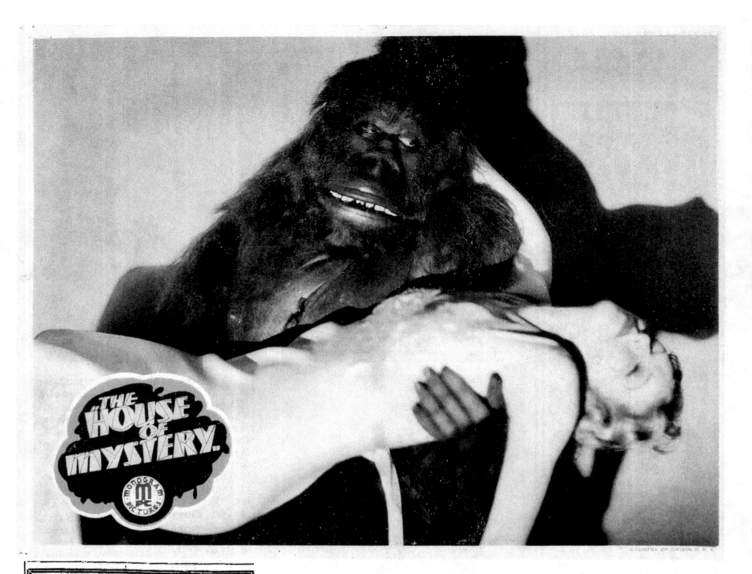

"Spook Party" Saturday Night

Theatergoers in search of the unusual will be attracted by Syko's "Spook Party," to be presented at the Rivoli theater in a midnight show Saturday. The doors will open at 11 p. m. and the show will start at 11:30.

At that time the feature picture, "The House of Mystery," featuring Ed Lowry, Verna Hillie and Lya Joy, will be shown.

Then the "Spook Party" will start in earnest with ghostly writings, table rapping, talking skulls, and a ghost which will roam out over the audience, according to the management.

Children should be left at home, the Rivoli advises La Crosse folk planning to attend.

Chloe

Released U.S. April 1, 1934

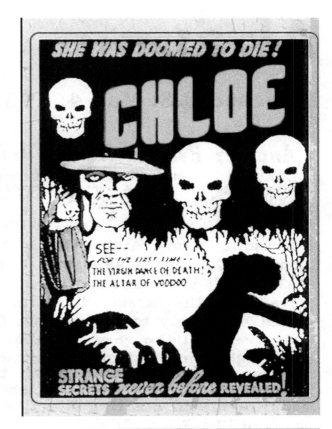

At the Theaters

Tonight

Fitchburg—"Mrs. Wiggs of the Cabbage Patch."

Strand—"Viva Villa" and "Social Register."

Universal—"His Greatest Gamble" and "Forgotten Men."

Shea's—"Gambling."

Cumings—"The Great Flirtation" and "Chloe Love Is Calling You."

Lyric—"Here Comes the Navy" and "City Park."

7L-8609   Chloe   Code SERBUR
Featuring Olive Borden and Mollie O'Day.

A beautiful modern drama of the Southland, directed by Marshall Neilan, and with superb musical accompaniment by Erno Rapee, featuring Olive Borden as Chloe, the supposed child of a colored mammy who practiced the Voodoo art to avenge the death of her husband.

But it transpires that Chloe, while a baby girl, had been stolen by Mandy, the Voodoo woman, after her own child had drowned. When her father discovers that Chloe is his long lost daughter, Betty Ann, the jealous Voodoo woman makes an unsuccessful attempt upon her life. The weird woodland night spectacle of the fanatical Voodoo rites will hold every spectator breathless. Beautiful photography and exquisite musical background. *56 min.*

Alraune

Released U.S. May 4, 1934

Another Brigitte Helm Film.

ALRAUNE, a dialogue film in German, with Brigitte Helm, Albert Bassermann, Agnes Straub, Harald Paulsen, Kaethe Haack and Bernhardt Goetzke; directed by Richard Oswald; an UFA production.

Persons unacquainted with the popular German novel upon which "Alraune," the current film at the Seventy-ninth Street Theatre, is based are likely to be kept on the qui vive until the very last reel of this highly interesting production. And even those familiar with the tale of the German scientist whose experiments in creating life finally led him to try his talent upon a human being no doubt will find considerable satisfaction in watching the action develop upon the screen.

Brigitte Helm, the versatile German actress, is the centre of the story, first as a dissolute cabaret entertainer and later as the charming 17-year-old result of the "greatest experiment." Her work is up to the high standard she has established in several foreign language pictures that have reached New York. Albert Bassermann, one of Germany's best veteran actors, is excellent as the scientist whose efforts to emulate the wonder-workers of the ancient days bring so much trouble upon nearly all involved in the affair, regardless of their innocence or guilt. The support is first class.

The name of the film is German for alruna, a plant the roots of which were credited by the early Teutons with magic properties. Although this picture was made almost four years ago, the sound reproduction and photography are clear. The direction is competent.

H. T. S.

Brigitte Helm
in dem Tonfilm
„Alraune"

„Ross" Verlag   Reproduction verboten

116

BRIGITTE HELM IN

Alraune

DEM MONUMENTALFILM NACH HANNS HEINZ EWERS

Brigitte Helm in:

Alraune

Beamten den Geheimrat verhaften wollen, finden sie — einen Toten. Sterbend noch hat er in teuflischer Voraussicht Frank Braun zum Vormund Alraunes bestellt, die seine Erbin ist. Nun will Frank, wer Vormund Alraunes ist, aber von ihr lassen, er zerstückelt die Sünde. In reiner Liebe ist es so stark, daß der Alraune erlöschen zu sein. Da erfährt das Mädchen der Frank ihrer Geburt. Ihr Entschluß steht fest. Wenn niemand ergründe gehen sah, will sie als er sein, nicht der Geheime. Schimmernd ziehen die Wogen des Flusses zum Meere. Eine Schuld wurde gesühnt, ein Fluch ausgelöscht.

urteilten Raub-
mörder und — ein
Weib! — Im Konzertcafé Ge-
Südstern zeigt Frank dem Geheimrat und seinem Assistenten das
Weib, Alma, die Dirne, die allabendlich
ihr Couplet „Komm, küß mich nochmal"
halb betrunken grölt. — Das Experiment
geht vor sich, die Fürstin assistiert. Sterbend gibt Alma einem Mädchen das Leben:
Alraune. — Die Jahre vergehen. Alraune
ist erwachsen, ahnungslos wer sie ist,
bildschön, aber von geheimnisvoll ver-
derblichem Reiz. Wer ihr verfällt, ist
verloren. Raspe, der Chauffeur, vermag
sich ebensowenig zu retten wie Wölf-
chen, der Sohn Petersens, der bei der
Verlobung der Tochter der Fürstin
tödlich verunglückt. — Schaudernd
wehrt sich ten Brinken gegen den
magischen, sinnbetörenden Reiz Alraunes. Immer mehr erliegt er der

ALRAUNE

„Ich weiß, warum die Schneider nähen, ich weiß, warum Maschinen gehen, Ich weiß, warum sich seinen Schädel zerbricht der Astronom im Bau — Alles wegen einem kleinen Mädel, alles wegen einer süßen Frau". — Jauchzend singen die Studenten den Refrain des Liedes, das Frank Braun am Klavier hämmert. Die Stimmung wird immer übermütiger, er muß doch noch seinem Onkel, dem berühmten Geheimrat ten Brinken, zum Geburtstag gratulieren. Das Wort ten Brinken zündet sofort, und die ganze angeheiterte Studentenschar macht sich unter Franks Führung auf zur Villa des Geheimrats. — Der ahnt noch nichts von seinem Glück. In seinem Arbeitszimmer steht die Fürstin Wolkonski und dankt für einen erwiesenen Dienst. Die Fürstin hatte sich so sehr ein Kind gewünscht, und ten Brinken, der skrupellose Zyniker, hatte Rat gewußt. Ein kleines Mädchen, die eben geborene Tochter Petersens, des Assistenten des Geheimrats, wurde einfach untergeschoben. Ein Scheck mit vielen Nullen ist der Lohn. Aber vergeblich fordert gleich darauf Petersen seinen Anteil. Ein eisiger Blick ten Brinkens, der das Geld für seine wissenschaftlichen Experi- mente braucht. — Während noch die Fürstin mit ten Brinkens Anwalt Manasse über die Versuche mit der künstlichen Befruchtung von Ratten plaudert, klingt von der Straße her der Lärm der Studenten, die dem Geheimrat eine Ovation bringen.

Black Moon

Out of the inferno of tropic madness comes the weirdest romance of our time!

Jack HOLT in BLACK MOON with FAY WRAY
Dorothy Burgess
From the Cosmopolitan Magazine novel by Clements Ripley
—PLUS—
Screen Souvenir
Flying Hockey
With
Grantland Rice
TODAY Mon. - Tues. QUEEN

LOVE BATTLING AGAINST THE SORCERY OF THE JUNGLE!

JACK HOLT in "BLACK MOON"
with FAY WRAY DOROTHY BURGESS
From the Cosmopolitan Magazine novel by Clements Ripley
Directed by ROY WILLIAM NEILL
A COLUMBIA PICTURE

"BLACK MOON"

Jungle drums beating . . . voodoo crazed blacks in an orgy of blood sacrifice . . . a man gazes horror-stricken at the scene . . . and sees . . . the leader of the savages is his wife!

There you have a sketchy idea of the thrills and suspense that await you in Jack Holt's new picture coming to the State tomorrow "Black Moon" delves into the weird religious practices of a tribe of black people.

The story tells of a white woman, the wife of Jack Holt, who returns to an island where she was born and becomes high priestess of the voodoo cult that still engages in blood sacrifices. Holt discovers his wife's dual personality just in time to prevent her from sacrificing their own child on the voodoo altar.

Dorothy Burgess and Fay Wray have the featured supporting roles, Miss Burgess playing the part of the wife. Little Cora Sue Collins appears as the daughter whose life is endangered by her mother's queer mania.

"Black Moon" reaches a high pitch of tension and suspense and maintains its speed and action at all times.

BLACK MOON

From the Cosmopolitan Magazine serial by Clements Ripley

Starring

JACK HOLT

A daring young sportsman and a beautiful girl—caught in the dark meshes of jungle superstition and danger—discover their love for each other in a blinding flash—in their hour of greatest need fate takes a hand. A vivid drama—flaming with romance—throbbing with thrills—full of the magic, tense mystery of the unknown!

Savage Band Leader Once Society Lass

Story For 'Black Moon' Cast In Background Of Voodooism

With Jack Holt in the stellar role a vividly dramatic one, Columbia's "Black Moon" comes to the Queen Theater today, Monday and Tuesday. "Black Moon" unfolds for the most part in Haiti, against the mystic background of voodooism. The story involves a white girl who rips the garments of civilization from her body and the thin veneer of convention from her soul to rule a savage band of blacks.

"Black Moon", which is an adaptation of Clement Ripley's Cosmopolitan magazine novelette, affords Holt one of the most colorful roles of his long career. As a staid New York business man, Holt learns that to his wife the beat of tomtoms was stronger than the love which beat in her heart. It enslaved her—overpowered her. Her flight to her native land, Haiti, to rule a black kingdom, and Holt's endeavors to fight his wife's strange actions, lead to a startling climax.

Holt, who has gained in popularity with each new film, was recently seen in "Whirlpool", "Master of Men", "Man Against Woman" and "The Woman I Stole."

Beautiful Fay Wray and Dorothy Burgess, fiery and raven-haired, are seen in Holt's support. Miss Burgess, is cast in the role of the wife, who, secretly, is the leader of a voodoo cult. Fay Wray has leaped to startling popularity in the last two years. Cast for a time only in "horror" roles, such as in "King Kong" she finally escaped from them in "Ann Carver's Profession." Other dramatic roles followed: "Once to Eevery Woman", "Viva Villa", "One Sunday Afternoon" and "The Bowery."

Miss Burgess, too, has come into her own recently. Her dark beauty "typed" her for a time in limited roles because of her outstanding characterization of a Latin in "Old Arizona". Recently, however, her fine acting took her out of the "type" class. Her latest pictures are "Modern Hero", "Circus Clown" and "Mr. Sweeney's Friend." With "Black Moon", this sterling young actress attains new heights.

The supporting cast includes Cora Sue Collins, the child who attained fame in "Queen Christina", Arnold Korff, Clarence Muse, Eleanore Wesselhoeft, Madame Sul-te-wan, Lawrence Criner and Lumsden Hare. Roy William Neill directed.

200 Colored Play in "Black Moon"

Two hundred and fifty colored people were taught voodoo dance routines during the making of the newest Jack Holt starring film produced by Columbia, "Black Moon," showing at the Carey Theatre next week.

The colored performers were instructed in the mysterious and supposedly devil-placating routines by Max Scheck, noted dance director, and Don Taylor, internationally known explorer, zoologist and ethnologist, who was engaged as technical director on the production.

Dorothy Burgess, who with Fay Wray is cast opposite Jack Holt, was taught a wild African dance which she is called upon to perform in the sequence where she is seen as the high priestess of a wild Haitian tribe of hill-men who still retain human sacrifice as part of their voodoo ritual.

Under instruction from Taylor, who spent many months in the hill country of Haiti disguised as a native, studying voodoo mysteries and the barbaric religious rites, Scheck instructed the players in the dances.

Outside of a few hardy explorers who have risked their lives in adventure, scarcely a handful of people have ever witnessed the originals of these pre-sacrifice dances such as will be seen in this production.

The story of "Black Moon" is a screen adaptation of the Clements Ripley Cosmopolitan magazine novelette, "Haiti Moon." The story was adapted to the screen by Wells Root.

In addition to Miss Wray and Miss Burgess, the supporting cast includes little Cora Sue Collins; Arnold Korff and the noted colored performer, Clarence Muse. Roy William Neill directed.

Jungle Madness!
Tropic Love!

JACK HOLT in

BLACK MOON

FAY WRAY   DOROTHY BURGESS

From the Cosmopolitan Magazine novel by CLEMENTS RIPLEY........

Directed by ROY WILLIAM NEILL.. a Columbia picture...

COLUMBIA PICTURES

NEWEST HOLT FILM IS THRILL-PACKED

DIXIE OFFERS RED-BLOODED ACTOR IN "BLACK MOON," A VOODOO STORY.

Laid against a background of the little known and mysterious voodoo worship of the West Indian Islands, Jack Holt's latest Columbia production, "Black Moon," opening today at the Dixie No. 1 Theater, is an exceptionally interesting picture.

The story is one of the strangest and most fascinating that this reviewer has seen in a long time. It presents Holt in one of the most dramatic roles of his career. With two leading ladies, Fay Wray and Dorothy Burgess, an excellent supporting cast, and the fine story by Clements Ripley, "Black Moon" can be chalked up as worthwhile entertainment.

Briefly the story tells of Stephen Lane, wealthy New Yorker, whose wife has been cold and distant, and pining for a visit to her childhood home, an island in the West Indies. She is overcome with joy when her husband consents to her spending a few months there.

With her child and her secretary, Gail, she visits the island. Within a few weeks Lane receives a radiogram from Gail, saying that there is something mysterious and menacing threatening them all. Lane hurries to the island.

He finds that his wife's behavior has been very strange. His child's nurse has been murdered, as has the wireless operator who has summoned him to the island. He follows his wife when she creeps out of the house at night, and discovers the horrid truth: that his wife

THE 15¢

LAST DAY GEORGE RAFT in BOLERO ALSO LITTLE WOMEN WITH KATHARINE HEPBURN

FRIDAY & SATURDAY MARGARET SULLAVAN in LITTLE MAN WHAT NOW? ALSO JACK HOLT in BLACK MOON

Jack HOLT FAY WRAY in "BLACK MOON"
A COLUMBIA PICTURE

Out of the inferno of tropic madness comes the weirdest romance of our time!

Jack HOLT in BLACK MOON
with FAY WRAY
Dorothy Burgess

Now Playing

DIXIE No. 1

PLUS SELECTED SHORT SUB

Vampyr

Released U.S. August 14, 1934

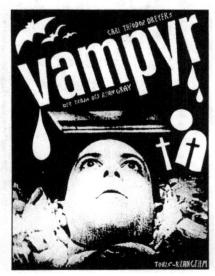

Maniac

Released U.S. September 11, 1934

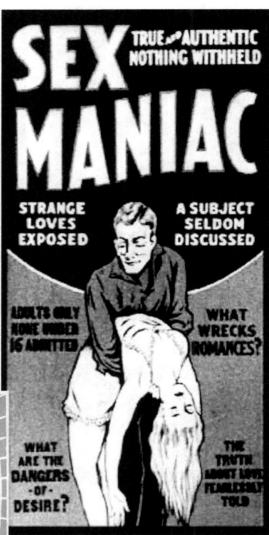

126

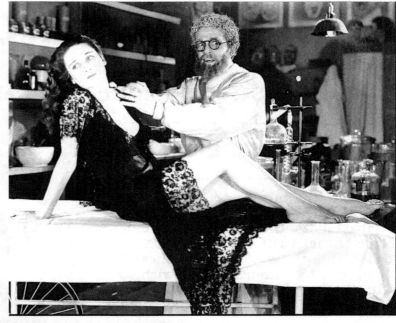

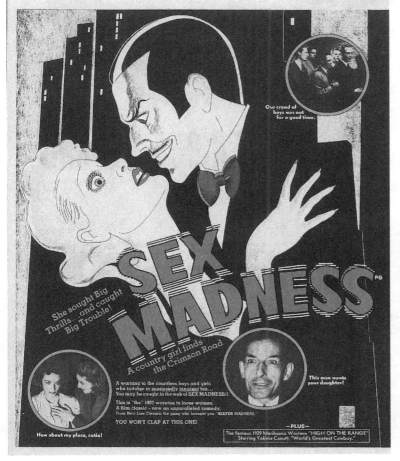

SEX MADNESS PG

She sought Big Thrills...and caught Big Trouble!

Our crowd of boys was out for a good time.

A country girl finds the Crimson Road

A warning to the countless boys and girls who indulge in supposedly innocent fun... You may be caught in the web of SEX MADNESS!!

This is "the" 1937 warning to loose women. A film classic—now an unparalleled comedy. From New Line Cinema, the gang who brought you "REEFER MADNESS."

YOU WON'T CLAP AT THIS ONE!

This man wants your daughter!

How about my place, cutie!

—PLUS—

The famous 1929 Marihuana Western "HIGH ON THE RANGE" Starring Yakima Canutt, "World's Greatest Cowboy."

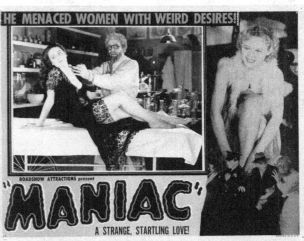

HE MENACED WOMEN WITH WEIRD DESIRES!

ROADSHOW ATTRACTIONS present

"MANIAC"

A STRANGE, STARTLING LOVE!

The Return of Chandu

12-Chapter Serial, First Chapter Released U.S. October 1, 1934

Ambassador

Tango, the new screeno game has caught the popular fancy at the Ambassador theatre on Division street near Austin, and each Tuesday evening at 9 o'clock the theatre is packed by hundreds who wish to win their share of fifty dollars in cash prizes and the grand door prize.

Tonight (Thursday) and Friday, another big three feature program is offered including the mystery picture, "The Perfect Clue,", Sally Blane in "City Park," and Kermit Maynard in "Frontier."

Saturday, "Charlie Chan in Paris" with Warner Oland and Mary Brian is the main picture, with chapter five of Ken Maynard in "Mystery Mountain" and a variety of shorts. Beginning this coming Saturday night has been slated as Amateur Night, with Sam Herman as master of ceremonies. Cash prizes are offered the winners and plenty of entertainment and fun is promised. Ossie's Litle German band, with novelty German music is also an added attraction.

A double feature is advertised for Sunday and Monday. The great adventure picture, "Lives of a Bengal Lancer," with Gray Cooper, Katheryn Burke, supported by a big cast, and Laurel and Hardy in "Live Ghosts." Also latest chapter of "Return of Chandu."

On Tuesday and Wednesday, Clark Gable, Joan Crawford and Robert Montgomery are cast in "Forsaking All Others."

SOL LESSER *presents*

BELA LUGOSI *in*

"THE RETURN OF CHANDU"

(THE MAGICIAN)

COUNTRY OF ORIGIN U.S.A.

EPISODE No. 6
CHANDU'S FALSE STEP

Distributed by PRINCIPAL DISTRIBUTING CORP.

WARNER BROS.
PLAZA
——Last Two Days——
Loretta Young
Ronald Colman
"BULLDOG DRUMMOND
STRIKES BACK"

Bela   Maria
Lugosi   Alba
"THE RETURN OF CHANDU"

SUNDAY
Paul Lukas
"The Casino Murder Case"

James Cagney
"THE ST. LOUIS KID"

132

TODAY 1 TO 11 P.M.

Fearless Riding, Desperate Fights, Blazing Guns.. A Tornado of Action

NOAH BEERY, Jr. in **"FIVE BAD MEN"**

Featuring
BILL PATTON · BUFFALO BILL, Jr.
WALLY WALES · ART MIX
PETE MORRISON

Directed by CLIFFORD S. SMITH

—EXTRA—
Chapter No. 11
"RETURN OF CHANDU"
and Cartoon

OPERA HOUSE
★

Brieviews

About the Talking Pictures and Those Who Are In Them At Local Theaters.

AT WARNER'S PLAZA

"THE RETURN OF CHANDU"—This film presentation of Oriental hocus-pocus is interesting, with Bela Lugosi aptly depicting the character of Chandu.

Lugosi returns from the Orient to California, where Princess Nadji (Maria Alba) is in grave danger from the cohorts of Vindhyan (Lucien Prival), who would make a sacrifice of the princess. Interesting captures of the princess and escapes engineered by Lugosi form the nucleus of the flicker, featured by the eternal conflict of two brands of black magic, that of Lugosi and Vindhyan, and of these two themselves. Oriental drums and strange musical notes accompany, along with appropriate disappearances by Lugosi in the face of danger after rubbing his mystic ring. Poison darts, drugged flowers and hypotism add to the melodrama.

"BULLDOG DRUMMOND STRIKES BACK" — Second-run featuring Ronald Colman with Loretta Young and Warner Oland. Colman's dramatic difficulties start when he becomes lost in a London fog, strays into a deserted house and finds a murdered man.

The program changes Sunday. It also includes a water rodeo short with Ted Husing, and a cartoon. The bill is satisfactory melodrama.—R. F. B.

Loew's RICHMOND

TODAY and WED.!

ANN HARDING

in the story of a wife who dared to ask herself, "What is fidelity?"

"THE FOUNTAIN"

From Charles Morgan's celebrated novel

with

**BRIAN AHERNE
PAUL LUKAS
JEAN HERSHOLT**

Also:
"THE RETURN OF CHANDU"
(THE MAGICIAN)

STARTS THURS.!

THE "SCREAM" VERSION OF THE LAUGH HIT OF THE STAGE!
"BY YOUR LEAVE"
WITH
**FRANK MORGAN
GENEVIEVE TOBIN**

SOL LESSER Presents
Bela LUGOSI in
THE RETURN OF CHANDU
(THE MAGICIAN)
with **MARIA ALBA**

Directed by RAY TAYLOR

EPISODE No. 12

THE KNIFE DESCENDS

Distributed by PRINCIPAL DISTRIBUTING CORP.

TODAY 1 TO 11 P.M.

COURAGE of the NORTH

with
John Preston as
MORTON OF THE MOUNTIE
and
William Desmond
Tom London
June Love
White Feather

DYNAMITE
CAPTAIN

Starts **MONDAY**
Louisa May Alcott's
'LITTLE MEN'

ADDED!
"Return of Chandu"
chapter no. 7
POPEYE CARTOON

WARNER BROS.
OPERA HOUSE
ALL SEATS 15c TILL 6 P.M.

MATINEE 2 P. M.—10c TO ALL
3 SHOWS TONITE START 5.45 P. M.
TODAY AND TOMORROW

STRAND

Joseph M. Schenck presents
WALLACE BEERY
in DARRYL F. ZANUCK'S PRODUCTION
THE MIGHTY BARNUM
ADOLPHE MENJOU · VIRGINIA BRUCE

APOLLO KAY FRANCIS—WARREN WILLIAM in "DR. MONICA"
TODAY—AND THE 7TH CHAPTER "RETURN OF CHANDU"
EVENINGS, 10c & 15c

SOL LESSER Presents
BELA LUGOSI in
The RETURN of CHANDU
(THE MAGICIAN)
WITH MARIA ALBA
DIRECTED BY RAY TAYLOR

THE LONG AWAITED THRILL IS HERE! "CHANDU" The Master of Magic and Thrills in a new series of nerve-tingling adventures, baffling mystery and necromancy. YOU OWE YOURSELF A THRILL! "CHANDU" WILL PAY YOU A HUNDREDFOLD!

A PRINCIPAL PICTURE

SOL LESSER Presents
BELA LUGOSI in
THE RETURN OF CHANDU
(THE MAGICIAN)
EPISODE No. 12
THE KNIFE DESCENDS
Distributed by PRINCIPAL DISTRIBUTING CORP.

PHIL S. LEWIS Presents

BELA LUGOSI

in CHANDU on the MAGIC ISLAND

SOL LESSER presents

BELA LUGOSI with MARIA ALBA in

CHANDU ON THE MAGIC ISLAND

DIRECTED BY RAY TAYLOR

DISTRIBUTED BY
PRINCIPAL PICTURES CORPORATION

SOL LESSER presents

BELA LUGOSI in

CHANDU ON THE MAGIC ISLAND

Distributed by PRINCIPAL DISTRIBUTING CORP

FLASH

ACCESSORIES TO SELL YOUR SHOW

SIX SHEET

THREE SHEET

ONE SHEET

SET OF TWO
22 x 28 LOBBY
DISPLAYS
IN FULL COLOR

SET OF EIGHT
11 x 14 LOBBY
DISPLAYS
IN FULL COLOR

SET OF THIRTY
8 x 10 STILLS

SPECIAL TRAILER $10.00
Order from
PRINCIPAL DISTRIBUTING CORP.
1501 Broadway, New York City

COLORED SLIDE
AVAILABLE

ORDER ALL CUTS
AND MATS BY
NUMBER

CATCHLINES

SEE — The Master Magician Chandu in new breath-taking adventures.

Chandu pits his skill and magic against the black art of the monstrous Cat-men.

The magic of Chandu against the Black Art of Vistra Master Magician of the Cat Worshippers.

SEE — Chandu in his death-defying struggle with the Sacred Tiger.

SEE — Chandu in his breath-taking escape from the torture chamber.

SEE — Chandu use the power of invisibility to rescue the helpless victim from the sacrificial blade.

SEE — Chandu combat the Monstrous Cat Men, the Evil Vistra, and escape from the Cove of the Crushing Rock.

SEE — Chandu pierce the invisible barrier of Black Magic!

**WEIRD! MYSTERIOUS! BAFFLING!
More Exciting and Thrilling Than Ever!**

PRINCIPAL DISTRIBUTING CORPORATION
Paramount Building, 1501 Broadway, New York City

Foreign Distributor—British & Continental
Trading Co., Inc., 1540 Broadway, N. Y.

Cable Address — "Bernsfilm"

The Man Who Reclamied His Head
Released U.S. December 24, 1934

The Phantom Mystery Show
WEIRD... EERIE... SPELLBINDING!

THE MAN WHO RECLAIMED HIS HEAD

Starring

Claude RAINS

Joan BENNETT

Lionel ATWILL

A *Rexford Picture*
Released by
FILM CLASSICS, INC.

"THE INVISIBLE MAN" becomes "The Man Who Reclaimed His Head."

Quite a feat—but when Claude Rains is the man, anything is possible. He emerges from invisibility in a fashion that will cause every lover of drama to insist that this actor rates as one of the screen's top-notch artists.

"The Man Who Reclaimed His Head" qualifies as the highest type of dramatic technique, and in the unfoldment of story and plot is the season's finest psychological study of soul in mental torment. Rains endows the character with a feeling and intensity that vitalizes every thought and move and distinguishes himself in a role that might easily have been bungled.

Although highly dramatic and almost devoid of lightness, the picture has been so expertly handled by cast, director and authors that it provides entertaining fare for any but juvenile audiences. The star alone makes the production a noteworthy event, and he finds most capable support in Lionel Atwill, Joan Bennett and Baby Jane, to mention only the principals.

Briefly, Rains is a French political journalist with one of the finest and most penetrating minds in France. Financial returns mean less to him than retaining his identity as an individual.

When a newspaper publisher (Atwill), ambitious for power, offers him a large sum of money for his editorials, to be published under the publisher's name, Rains consents to the proposition, against his will, knowing that his wife (Miss Bennett) yearns for the luxuries and pleasures of life.

In so disposing of his brain to the publisher—his head, as it were—the full significance of the title is made clear. In a fit of temporary insanity, he reclaims his head—in the goriest manner imaginable!

Pretty sordid stuff, you might say, away over the heads of the theater-going public. In the telling, the story does sound beyond the realm of reason. On the screen, it is marked by extraordinary interest; it grips you and it holds you.

The man who made such a treat for you in "The Invisible Man"—even though you saw his face only once—duplicates his previous success. Thoroughly at home in dramatic characters and particularly in spectacular situations, he moulds the part with a master's hand. The screen needs more actors of Rains' caliber.

Both Miss Bennett and Atwill contribute splendid performances, the latter in particular offering a characterization of rugged strength. As the publisher who uses Rains for his own aims and ambitions, and finally betrays him, he turns out what many will declare to be his outstanding screen portrayal. Certainly his work carries every ounce that could be injected into the part.

Miss Bennett's interpretation is tempered with laudable restraint. She engages the interest, as does Baby Jane, too, to a surprising degree. This child is rapidly assuming an important place on the screen and unquestionably possesses talents far beyond the average child actress of her age.

Others to be commended for their acting include Henry O'Neill, Henry Armetta, Gilbert Emery and Bessie Barriscale.

At the Ritz

Residents of Oak Park and vicinity who are devotees of vaudeville and stage shows will find entertainment to their liking in the stage and vaudeville show offered at the Ritz theatre, on Roosevelt road near Ridgeland, every Sunday matinee and night.

This showhouse also offers the best available programs in pictures. Tonight (Thursday), for the first time in this vicinity will be shown the "Man Who Reclaimed His Head," featuring Claude Rains and Joan Bennett, which is a dramatic picture, which gives Claude Rains the opportunity for portraying one of his best character roles.

Friday and Saturday, all the family will enjoy Jackie Cooper in "Peck's Bad Boy."

Sunday and Monday, Dick Powell has the lead in "Happiness Ahead," also the regular stage and vaudeville show Sunday, matinee and night.

"What Every Woman Knows," with Helen Hayes in the title role, will be shown Tuesday and Wednesday.

Rialto 5 till 6:30

LORETTA YOUNG and CARY GRANT in

BORN TO BE BAD

—2nd Feature—
"THE MAN WHO RECLAIMED HIS HEAD"
JOAN BENNETT   CLAUDE RAINS

CLAUDE RAINS
("THE INVISIBLE MAN")
JOAN BENNETT
LIONEL ATWILL

BABY JANE
HENRY O'NEILL
HENRY ARMETTA
LLOYD HUGHES
BESSIE BARRISCALE
CAROL COOMBE

in
The MAN WHO RECLAIMED HIS HEAD

from the exciting play by JEAN BART
Directed by EDWARD LUDWIG
Produced by CARL LAEMMLE Jr.
Presented by CARL LAEMMLE

A UNIVERSAL PICTURE

Claude RAINS
Joan BENNETT

MANNEN SOM SÅLDE SITT HUVUD
En UNIVERSAL film

Thursday, Friday and Saturday—A timely story is told by "The Man Who Reclaimed His Head," on the double feature bill. It exposes the activities of the international munitions manufacturers in fomenting war. Claude Rains, Joan Bennett and Lionel Atwill head the cast. The story presents Rains as a plodding writer, finally achieving prosperity when he writes articles against war which appear under Atwill's name in his "Pacifist Journal." Atwill secretly works with the munitions makers. On the declaration of war Rains is sent to the front. The publisher's influence keeps the war-hating soldier in the trenches, while he himself proceeds to a conquest of the writer's wife. The climax is said to be a thrilling one. Beautiful voices, stirring music and Laurel and Hardy's comedy make "Babes in Toyland," the other feature on the bill, the M-G-M production of Victor Herbert's delightful operetta, an entertaining film. The characters move through gorgeous sets and present a story interesting to both grown-ups and youngsters. Highlights are the rendition of "March of the Toys," "Castle in Spain" and "Go to Sleep, Slumber Deep." Charlotte Henry is Bo-Peep. Henry Kleinbach, Felix Knight, Atwater Kent radio finalist, and Virginia Karns, are in the cast.

Claude Rains Does Interesting Character as 'Man Who Reclaimed His Head'

By WOOD SOANES

PSYCHOLOGICAL drama seems to be the most difficult hurdle that Hollywood has to leap and yet it continues to try, as witness "The Man Who Reclaimed His Head" at the Roxie with Claude Rains in the stellar role.

In this case the failure, or the lack of absolute success to be precise, lies not so much with the producer as with the author and the star. There is too much indecision about the story, too much determination to get from drama of the mind to drama of the emotions. Yet despite the fact that "The Man Who Reclaimed His Head" does not achieve what it sets about, it does make its presence felt as entertainment on a double bill and it does add laurels to the crown of Rains. I cannot yet subscribe to the theory that he is a great actor, but he is an interesting one.

In "The Man Who Reclaimed His Head" he is a brainy man with a peace complex. Something of a genius, he regards himself in that light and finds one man at least to agree. The man, played with consumate skill by Lionel Atwill, is a publisher who has all it needs for success except political shrewdness and the talent for writing.

So Atwill convinces Rains, through the latter's ambitious young wife, Joan Bennett, to combine forces. He will publish the writings of Rains under his own name. He will get the fame that Rains doesn't seek; Rain will have the satisfaction of giving universal voice to his theories. The scheme works perfectly until Atwill has a chance to improve his status by changing his coat.

What Jean Bart apparently wanted to do in the beginning was write a purely intellectual drama using as contrasts brain, represented by the pen, and brawn, as represented by money. But she drifted off into an outcry on the munitions business, retraced her steps to delve into domestic affairs. Then Universal conceived the brilliant idea of dragging in a new Shirley Temple by the heels in little Baby Jane.

THE
MAN WHO
RECLAIMED
HIS HEAD

Claude   Joan
RAINS BENNETT
Lionel ATWILL

SIGMA

The voice which made a screen star overnight has returned to Hollywood, direct from a triumphant engagement on the New York stage. The owner of that voice is Claude Rains, who was heard but not seen in "The Invisible Man." It is a coincidence that his latest picture, now at the Sigma is "The Man Who Reclaimed His Head." It is a most absorbing drama, not the least interesting feature of which is a detailed expose of the nefarious practices of the international munitions ring in fomenting unrest and actual war between nations. In the supporting cast are Joan Bennett, Lionel Atwill and three-year-old Baby Jane.

1935

Phantom Empire
Night Life of the Gods
Phantom of the Convent
Mark of the Vampire
Mad Love
She
Condemned to Live
The Crime of Dr. Crespi
The Black Room
Transatlantic Tunnel

The Phantom Empire

12-Chapter Serial, First Chapter Released U.S. January 7, 1939

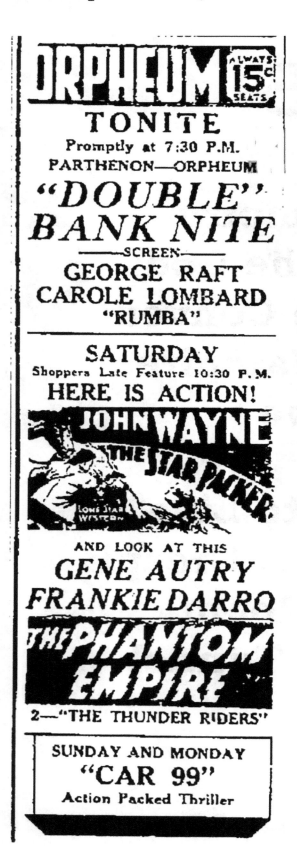

MYSTERY AND ACTION FILL DOUBLE FEATURE PROGRAM AT GRAND

Thrilling excitement, mystery and slam-bang action fill the double feature program at the Grand today and tomorrow, with Edmund Gwenn, Maureen O'Sullivan, "The Bishop Misbehaves" starring Lucille Watson, Reginald Owen, Dudley Digges and Norman Foster heading the program; and Bill Cody in "The Frontier Days" as the associate attraction; plus the fourth chapter of "The Phantom Empire."

Sherlock Holmes, The Thin Man and Philo Vance have nothing on the Bishop. He can spot a clue with the best. He can match wits with the underworld's most desperate, and he can win laughs when he mixes sleuthing and match making in the new season's brightest comedy mystery.

"Frontier Days" is a thrilling drama of the wild west with heroism, romance and adventure blended into a fast moving screenization of the colorful west.

Gene Autry, Frankie Darrow and Betsy Ross King star in "The Phantom Broadcast," the fourth chapter of "Phantom Empire."

NAT LEVINE presents

GENE AUTRY

THE WORLD FAMED STAR OF RADIO AND SCREEN

in 'the PHANTOM EMPIRE'

with FRANKIE DARRO
BETSY KING ROSS

Directed by
OTTO BROWER and B. REEVES EASON

Supervised by
ARMAND SCHAEFER

A MASCOT MASTER SERIAL

CHAPTER 5 BENEATH the EARTH

MASCOT SERIALS

"BLAZING THE TRAIL"

COUNTRY OF ORIGIN U·S·A

Matinee 2:20 — Evening 6:30-9

GRAND

TODAY -- TOMORROW

He dropped his A-men to join the G-men and solve a mystery!

the BISHOP MISBEHAVES

EDMOND GWENN
MAUREEN O'SULLIVAN
NORMAN FOSTER
REGINALD OWEN
DUDLEY DIGGES

From the Howling Broadway Stage Hit!

PLUS

BILL CODY

in a thrilling actionful saga of the wild and wooly west in the stage coach days!

"FRONTIER DAYS"

EXTRA

"The Phantom Broadcast"
Chapter 4 of
"THE PHANTOM EMPIRE"

THE PHANTOM EMPIRE

MOST SPECTACULAR SERIAL OF THE AGE

Gene AUTRY
Frankie DARRO
Betsy King ROSS

LA REINE DE L'EMPIRE FANTOME
DE KONINGIN van 'T SPOOKENRIJK

ORPHEUM

ALWAYS 15c SEATS

Today --- BOB STEELE
"SMOKEY SMITH"

PLUS TWO FAVORITES

GENE   FRANKIE
AUTRY   DARRO

"Phantom Empire"

Shoppers' Late Feature 10:30 P.M.

Sunday and Monday

HERE THEY ARE -- IN THEIR FIRST GREAT HIT TOGETHER!

AL JOLSON
Ruby KEELER

in

"GO INTO YOUR DANCE"

NOTICE! TUESDAY

CASH   CASH
SCREENO   FORTUNE

"THE PHANTOM EMPIRE"

From
The Mascot Motion Picture Serial
In Twelve Thrilling Chapters

Chapter 12
"THE END OF MURANIA"

"He-elp!"

The cry grew fainter as Gene Autry weakened under the withering ray of Murania's most dreaded invention, the Disintegrator.

He was alone, helpless, in the room of death. Queen Tika had fled, pursued by Argo. But suddenly the trapdoor above Gene opened and two very surprised gentlemen tumbled through. They were Pete and Oscar.

"Quick—shut off the ray!" Pete sprang to the controls.

A moment later Gene was saved. But there was scant time for thanks, as the rebels returned at the same instant with Tika, again a captive.

Forgetting his fatigue and wounds, Gene Autry led the attack on the warriors. The earth-men's onslaught was irresistible. With the Muranians stretched upon the floor they were just about to leave the room when another group of enemies charged through the door, led by chancellor Argo himself.

Gene was at the helm of the Disintegrator now. Quickly he covered Argo's party with its deadly rays and led Tika, Pete, and Oscar out. They locked the metal door behind them.

Back in the control room after a battle in the streets, they trained the central television set upon the chamber they had just left. To their amazement Argo and his henchmen, very much alive, had mastered the Disintegrator machine and turned it full tilt upon the door that barred their egress. But suddenly as Argo, impatient, gave the dread contrivance too much power, it went wild and threw its tremendous rays in all directions.

Argo and the other Muranian rebels went down like ten-pins. Then the walls—the whole building—began to disintegrate!

"It is the end of Murania!" Queen Tika cried, and Gene knew instinctively that she spoke truth.

No man could approach that horrible machine to shut it off.

"Escape while you can," Tika begged, "I will stay here and open the cave door on the surface!"

"No," Gene declared, "I won't leave you!"

150

Night Life of the Gods

Released U.S. March 1, 1935

BALET
BLAY
presenta

Marte ataca
a la Tierra

Larry (Buster)
Grabbe
Joan
Rogers
Charles
Middleton
Diana
Shannon

Directores: Ford Beey, Robert Hill

By WOOD SOANES

THORNE SMITH'S maniac tale concerning the adventures of Hunter Hawk, the scientist, when he discovered his ability to turn live men into stone and revivify marble statues at will, "Night Life of the Gods" started its run at the Roxie yesterday, affording many a chuckle.

Curiously enough the prospect of a film based on the Smith whimsey was more hilarious than the finished product. Occasionally the movie folks were able to catch the antic spirit of the author and keep it sustained but the effort seemed too great.

As a result "Night Life of the Gods" is by turns side-splitting, dull, despite the yeoman efforts of Alan Mowbray who turns in a capital comedy performance as the eccentric young scientist. Heretofore Mowbray has been identified only with villainy, which seems to have been an error.

✿ ✿ ✿

Alone of all the cast, with the exception of the late Lowell Sherman, who directed the opus, Mowbray seemed to catch the spirit of the frolic. His serious outlook on life in the midst of the most bewildering circumstances is a masterpiece of sustained light comedy.

"Night Life of the Gods" has to do with this troubled scientist who while trying to discover a new explosive, happens upon a magic ray that does things to people. He tries it out with great success on a houseful of unpleasant relatives and then sallies forth to have fun with a 900-year-old ingenue he picks up on the way.

His trail leads eventually to the Metropolitan Art Museum where he decides to bring the statues of the gods back to life and let them see what New York in the twentieth century has to offer. In no time at all Hunter Hawk and his friends from Olympus are in the midst of a very wild evening on the Rialto.

✿ ✿ ✿

○ ○ ○

"Night Life of the Gods" doesn't pause long for romance, which is just as well. What little there is is taken care of by Mowbray and Florine McKinney, the aged flapper, in their comedy stride. The humans in the cast have little to do aside from this pair, but the gods have their moments with George Hassell, Robert Warwick and Geneva Mitchell standing out.

Hassell as Bacchus has a fine chance to show his comedy wares; Warwick gets a lot of fun out of Neptune and Miss Mitchell lends both beauty and a sense of humor to Hebe. One other good performance is that furnished by Gilbert Emery, whose portrait of the sane butler in an insane household is delightful.

The supporting bill has to do with lessons in wrestling by Londos and other experts; a musical short featuring Olga Baclanova and other radio and stage favorites; and a colored cartoon. All told it's light fare, likely to have a sustained run but certain to provide amusement for those who like burlesque and antics mixed.

Statues Take Life In Palace Film

"NIGHT LIFE OF THE GODS" is the current offering of the Palace Theater on a double bill with "Reckless," starring William Powell and Jean Harlow.

Alan Mowbray and Florine McKinney play in the former picture, a story of an eccentric young scientist who finds a way to turn human beings into statues and vice versa.

What happens when Mowbray's vitalized statues start talking and walking forms the basis of an amusing story.

Monday and Tuesday the Palace will offer "One More Spring," with Janet Gaynor and Warner Baxter. "Naughty Marietta" will return Wednesday to play through Friday, with Jeanette MacDonald and Nelson Eddy.

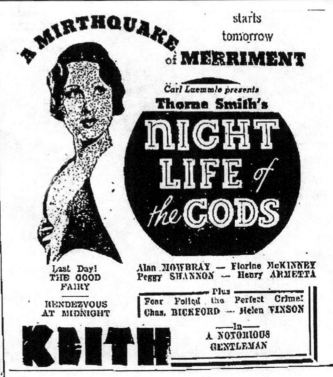

Phantom of the Convent (El Fantasma del Convento)

Released U.S. April 21, 1935

El Lunes y Martes, se presentará en el Teatro México, Radio Johnny Wise, el Mago del Teclado conocido por todo el país como el Paderewsky Americano, tocando el piano con una mano y el órgano con la otra. Una verdadera atracción. Noche de gala. En la pantalla se exhibirá la película El Fantasma del Convento con Enrique del Campo y Carlos Villatoro.

154

Mark of the Vampire

Released U.S. April 26, 1935

"MARK OF THE VAMPIRE" THRILLING, CHILLING AND SHOCKING MURDER MYSTERY

Uncanny mystery, weird "undead" vampires figuring in blood-chilling thrills, and a strange romance told against a background of sinister shadows are the highlights of "Mark of the Vampire," Metro-Goldwyn-Mayer's new detective-terror drama, playing Sunday, Monday and Tuesday at the Orpheum theater.

Directed by Tod Browning, creator of "Dracula" and similar thrillers, it deals with an amazing murder case, and a detective pitted against an uncanny vampire cult. Strange shadows, fantastic clouds, bats that turn to human beings, the weird "vampire girl" and other hair-raising detail surrounds the baffling mystery plot.

Lionel Barrymore as the strange Professor Zelen, student of demonology, plays the outstanding character role in the new picture, and the horrific Count Mora, vampire menace, is enacted with gruesome exactitude by Bela Lugosi of "Dracula" fame. He is teamed with Carol Borland, newly discovered "Vampire Girl," who is seen as his daughter Luna. Holmes Herbert and James Bradbury, Jr., play two other "un-dead" terror characters in the weird story.

Furnish Love Interest

The love interest is in Elizabeth Allan, as daughter of the victim of a vampire attack, and Henry Wadsworth, playing her sweetheart, Fedor. They enact dramatic roles, in which they are under the vampire menace, skillfully and convincingly. Lionel Atwill makes a perfect detective, and Jean Hersholt gives a splendid performance as the enigmatic Baron Otto. Other clever players in the cast are Donald Meek, Jessie Ralph, Leila Bennett and Ivan Simpson.

The weird story was written by Guy Endore, author of "Werewolf of Paris" and "Babouk," and Bernard Schubert.

Das Zeichen des Vampyrs

YOU WILL NOT DARE BELIEVE . . . WHAT YOUR EYES SEE!

Lionel BARRYMORE in MARK OF THE VAMPIRE

with

ELIZABETH ALLAN
LIONEL ATWILL
BELA LUGOSI
JEAN HERSHOLT

THE CRUELEST WOMAN IN TWO WORLDS!

A beauty from out of the shadow of doom . . . a dread temptress who lured her victims to the hiding-place of her maniacal master. Together they ruled the realm of the "undead" . . . their symbols of death menaced the living! You will shudder . . . but you'll be fascinated by the strangest story ever told on the screen!

IMPORTANT!

Do not divulge the secret of "Mark of the Vampire" to your friends . . . let them be mystified . . . and thrilled!

TOD BROWNING'S PRODUCTION
A Metro-Goldwyn-Mayer Picture

Lionel Barrymore as Prof. Zelen. His scientific mind fights the forces of evil.

158

Undead...
yet living
on the Kisses
of Youth!

SUITABLE ONLY FOR ADULTS

Lionel
Barrymore
in

MARK of the VAMPIRE

WITH

ELIZABETH ALLAN
BELA LUGOSI
LIONEL ATWILL
JEAN HERSHOLT

A Metro-Goldwyn-Mayer PICTURE

IN MURDER SHOCKER

BELA LUGOSI AND CAROL BORLAND
Above is the way a prominent artist sees Bela Lugosi and Carol Borland in one of the startling scenes from "Mark of the Vampire," which will be presented as a pre-release feature in midnight matinee Saturday night at the Fair Theater. Lionel Barrymore and Elizabeth Allan are also prominently cast in this feature to which children will not be admitted.

Bela Lugosi, of "Dracula" Tells Of Experience With Human Vampire

The strangest creature in America is living today in Hollywood, surrounded by a brooding atmosphere of horror and madness. A tall, straight figure of a man, he goes among his fellows with a strange aloofness that marks him as a man apart. Unfathomable thoughts gleam behind his deep-set eyes and on his throat he bears two tiny wounds that prove a terrible attack by a human vampire.

Bela Lugosi is the name of this strangest of men, a Hungarian born amid the black, mysterious mountains where vampires take a heavy toll among the natives, and the whole countryside lives in terror of the night. For it is only after sunset that these strange undead creatures rise from their graves.

Lugosi is loath to discuss his terrifying experience in his native land. "It is all a terrible nightmare which I am destined never to forget," he says, "until a certain woman in Hungary shall go to a peaceful and lasting death. She is an actress with no more than usual amount of feminine charm, but many men are her abject slaves, because within her smoulders the burning flame of the vampires.

"It was her sharply pointed teeth which made these wounds in my throat, and it was her unspoken but irresistible commands which caused me to visit her again and again. At length my mother noticed that I was rapidly losing weight, and she soon divined the cause. I had fallen under the influence of a vampire. Shortly afterward, at my mother's insistence, I fled the country—and I shall probably never go back .

"But even now I dare not sleep at night. This is the time when we feel the thought impulses of the vampires, and I dare not lose consciousness during the hours of darkness. With a light burning low in my bedroom, I read and pace the floor—and think. If I rest at all, it must be during the day.

"I had been an actor in Hungary, and when I fled to New York one of the first parts offered me was the role of Count Dracula in the play, 'Dracula,' which was then about to be produced for the first time. And, most strangely, this story dealt with the very subject which has caused me to leave my native country—vampires of the night, and the strange Legion of the Undead. Possibly because I was so strongly drawn to the subject, and had not been able to escape from the menace which constantly hung over me, I took the part, and appeared in the play for more than two years. Literally fascinated by the role, I lived in another world, and I actually seemed to have become Dracula himself.

"And when I learned that Tod Browning was at Universal to make 'Dracula' into a talking picture, this strange fascination drew me to the studio. I have played the role on the screen, and I often sit in dark theaters, watching and wondering if the sinister character in the picture is Bela Lugoso—or Dracula."

The cast of "Dracula", which comes to the Orpheum Theatre Sunday, Monday and Tuesday, also includes Helen Chandler, David Manners, Edward Van Sloan, Dwight Frye, Frances Dade, Herbert Bunston, Joan Standing and Charles Gerrard.

TOO MUCH HORROR FOR ONE THEATRE
World Premiere Tonight at 6:00

RIALTO AT BOTH THEATRES **MAYFAIR**
Broadway & 42nd St Broadway & 47th St

NOT FOR WEAK HEARTS!

For your nerves' sake, no standing will be permitted in either theatre. The capacity of two theatres assures seats for every one. The terrifying suspense of this picture demands that you be seated from beginning to end. Please don't tell your friends the thrilling climax!

"MARK OF THE VAMPIRE"

An M-G-M Picture with

BELA (Dracula) LUGOSI
LIONEL BARRYMORE
LIONEL ATWILL · JEAN HERSHOLT
ELIZABETH ALLEN · A Tod Browning Production

Come at six or after for last showings of current attraction plus preview of "Mark of the Vampire"

"MARK OF THE VAMPIRE"

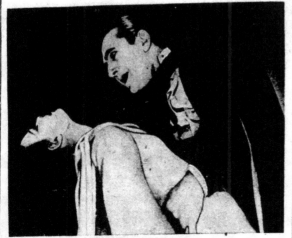

Bela Lugosi with one of his victims in "Mark of the Vampire" mystery thriller, with Lionel Barrymore, Elizabeth Allan, showing Wednesday and Thursday at the Capitol, Brownsville.

TODAY — "BEHIND GREEN LIGHTS" AND "ONCE TO EVERY BACHELOR"

15c
UNTIL
6.30 p.m.

GARDEN
Indiana Harbor
First Run Pictures

DOORS
OPEN
SUNDAY
12:30
NOON

STARTING SUNDAY FOR 3 DAYS
THE SUPREME THRILLER OF THE YEAR
COME EARLY AND AVOID THE CROWDS

WOMAN or VAMPIRE?
Beautiful ... alluring ... hiding behind a dread mask of unearthly terror! The picture you'll love to shudder at!

LIONEL Barrymore
with
ELIZABETH ALLAN
LIONEL ATWILL
BELA LUGOSI
JEAN HERSHOLT
Tod Browning Production

Metro-Goldwyn-Mayer PICTURE

MARK OF THE VAMPIRE

PLEASE!
Let your friends learn the thrilling climax for themselves!

— ALSO —
LATEST "OUR GANG" COMEDY SCREAM
COLORED CARTOON · METROTONE NEWS

Mark of the Vampire With Bela Lugosi and Lionel Barrymore at the Garden Sunday

Sinister shadows, vampires that roam in the night, terror in its ultimate intensity, blend with suspense, thrills, romance and comedy

Carol Borland and Bela Lugosi in "Mark of the Vampire"

in "Mark of the Vampire," Metro-Goldwyn-Mayer's amazing detective thriller at the Garden theater Sunday.

CAPITOL
BROWNSVILLE
Wednesday and Thursday

A Beautiful Girl Enslaved by a Sinister Weird Thing!

LIONEL BARRYMORE

in

"MARK OF THE VAMPIRE"

with

ELIZABETH ALLAN
BELA LUGOSI

M-G-M Spine-tingling Hair-raising Murder Mystery!!

On the Stage
Thursday Night—

'Amateur NIGHT'

6 Good Amateur Talent Acts . . . And the Old Fashioned Band

LA MARQUE DU VAMPIRE
MARK OF THE VAMPIRE

1935
U.S.A.
FANTASTIQUE

RÉALISATEUR
Tod Browning

Lionel **Barrymore**
in
MARK OF THE VAMPIRE

Today Only

CAPITOL
BROWNSVILLE

Mad Love

Released U.S. July 12, 1935

NEW STAR APPEARS IN PLAZA FEATURE

"Mad Love," new drama which introduces a new personality too the American screen in Peter Lorre, comes tomorrow to the Plaza theater. The action ranges from a Grand Guignol horror theater in Paris, to the weird surgery, where the mad doctor and his Oriental assistant work out their scientific wonders. Frances Drake plays the heroine Yvonne, and Colin Clive is Orlac, her husband. Edward Brophy and Isabel Jewell are also in the cast. Also on the same program are Clark Gable and Constance Bennett in "After Office Hours."

MONDAY, TUESDAY, SEPT. 30, OCT. 1

TWO BIG DAYS

PETER LORRE

in "MAD LOVE"

PETER LORRE

with

FRANCES DRAKE

COLIN CLIVE
TED HEALY
ISABEL JEWELL

•

Directed by
KARL FREUND

A Metro • GOLDWYN • Mayer PICTURE

the Hands of Orlac

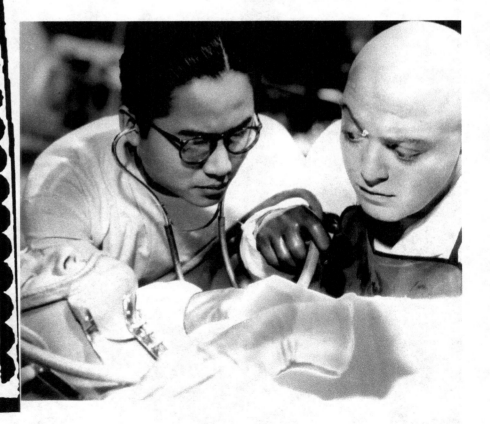

"Mad Love"

An amazing new kind of mystery picture, with an amazing new kind of villain, is on the State's screen this Tuesday with the showing of "Mad Love." It introduces to the American screen Peter Lorre, European star of "M," one of the greatest European mysteries ever filmed. Lorre is an astonishing new personality. Charlie Chaplin calls him the world's greatest character actor.

The story deals with a great surgeon who, when he covets the wife of a pianist, sets about ruining the other man's life and driving him mad. Played with fantastic shadows and lights, it shows weird surgical experiments and other amazing detail, introduces the Paris Grand Guignol horror theatre, and a romantic development against this macabre background.

An all-star revue called "The Infernal Triangle," the latest screen snapshots and a new Pathe News are short reels on the same bill at the State this Tuesday with "Mad Love."

Released by Metro-Goldwyn-Mayer, directed by Karl Freund, featuring Peter Lorre, Frances Drake, Colin Clive.

◇ ◇ ◇

Flabby-faced Peter Lorre can tell more in one look than one half of Hollywood's pictures, all its publicity. He makes a real madman in this picture, turns the show into one which really has the element of shock.

It is not only his looks, but that subtle ability to say things, as Charles Laughton does, without speaking a word. One need not watch him long before deciding he is mad, expect him to do something appropriate. He does.

He falls in love with Yvonne Orlac (Frances Drake), a semi-actress, and takes home a wax statue of her to love when he cannot win the woman.

The facile fingers of Yvonne's husband, Stephen (Colin Clive), are crushed in a train wreck. Amputate, says one doctor, but the faithful hopeful wife thinks of Doctor Gogol (Lorre) and hopes that he can saves the hands of a pianist husband.

Lorre takes the hands of a criminal guillotined that day, grafts them to Stephen's arms. The criminal, Rollo, found death because he gave it—with his hands and knives.

Recovered, Stephen finds he can no longer play the piano, but can throw knives, as their first owner did. His step-father is murdered, and the efficient French police arrest Stephan. The step-father ha been stabbed.

Then comes a gruesome scene, or to send shivers, make "Mad Love the best horror picture of the yea —so far. Dr. Gogol is mad an proves it when he starts stranglin Yvonne with the braids of her hai

A moment later the hands h grafted open a window slot, flash knife into his back.

You will be frightened by Lorr but you will like him for his part He, as with few others in Holly wood, can wrap the word "unique around his bald brow.

Now current at the State theater and heading the double bill is "Ivory Handled Guns," and "Mad Love" as the second feature. The serial, "The Roaring West," is also on the program.

"Ivory Handled Guns," starring Buck Jones, is the story of two relentless figures of the great open spaces, one with the forces of right on his side and the other masquerading under the guise of decent society, struggling for possession of an ivory-handled gun, one of a pair. Mere ownership of the weapon is not the issue at stake but for the one it represents a high principle and for the other, it is a pawn of power and vicious corruption.

The story of "Mad Love," starring Peter Lorre and Frances Drake, deals with a great surgeon who, when he covets the wife of a pianist, sets about ruining the other man's life and driving him mad.

Miss Drake is the wife of the pianist, Colin Clive, while Lorre plays the mad surgeon. Others in the cast are Henry Kolker, Ted Healy, Edward Brophy and many others.

DEAD HANDS THAT LIVE...AND LOVE...AND KILL!

MAD LOVE

STARRING

Peter **LORRE**

FRANCES DRAKE
COLIN CLIVE
TED HEALY
ISABEL JEWELL

A Metro-Goldwyn-Mayer PICTURE

NILE
19th YEAR of M. 947
COOL and COMFORTABLE

2 BIG HITS TONIGHT 7 P.M.

Elisabeth Bergner in
UNITED ARTIST'S RELEASE
ESCAPE ME NEVER

—AND—

PETER LORRE in "MAD LOVE"

TODAY
See How The French Police Exposed

THE MOST BAFFLING LOVE CRIME EVER CONCEIVED!

"MAD LOVE"

With Dynamic M-G-M Character Star
PETER LORRE
FRANCES DRAKE — TED HEALY
COLIN CLIVE — ISABEL JEWELL

Plus
"The Valient Tailor" Color Cartoon   Chapter No. 9 "Return of Chan Du"

STATE

WARNER BROS.
PLAZA   ALL SEATS
16c   Tax Incl.

—Last Day—
"MY HEART IS CALLING"
"$20 A WEEK"

Tomorrow!
CLARK GABLE
CONSTANCE BENNETT
'AFTER OFFICE HOURS'
—Also—
PETER LORRE
"MAD LOVE"

"Mad Love" was originally "The Hands of Orlac," a fantastic story of how the concert pianist became a murderer with a flair for knife throwing when he lost his own hands and had another's grafted onto his wrists. The studio has seen fit to concentrate more on the doctor than the patient and the story suffers as a result.

The picture is designed for special audiences only as it is too horrific even for the average horror enthusiasts and just the sort of thing to send sensitive juvenile audiences into hysterical nightmares. But it has a definite place in the Lorre gallery of psychopathic cinema cases and is worthy of the student's time.—WOOD SOANES.

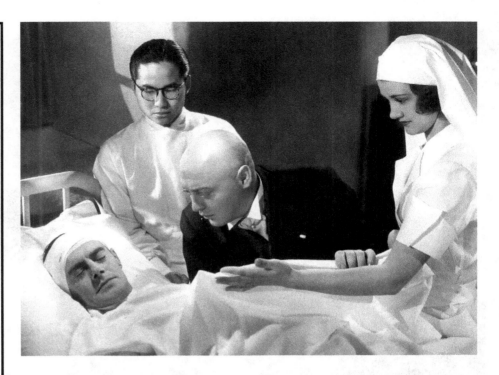

On the same bill Peter Lorre, Hungarian actor, makes his American picture debut as the mad surgeon, Doctor Gogol in "Mad Love," a film that provides a completely new set of shudders for those who like different kinds of chills than the theater's cooling system provides. It is an entirely new type of horror picture. Mr. Lorre establishes himself as an expert actor and promises to be an adequate candidate for Lon Chaney's long-vacant throne because he is no surface performer of human grotesqueries but manages to leave human distortion somewhat human. Frances Drake, Colin Clive, Ted Healy and Henry Kolker give excellent support. May Beatty is excellent as the tipsy housekeeper. Karl Freund is the director. The story is taken from the novel "Les Mains D' Orlac" by Maurine Renard.

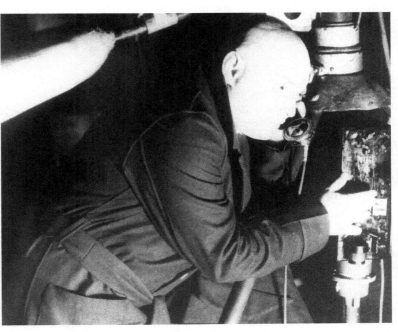

173

She

Released U.S. July 12, 1935

H. RIDER HAGGARD'S Great Novel

"SHE"

HELEN GAHAGAN • RANDOLPH SCOTT
HELEN MACK • NIGEL BRUCE • AND A CAST OF THOUSANDS

Directed by IRVING PICHEL and LANSING C. HOLDEN

MERIAN C. COOPER PRODUCTION

R K O RADIO PICTURES

Cooper Prefers Color

Watching the proceedings is Meriam C. Cooper, the producer. He says he thinks "She" will be a good picture in black-and-white, but it would be better in color. He wanted to do this in the new color process, but R. K. O., for whom he is making the film, thought otherwise. After "She" and "The Last Days of Pompeii" for R. K. O., Cooper enters upon his duties as executive vice-president of John Hay Whitney's Pioneer company. He then will make no more pictures in black-and-white.

"She" is a combination of adventure, romance and weird fantasy. Helen Gahagan's role is that of a princess endowed with eternal youth. In search of her secret goes the young scientist (Randolph Scott).

Fantasy is material at which most producers shy, and Cooper concedes that it is "dangerous" from the box-office standpoint at best, but he is applying to "She" his pet formula: "Make it so real that audiences will believe in it."

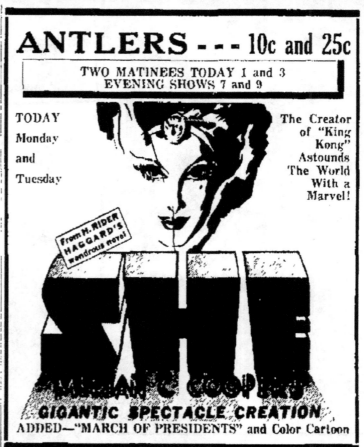

A MERIAN C. COOPER PRODUCTION

A WONDER OF STAGECRAFT!

SHE

H. Rider Haggard's amazing character comes thrillingly to life in one of the most gigantic spectacle dramas ever filmed.

Portrayed by a cast of 5,000 including
HELEN GAHAGAN
RANDOLPH SCOTT
HELEN MACK • NIGEL BRUCE
Directed by Irving Pichel and Lansing C. Holden

HOLLYWOOD
SIGHTS AND SOUNDS

By Robbin Coons

Hollywood, April 4—When Hollywood becomes as thoroughly "color-conscious" as the color camera proponents predict, scenes like this no longer will be fed to the prosaic black-and-white film:

A great ceremonial hall in the Kingdom of Kor covers the entire sound stage. Beyond an expanse of dark green polished floor—for this is a "long shot"—is the "jeweled throne" of She, heroine of H. Rider Haggard's fantastic novel. The walls are high, severe, gray, and the tall throne, with its background of patterned mirrors, is lilliputian against them.

Riot Of Brilliance

Before the throne, on a circular dais, are the fire priests, clad in somber robes of gray or black; some of them wear golden masks. She (Helen Gahagan) sits on the throne, a costume of yellow and orange-gold flowing in folds about her.

Courtiers, guards, priests, soldiers are scattered about the steps leading up to the throne. Yellow and orange-gold must be the royal colors, for the guards, stationed sentinel-like at intervals, wear helmets in the shape of eagle-heads, orange-gold and yellow.

The whole effect is one of striking spectacle and color. The camera will catch the spectacle, but the colors will be lost.

MERIAN C. COOPER creator of "King Kong" startles the world again!

SHE

H. Rider Haggard's amazing character comes thrillingly to life in one of the most gigantic spectacle dramas ever filmed.

"SHE"

H. Rider Haggard's famous novel, "She," comes to the Majestic theater screen today in its movie version, produced by Merian C. Cooper, who turned out "King Kong" and other weird thrillers.

The story takes two English scientists into the mysterious kingdom of Kor at the North Pole in a search for the source of eternal life. The drama resolves itself into a romantic battle between the immortal empress ("She") and the mortal Tanya, daughter of a trader, with Leo (the hero) as the object of their affections.

Helen Gahagan, Broadway star, makes her motion picture debut as She, with Helen Mack, Randolph Scott and Nigel Bruce in the other leading roles.

The Black Room

Released U.S. July 15, 1935

KISS HIM... AND DIE!

BORIS KARLOFF
THE BLACK ROOM

WITH
MARIAN MARSH
ROBERT ALLEN
KATHERINE DeMILLE

DIRECTED BY
ROY WILLIAM NEILL

COLUMBIA REPRINT

QUITE A CHANGE, KARLOFF SCARED

Frightens Himself in Garrick Film and Fans Grin in Great Glee

HAVING been scared half out of their senses in certain pictures by Boris Karloff, supreme menace of the screen, fans may sit back in their seats at the Garrick theatre and chortle—if they have sufficient breath—at Karloff scaring himself for a change, in "The Black Room." He has a dual role, one part of which is that of an inhuman monster, a baron through whose machinations many young women disappear, and the other his twin brother, a lovable personality. This is no film for nervous persons; it is a horror picture but is set in aristocratic surroundings in the early part of the 19th century.

The theme is, that, hundreds of years previously, the younger of twin brothers killed the firstborn in a black room, and the legend grew that the line would end when another son killed his older twin brother. Through a twisting plot the story is well developed and is carried through with consummate ability to its dread conclusion, when prophecy is fulfilled in unexpected fashion, though the younger twin is already dead.

Master of the house of terror! Monster of the room of doom! His kiss is the password to oblivion— and, dead or alive, he can kill!

The man characterized in the foregoing is Karloff in "The Black Room."

Karloff's latest horror role is that of a ruthless killer, a bluebeard, who entices beautiful girls into the Black Room of his castle, only to take their lives. He himself lives under the dread malediction that he is to meet death at the hands of his twin. Finally, he murders his brother in an attempt to defy the curse—but he ultimately meets death at the hands of the corpse. Marian Marsh, Thurston Hall, Robert Allen, Katherine DeMille and a host of others are in support of the star.

180

KARLOFF REVEALS...
WHAT THE GRAVE CONCEALS!

BORIS KARLOFF

THE BLACK ROOM

Marion MARSH · Robert ALLEN · Katherine DeMILLE

Directed by ROY WILLIAM NEILL

Condemed to Live

Released U.S. September 11, 1935

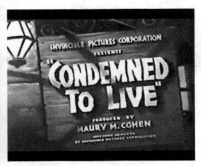

"Condemned To Live"

A noted scientist is afflicted with a dread disease which creates the necessity for his committing atrocious crimes. Mystery and terror run rampant in "Condemned to Live," State theater feature Friday only with Ralph Morgan, Maxine Doyle,, Russell Gleason and Mischa Auer in leading roles.

— Wednesday and Thursday —

SAINT OR SATAN?
MAN OR MONSTER?
What was this creature that DEATH could not claim?

**"CONDEMNED
TO LIVE"**

— Plus —

BUD'N BEN WESTERN
"CLANCY AT THE BAT"

**TWO FEATURE BILL
PLAYING IN GRAND**

Out of a maze of western stories comes Spectrum's picture "Frontier Days," to shine and bristle on the screen of the Grand theater today and Saturday to the keen delight of young and old.

A thrilling tale of adventure and romance packed with action in a well-told story of the stage coach days.

Ralph Morgan is stepping out of his usual gay character these days to shoot chills up and down your spine. Bela (Dracula) Lugosi and Boris (Frankenstein) Karloff had better look to their laurels for Comedian Ralph Morgan has called forth some unexpected talent.

"Condemned To Live" plays on the same program with "Frontier Days."

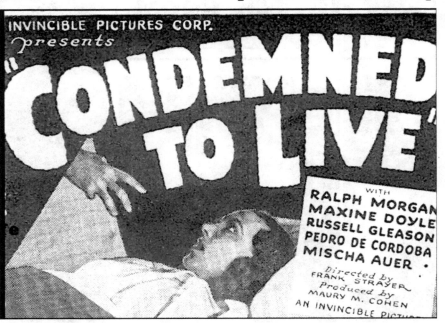

182

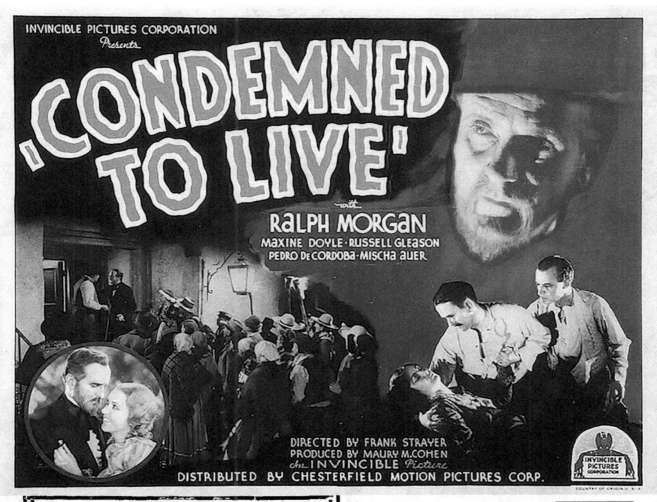

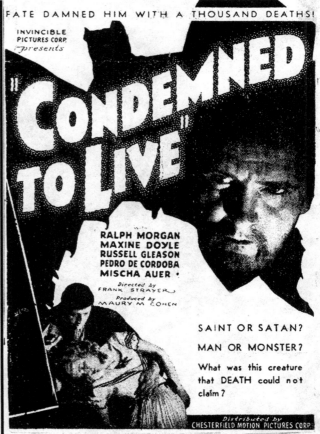

The Crime of Dr. Crespi

Released U.S. September 24, 1935

GREAT SURGEON OR INHUMAN FIEND?

Maddened by a jealous hate, the famous Dr. Crespi prepared a horrible torture for his rival. An auto crash placed the victim in his vicious power—Buried as dead, in reality alive — seeing hearing, feeling, suffering. The man you love to hate. Eric Von Stroheim, in "The Crime of Dr. Crespi" showing at the 4th Street Tuesday only. (Bargain Night). Two passes at the 4th Street B. O. for J. B. Holman today.

Crespi takes a selfie!!!

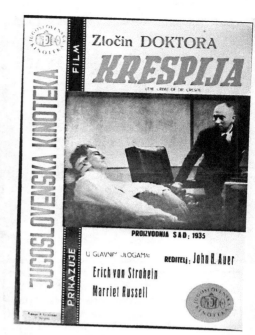

ORPHEUM.

A thriller based on an Edgar Allen Poe story is showing at the Orpheum today and tomorrow, with Eric Von Stroheim in the title role of "The Crime of Dr. Crespi." Harriett Russell as the innocent cause of his sentence of living death on her husband and Dwight Frye have prominent role.

When Dwight Frye doesn't die in a picture, the fans will agree that that's news! In the new Eric Von Stroheim thriller, "The Crime of Dr. Crespie," which will play at the Texas Theater tomorrow night only, the player who has gasped his last in such famous films as "Dracula," "The Vampire Bat," "Frankenstein," "Doorway to Hell" and "The Maltese Falcon," actually is up and on his feet as the last reel comes to its final fide-out.

Hitherto, Frye has met with violent death in every feature in which he has been seen. He has been stabbed, poisoned, hanged, thrown from speeding trains, tossed over cliffs, drowned and torn to bits by wild animals . . . all for the sake of film art. "The Crime of Dr. Crespi" spares him, however, even though Eric Von Stroheim — the hate-maddened surgeon of Edgar Allan Poe's amazing story—tries to put him out of the way. Instead it is Crespi who comes to a violent end.

Frye doesn't escape the "neurotic" type of role even though he manages to survive. The "man who has died a thousand deaths" enacts the part of Dr. Thomas in the film, a nervously capable medico who suspects Crespi of a foul plot and succeeds in running him down.

Edgar Allan Poe's fantastic tale, "The Premature Burial" depicts the blood-chilling situation which suggested the new horror film "The Crime of Dr. Crespi," in which Eric Van Stroheim stars in the brilliant role of the vengeful surgeon who plots a revenge on the man who married his former sweetheart.

STARTS MONDAY!!

Bravery and bullets make this outdoor action story outstanding!

Rearing action on the range! Zane Grey's 'DRIFT FENCE, with LARRY CRABBE Katherine DeMille Tom Keene

A Paramount Picture

2—Big Features—2

ERIC VON STROHEIM The man you love to hate..! in "The CRIME OF Dr. Crespi"

EDGAR ALLEN POE'S MARROW CHILLING MASTERPIECE

MON. 16c Till Six! Then 26c

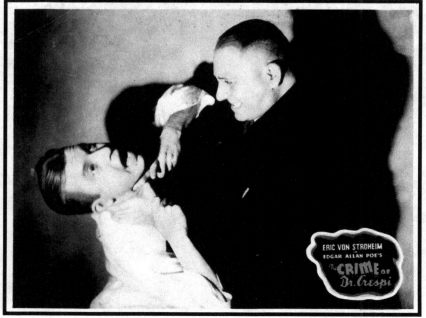

ERIC VON STROHEIM EDGAR ALLAN POE'S The CRIME OF Dr. Crespi

MIDNIGHT HYPNOTIC FROLIC!

Tonight
11:15 o'Clock

Spook Show

More Fun Than 100
Circuses!
Such Hilarity
Is Only For
Midnight

Karston

Sensational Magician presents

HISTORY'S MOST
COLOSSAL
EXPOSITION
WONDERS

MIRACLES
FROM ALL
PARTS OF
THE WORLD

See...

THE $50,000 PHANTOM
SOLDIER ILLUSION
12 PEOPLE VANISH
BEFORE YOUR EYES
A 2000 YEAR OLD
MUMMY COMES TO LIFE
GIRL DISAPPEARS into PUMPKIN
THE $10,000 RADIO
CABINET MYSTERY
SPIRIT PAINTINGS
AND 1001 OTHER GREAT
SUPER SPECTACLES

On the Screen

An Epic of Horror
Edgar Allan Poe's

"THE CRIME OF
DR. CRESPI"

With

Eric Von Stroheim

(The Man You Love to Hate)

Tonight 11:15

KiMo

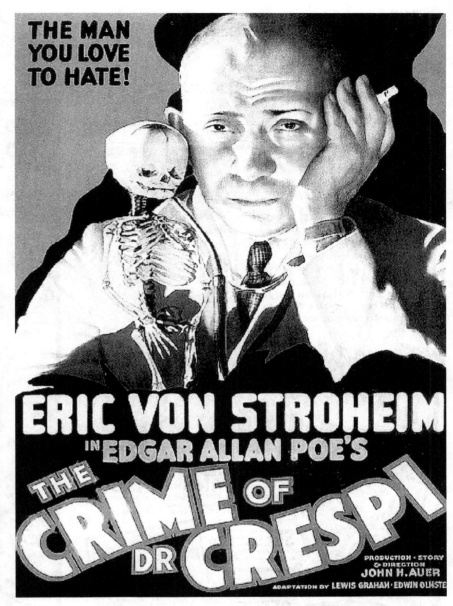

THE MAN
YOU LOVE
TO HATE!

ERIC VON STROHEIM
IN EDGAR ALLAN POE'S

THE CRIME OF DR CRESPI

PRODUCTION · STORY
& DIRECTION
JOHN H. AUER

ADAPTATION BY LEWIS GRAHAM · EDWIN OLMSTE

The Greenbrier
Corner · Summers & State

TODAY — DOUBLE FEATURE PROGRAM

"PECK'S BAD BOY" | "NO MAN'S RANGE"
With | With
JACKIE COOPER | BOB STEELE

TWO BIG FEATURES

Mon. Tues.	"Crime of Dr. Crespi"
	With
	ERIC VON STROHEIM
First Run Program	PLUS
	"Racing Luck"
	With
	BILL BOYD
	Also First Run Pathe News

Rest of Week—Wednesday—"Count of Monte Cristo;" Thursday—
"Daring Young Man" and "Our Daily Bread;" Friday—"Doubting
Thomas" and "Folies Bergere;" Saturday—"His Fighting Blood"
and Chapter Eight Rustlers of Red Dog.

BARGAIN MATINEE — EVERYBODY 10c

If It's A Good Picture It Will Be Shown At The

GRAND......

Not Occasionally — But Always A Good Show

FRI - SAT. - 2 BIG FEATURES

FIRST TIME SHOWN IN STAMFORD

NUMBER 1—
—Another swell Zane
Grey picture rides into
town! Rip-roaring action
—Romance amid scenic
beauty.

Adolph Zukor presents

ZANE GREYS

Nevada

With Buster Crabbe,
Kathleen Burke, Monte
Blue, Raymond Hatton.

NUMBER 5—
"Stars of Tomorrow"
Comedy

NUMBER 2—
The Man You Love To Hate
Eric Von Stroheim
—in—
EDGAR ALLEN POE'S
"THE CRIME OF
DR. CRESPI"

NUMBER 3—

THE
**FIGHTING
MARINES**

NUMBER 4—
Betty Boop Cartoon-
Comedy

THE CRIME OF DR. CRESPI—
Eric Von Stroheim back again
in the wildest kind of horror
shocker.

The "man you love to hate,"
Eric Von Stroheim, returns to the
screen in "The Crime of Dr.
Crespi," at the 4th Street Tuesday, a film that runs the gamut
of all the things Hollywood
thinks should make cinemaddicts
swoon with extroverted terror.

"The Crime of Dr. Crespi" has
been publicized as an Edgar Allen Poe story "suggested" by his
short story of live funerals, "The
Premature Burial." As a matter
of record—any student of Poe
will find it out the minute he
steps into the theater, anyway—
the only connection between the
two is that both have something
to do with cemeteries.

Von Stroheim, minus his mono-
cle, is the same man theater-
goers snarled at in "The Wedding March," some twelve years
ago. Others in the cast are
Dwight Frye, Paul Guilfoyle,
Harriet Russell and John Bohn.
John H. Auer wrote, directed
and produced this independent.

Transatlantic Tunnel

Released U.S. October 27, 1935

Helen Vinson, who has been working at the Gaumont British studios in London on "King of the Damned," with Conrad Veidt and Noah Beery, and in "Transatlantic Tunnel," in which she is featured with Richard Dix, Madge Evans, Leslie Banks and C. Aubrey Smith, will arrive here on Aug. 27 aboard the Ile de France.

* * *

There seems to be some doubt over at the Center Theatre in Radio City about whether "Way Down East" will continue for a second week. If it does not, the house will have a new one on Wednesday, but what no one seemed to know. . . . "Transatlantic Tunnel" may continue for a third week at the Roxy. If not, set aside Friday for Universal's "Three Kids and a Queen." . . . The Paramount expects to retain "Hands Across the Table" for an additional seven days, beginning Friday. In case there is a last-minute change in plans put down "Mary Burns, Fugitive," with Sylvia Sidney in the title rôle. It is a Walter Wanger production directed by William K. Howard.

The first of a series of three Sunday night travel talks, illustrated by motion pictures, will be offered tonight at Carnegie Hall by E. M. Newman. Tonight's subject will be "Italy."

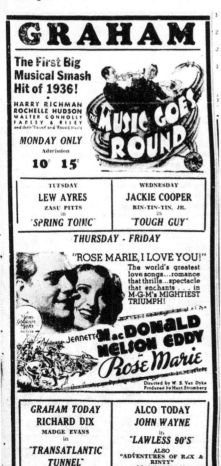

T-52.

GB's EIGHT STAR SPECIAL

TRANSATLANTIC TUNNEL

NEW YORK TO LONDON

Richard **DIX**   Madge **EVANS**   Leslie **BANKS**   Helen **VINSON**   C. Aubrey **SMITH**   Basil **SYDNEY**

Based upon the novel "THE TUNNEL"
by B. KELLERMANN
Directed by MAURICE ELVEY

A **GB** PRODUCTION

Special Portrayals by
GEORGE ARLISS
AND
WALTER HUSTON

SCREEN NOTES

"Hands Across the Table," with Carole Lombard and Fred MacMurray, will open today at the Paramount.

Kay Francis's new picture, "I Found Stella Parish," succeeds "Shipmates Forever" tonight at the Strand.

"The Rainmakers," a new Wheeler and Woolsey comedy, will move into the RKO Palace today. "Metropolitan," with Lawrence Tibbett, also is on the program.

"Rendezvous," with William Powell, has been held over for a second week at the Capitol, and "Transatlantic Tunnel," with Richard Dix, will enter its second week today at the Roxy.

Paramount's film production of "Peter Ibbetson," co-featuring Gary Cooper and Ann Harding, will be at the Music Hall on and after Thursday.

Arthur K. Kelly, vice president in charge of sales for United Artists, left yesterday for the coast.

Gaumont British will show "Transatlantic Tunnel" to the sandhogs and engineers working on the Thirty-eighth Street Midtown Tunnel. The screening will take place on Monday afternoon in the New Jersey end of the tunnel.

Arthur Rosenstein, accompanist for Geraldine Farrar and other Metropolitan Opera stars, has joined Metro-Goldwyn-Mayer as musical instructor and coach. He will leave for Hollywood today.

The film rights to W. Somerset Maugham's novel and play "Caesar's Wife" have been bought by Warner Brothers.

Rochelle Hudson will appear opposite Harry Richman in "Rolling Along," which Columbia will produce.

Charles Boyer and his wife, Pat Patterson, left yesterday for the West Coast.

"Where are we?" she asked of the Hatter.

"Sh!" he whispered. "This is the preview of Francis Lederer's new picture at the Waldorf-Astoria. That's Mr. Lederer in the bellboy's uniform."

"This ridiculous uniform was not my idea," Mr. Lederer was saying, "blame it on the Fox publicity office."

"I don't believe a word of it," hissed the Duchess.

Mr. Lederer went on to tell how Lucius Boomer, president of the Waldorf, had objected to a scene in the picture in which a hotel manager peeps over the transom of a guest's room. It was quite innocent, said Mr. Lederer, but—on Mr. Boomer's word that it might damage~ hotel prestige—the scene was stricken out.

"So you see," he continued," the film industry is courteous to every one so I hope you newspaper critics will be just as considerate of us."

"Where's the connection?" asked Alice.

"No connection," snapped the Duchess. "Off with his head!"

Alice wanted to warn Mr. Lederer when he came around later and was kissing every one's hand, but she hadn't the time and suddenly found herself at the Helen Vinson party in the Gaumont-British office. Miss Vinson had just returned from England where she had made "Transatlantic Tunnel" and "King of the Damned." She had been abroad for four months, but almost every one was more interested in her reported romance with Fred Perry, the British tennis champion, than in her reaction to English film-making.

"The proof of my liking for English pictures," Miss Vinson was saying, "is that I plan to return in January for 'The King's Pajamas.' "

BRITISH ALIANZA FILMS
presenta
EL TUNEL TRANSATLANTICO
con
RICHARD DIX
MADGE EVANS
LESLIE BANKS
HELEN VINSON
C. AUBREY SMITH
GEORGE ARLISS
WALTER HUSTON
DIRIGIO
MAURICE ELVEY

TRANSATLANTIC TUNNEL
NEW YORK to LONDON

GB's Eight Star Special
Richard DIX
Leslie BANKS
Madge EVANS
Helen VINSON
C. Aubrey SMITH
Basil SYDNEY

Special portrayals by Mr. George Arliss and Mr. Walter Huston

GB PRODUCTION

DIRECTED BY MAURICE ELVEY

Death, in fact, is a euphemism for what Karloff impressed a few nervous individuals as being in "Frankenstein," for Death, after all, is dead, whereas Mr. Karloff, inexplicably, lives. The hollow-eyed, ashen-gray mask of his face, materializing against a backdrop of night and the infinite, was enough to send paying customers shrieking toward the exits. Perversely enough, Universal has found that it actually draws them to the box office, like flies to a syrup barrel.

It is a standing vogue in Hollywood to be, "in person" quite unlike the rôles one plays on the screen. Some players strive very hard for this antipodal effect, but Karloff doesn't have to. No one could possibly be like Dr. Frankenstein's monster or the mummy even if he wanted to be. The monster itself and the mummy, too (if they really existed), would rather be like Bing Crosby if they had any say so in the matter. The tragedy is that they haven't any.

1936

Ouanga
3 Live Ghosts
The Golem
Flash Gordon
Undersea Kingdom
The Devil Doll
Things To Come
The Man Who Lived Again

Ouanga

Released U.S. 1936

REAL LIFE DRAMAS
presents

THE LOVE WANGA

A story of Voodoo filmed in its entirety in the West Indies

COPYRIGHTED IN MONTREAL, CANADA

APPROVED CERTIFICATE No. 7703

PASSED BY THE NATIONAL BOARD OF REVIEW

LET VOODOO RELIEVE YOUR FRUSTRATIONS

Take them out on a real authentic Voodoo Kit. Imported from Haiti, this Black Magic Kit comes complete with Voodoo Doll, Lodestone, Pins, Magic Powders, directions and even name tags. If you want to give a different kind of a gift, THIS IS IT. Only $2.00 each plus 25c to cover mailing & handling charges. Send Cash, Check or money order (no C.O.D.) to

VOODOO
P. O. BOX
Chicago

if you dare

Bojangles and Fredi Open at the Fremont

Fredi Washington and Bill (Bojangles) Robinson have featured roles in the picture, "One Mile from Heaven," which opens at the Fremont Theatre, Monday, and continues through Tuesday.

Bojangles has the part of a kindly tap-dancing cop, and Fredi Washington plays the part of a mother who has adopted a white child. Sally Blaine is the child's real mother.

The story is packed with thrills and excitement, but finally comes — to a novel and exciting ending.

For Wednesday and Thursday, the picture will be "New Faces of 1937," featuring the Chocolateers and other colored players.

GEO. W. TERWILLIGER
Director Lubin Co.

Motion Pictures
"POCOMANIA" COMES TO PALACE TONIGHT

Everyone remembers that recently a picture was taken in its entirety in this island. The picture was a Lenwal production and was produced and directed by Arthur Leonard from an original story by George Terwilliger. This picture has been called POCOMANIA.

It will also be remembered that Nina Mae McKinney, celebrated coloured star together with Jack Carter, Ida James, Hamtree Harrington, Willa Mae Lane and Emmett Wallace all made a personal appearance on the stage of the Palace before production commenced. The dancers, extras and crowds were natives of this island and the picture is the first to have been successfully filmed in this island and to receive the acclaim of New York critics.

POCOMANIA takes full advantage of the natural beauties and background of this island by weaving the story within the framework of a travelogue, which opens the picture and leads the story. The travelogue shows the famous Myrtle Bank Hotel, the Glass Bucket Club, colourful Spanish Town, and shows bananas being loaded on the ships at the docks and presents the Linstead Market dancers in Jamaica's well known folk song "Sweetie Charlie."

POCOMANIA ran into a certain amount of trouble with the Censors but has eventually been passed on the understanding that it will be made clear to the public of Jamaica that it has been allowed for the purpose of showing up the stupidity and wickedness of Pocomania and other pagan rites.

POCOMANIA is a picture that no Jamaican should miss.

SHELDON LEONARD AND THE SHOW GOES ON

BROADWAY AND HOLLYWOOD ADVENTURES

3 Live Ghosts
Released U.S. January 10, 1936

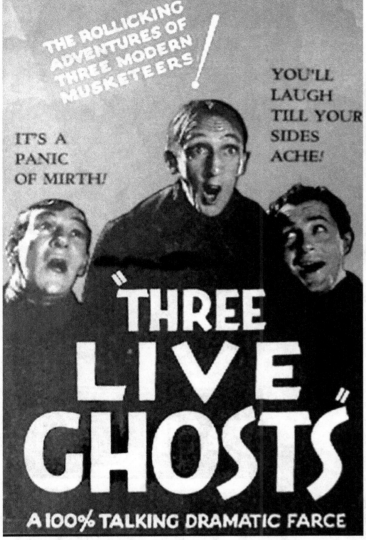

THE ROLLICKING ADVENTURES OF THREE MODERN MUSKETEERS!

IT'S A PANIC OF MIRTH!

YOU'LL LAUGH TILL YOUR SIDES ACHE!

"THREE LIVE GHOSTS"

A 100% TALKING DRAMATIC FARCE

3 LEVANDE SPÖKEN

OMEDI I 6 AKTER MED ANNA Q. NILSSON I HUVUDROLLEN REGI GEORGE FITZMAURICE OFFIGIN PARAMOUNT

They'll haunt you with laughter!!!

THREE LIVE GHOSTS

RICHARD ARLEN
CLAUDE ALLISTER
BERYL MERCER
Dudley Diggs

M-G-M HIT

Wednesday And THURSDAY

QUEEN BROWNSVILLE

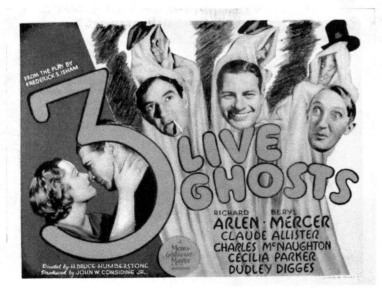

FROM THE PLAY BY FREDERICK S. ISHAM

3 LIVE GHOSTS

RICHARD ARLEN · BERYL MERCER
CLAUDE ALLISTER
CHARLES McNAUGHTON
CECILIA PARKER
DUDLEY DIGGES

Directed by H. BRUCE HUMBERSTONE
Produced by JOHN W. CONSIDINE JR.

JOSEPH M. SCHENCK presents

"Three Live Ghosts"

Directed by THORNTON FREELAND

MAX MARCIN Production

Based on the Stage Play "Three Live Ghosts" by Frederick S. Isham

UNITED ARTISTS PICTURE

NOMINATED FOR THE LAUGH PRIZE OF 1936!

THREE LIVE GHOSTS

From the play by FREDERICK S. ISHAM
Directed by H. BRUCE HUMBERSTONE
Produced by JOHN W. CONSIDINE, Jr.

While their friends were singing 'The Cemetery Blues'...the 3 LIVE GHOSTS were singing 'Hail Hail The Gang's All Here'.

The grand stage comedy that millions have laughed at...is now a howling romantic delight!

with RICHARD ARLEN BERYL MERCER

Claude Allister
Charles MacNaughton
Cecilia Parker
Dudley Digges

A Metro-Goldwyn-Mayer PICTURE

M-G-M, producers of "A Night at the Opera", know how to put you in good humor with gay comedies.......
.....Here's their latest laughing hit!

Shows Nightly 7:30 - 9:30
Matinees Sundays and Holidays at 3:00

FAMILY THEATRE EAST TAWAS

Good Selections Of Short Features With All Programs

WED THU   FEB 5 - 6
SPEND AN EVENING OF THRILLS AND LAUGHTER WITH

3 LIVE GHOSTS
RICHARD ARLEN - BERYL MERCER
CLAUDE ALLISTER

FRI SAT   FEB 7 - 8
IT'S TIPSY WITH TIP - TOP MERRIMENT
EDWARD EVERETT HORTON
YOUR UNCLE DUDLEY
LOIS WILSON & ALAN DINEHART

SUN MON TUE   FEB 9 - 10 - 11
HIGH FLIERS! BROKEN WINGS!
JAMES CAGNEY - PAT O'BRIEN
CEILING ZERO
ISABEL JEWELL & B. MacLANE

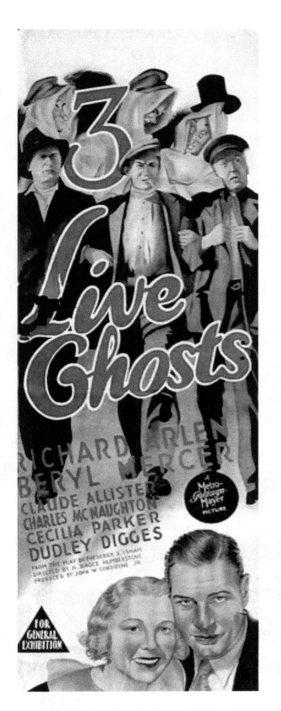

The Golem

Released U.S. March 21, 1936

Small Talk About Stage And Screen

By H. M. LEVY

Best film in town over the weekend—"The Buccaneer" ... Next best—"The Golem" ... To show, "You're a Sweetheart" ... Best role—Akim Tamiroff as Dominique You, the cannoneer ... Next best—Harry Baur as the mad emperor in "Golem." ...

A foreign list of bests, including the British importations, probably would begin with "The Eternal Mask." In quick succession would follow Russia's "The Last Night" and "The Thirteen," Alfred Hitchcock's "The Woman Alone" and then, in an untidy jumble, "The Man Who Could Work Miracles," the Viennese "Episode," the Knud Rasmussen "Wedding of Palo," the German "Amphitryon," the Russian "Beethoven Concerto" and the French "The Golem."

Theater-goers are deeply interested in the high standard of French films being presented in larger cities at present "Mayerling" "Golem" "Under Western Skies" are three productions which are attracting unusual attention and each of them has been accorded high praise Harry Baur leading man in 'Golem' is a fine actor

* * * *

CONCERNING THE GOLEM LEGEND

OF the many myths and legends surrounding the artificial creation of life, none has been more enduring than that of the Golem, which originated in the tortured, twisted ghetto of medieval Prague. Its archaic charm has persisted for three hundred years or more, and even Gustav Meyrink, an authority on the lore of the period, says in his novel, "Der Golem"—"I really do not know what the origin of the Golem legend is, but that somewhere something which cannot die haunts this quarter of the city (Prague) and is somehow connected with the legend, of that I am sure."

But this much we know. Rabbi Loew, a savant of the sixteenth century, a student of science and the Kabbala, created a being to which he gave human form, and which was endowed with colossal strength. The legend has it that through this learned man's profound knowledge of the Kabbala he was able to employ the mystic characters for the name of God so as to endow this figure with life. Bloch, in his "Legends of the Ghetto of Prague" explains that "* * * those, however, who do not believe in and deny any justification for the mystical and the occult, aver that we have here to deal with a symbol the allegorical meaning of which was eventually forgotten, because of the clearness and vividness of the symbol itself, which has consequently come down through the centuries with a sort of independent life of its own in the shape of a legend."

The Golem was formed of clay, it served its master dutifully and loyally; ultimately, however, it became mad and ran amuck, so that its master had to turn it back again into earth, which he did by taking away from it the "Shem," the sacred word, the life-principle. The Golem (meaning "strong") was created only incidentally as a servant. Its chief duty was to protect the ghetto of Prague from the many acts of persecution directed at it by the chancellor of Emperor Rudolph II. In 1610 Rabbi Loew died, returning the Golem to an inanimate state. It was then abandoned in the attic of the Altneu Synagogue. But both Rabbi Loew and the Golem became, in the eyes of the oppressed Jews, who believed in their ultimate liberation through the offices of rabbi and golem, a symbol of freedom. Without a doubt, the faith and unshakable confidence in a heaven-sent "deus ex machina" helped to strengthen the morale of the oppressed people and made the burden of their sufferings easier.

HARRY BAUR et **GERMAINE AUSSEY** dans **"LE GOLEM"**

UNITED ARTISTS

Flash Gordon

13 Chapter Serial, First Chapter Released U.S. April 6, 1936

THE BIG FEATURE SENSATION!

FROM ALEX RAYMOND'S FAMOUS NEWSPAPER

CARL LAEMMLE presents

BUSTER CRABBE as FLASH GORDON

with JEAN ROGERS as DALE ARDEN

CHARLES MIDDLETON as EMPEROR MING... PRISCILLA LAWSON as LURA
FRANK SHANNON as DR. ZARKOV ..... STANLEY J. SANFORD as VULTAN
RICHARD ALEXANDER as PRINCE ZARIN — AND — JAMES PIERCE · DUKE FORD JR. · LON POFF

DIRECTED BY FREDERICK STEPHANIE
SYNDICATED BY KING FEATURES
A UNIVERSAL PICTURE

AMAZING STRANGE WORLD ADVENTURES!

LAST TIMES TODAY LAUREL and HARDY in "THE BOHEMIAN GIRL"

STATE SUNDAY AND MONDAY

Watch Cassidy go into action when a prairie gang double-crosses his pal

Adolph Zukor presents

Clarence E. Mulford's
"CALL OF THE PRAIRIE"

BILL BOYD
JIMMY ELLISON.

SPECIAL EXTRA ADDED ATTRACTION

LARRY (BUSTER) CRABBE as
FLASH GORDON
IN
"THE PLANET OF PERIL"
FROM ALEX RAYMOND'S FAMOUS NEWSPAPER STRIP

MANOR
LAST DAY
FRED ASTAIRE · GINGER ROGERS
"FOLLOW THE FLEET"
FREE PARKING FOR OUR PATRONS
Mon. & Tues.- Ann Harding - Herbert Marshall in 'The Lady Consents'

BLIXT GORDON I NYA VÄRLDAR

LARRY "BUSTER" CRABBE.

JEAN ROGERS · CHARLES MIDDLETON · FRANK CHANNON.

THE TUNNEL OF TERROR

CHAPTER NO. 2

FLASH GORDON

FROM ALEX RAYMOND'S FAMOUS NEWSPAPER STRIP

BUSTER CRABBE as FLASH
JEAN ROGERS as DALE ARDEN

CHARLES MIDDLETON as EMPEROR MING
PRISCILLA LAWSON as LURA
FRANK SHANNON as DR. ZARKOV
JOHN LIPSON as VULTAN
RICHARD ALEXANDER as PRINCE ZARIN

A UNIVERSAL PICTURE

THE GIGANTIC SERIAL SPECTACLE!

Undersea Kingdom

13 Chapter Serial, First Chapter Released U.S. May 30, 1936

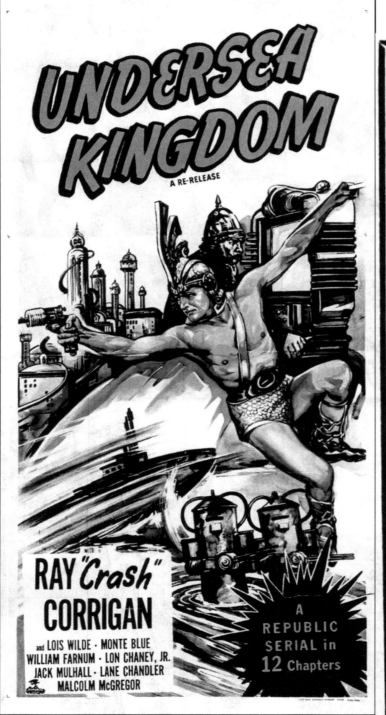

A REPUBLIC SERIAL *in* 12 AMAZING EPISODES

REPUBLIC PICTURES *presents*

UNDERSEA KINGDOM

with

RAY (CRASH) CORRIGAN

LOIS WILDE · MONTE BLUE · WILLIAM FARNUM
LON CHANEY JR. · LANE CHANDLER
JACK MULHALL · MALCOLM McGREGOR

PRODUCED *by* NAT LEVINE
DIRECTED *by* B. REEVES EASON · JOSEPH KANE
SCREEN PLAY *by* JOHN RATHMELL
MAURICE GERAGHTY · OLIVER DRAKE
ORIGINAL STORY *by* TRACY KNIGHT · JOHN RATHMELL

Chapter 1 BENEATH THE OCEAN FLOOR

A REPUBLIC SERIAL IN 12 AMAZING EPISODES *Chapter 12* ASCENT TO THE UPPERWORLD

REPUBLIC PICTURES *presents*
UNDERSEA KINGDOM

EMPTIED FAST

The bitter feuds that swept the west in the days of range warfare are brought back to life in a highly realistic form by Buck Jones in the picture, Empty Saddles, showing today and Monday at the Bijou theater. Buck buys the abandoned ranch and creates a dude ranch, although he is warned not to do so. Chapter three of the serial, Undersea Kingdom, will also be shown.

* * * *

ALCO

Last Times Today
John Wayne in "Lonely Trail", also "Undersea Kingdom."

Monday and Tuesday
Lewis Stone, James Gleason, and Bruce Cabot in "Don't Turn 'Em Loose."

Friday and Saturday
James Gleason and Helen Broderick in "Murder on a Bridle Path", also "Undersea Kingdom."

A REPUBLIC SERIAL IN 12 AMAZING EPISODES *Chapter* 7 THE SUBMARINE TRAP

REPUBLIC PICTURES present

UNDERSEA KINGDOM

REPUBLIC PICTURES present

"Undersea Kingdom"
RAY "CRASH" CORRIGAN

Episode 3
THE ARENA of DEATH

A REPUBLIC SERIAL

204

A REPUBLIC SERIAL IN 12 AMAZING EPISODES *Chapter 6 The Juggernaut Strikes*

REPUBLIC PICTURES *presents*

UNDERSEA KINGDOM

REPUBLIC
PICTURES

Undersea Kingdom

WITH

RAY "CRASH" CORRIGAN

LOIS WILDE · MONTE BLUE · WILLIAM FARNUM · LON CHANEY JR.
LANE CHANDLER · JACK MULHALL · MALCOLM McGREGOR

Episode 4
REVENGE of the VOLKITES
A REPUBLIC SERIAL

Produced by NAT LEVINE

THE NEW THEATRE
REISTERSTOWN, MARYLAND

Saturday, November 21st

BARTON MacLANE, JUNE TRAVIS
and WARREN HULL in

"BENGAL TIGER"

See the most ferocious tiger in captivity — when he meets
the best Cat Man in the Circus World.

Comedy—"Violets in Spring" News Acts

Also—"The Undersea Kingdom"

 **STATE** Now Showing

PLAY SCREENO
TONITE 9 P. M.

2 Ace Features—Serial

ROGER   GRACE
PRYOR   BRADLEY

Gay with gals . . . crammed
with comedy . . . the sky's
the limit for laughs!

"SITTING ON THE MOON"

Co-Feature

1st Showing in City

Kermit Maynard

James Oliver Curwood's
"Wildcat Trooper"

PLUS

LAST CHAPTER
"UNDERSEA KINGDOM"

 Kiddies
Look!
Special
Mat. Sat.

ONE HOUR OF COMEDIES

The Devil Doll

Released U.S. July 10, 1936

AT THE MARLOW

If you enjoy a really high-class, well-handled mystery thriller, then "The Devil Doll," current offering at the Marlow theater, is exactly the picture you're looking for. For, not since Lon Chaney turned in his greatest performance in "The Unholy Thief," has the screen had such a thoroughly enjoyable tale of this sort.

Dealing with a mad scheme of revenge through the employment of human beings that have been dwarfed to "dolls" of not over 13 inches in height, "The Devil Doll" is a cleverly worked out story. An insane scientist who has worked out the serum for the dwarfing of humans, employs his "dolls" for uncanny thefts of fabled jewels, as well as murders for vengeance.

Lionel Barrymore has one of his greatest roles in "The Devil Doll" and is ably supported by Maureen O'Sullivan and Frank Lawton in the romantic roles. A Popeye cartoon, "I Wanna Be a Lifeguard" is an added attraction of merit on this Marlow program, which continues through tomorrow.

The greatest thrill-mystery-romance since Lon Chaney's "The Unholy Three"!

There was a little old lady who ran a doll shop in Montmartre . . . but she wasn't a little old lady . . . and the dolls were not toys . . . they came to life to kill — to wreak the most amazing revenge that a human fiend ever conceived!

For the millions who thrilled to Lon Chaney's great triumphs, such as "The Unholy Three," a new and greater entertainment thrill now awaits!

The doll moves — it comes to life!

Off to kill. Hypnotically guided by an unknown master mind!

THE DEVIL DOLL

Starring

Lionel

BARRYMORE

Frank Lawton (you remember him as David Copperfield) and Maureen O'Sullivan are a grand romantic team. They take part in one of the most amazing, thrilling stories you have ever seen or read in your life.

as Paul Duval, who escaped from Devil's Island with the secret that baffled science!

MAUREEN O'SULLIVAN as Lorraine, the beautiful daughter of the doll woman.

FRANK LAWTON as Toto, who loves Lorraine but is suspicious of a strange, unnatural horror.

ROBERT GREIG as Coulvet, cracked Parisian banker, marked for death.

HENRY B. WALTHALL as Marcel, a half-mad scientist who discovers a formula to reduce living beings to one-sixth their normal size.

PEDRO DE CORDOVA as Matin, victim of a human 12-inch death messenger.

GRACE FORD as Lachna, a beautiful girl who became a devil-doll.

Directed by TOD BROWNING The man who made Lon Chaney's greatest screen hits!

The diamond-studded bracelet was almost as big as the doll-criminal!

CAPITOL

Lunes 28 de Marzo de 1938

ESTRENO

de la emocionante producción Metro, hablada en español,

Muñecos infernales

Interpretada por

Lionel Barrymore
Maureen O' Sullivan
y Frank Morgan

De los antros ignorados del más allá, surge una muñeca terrible... Tras sí, va la muerte, la destrucción, el terror, y el placer malsano de la venganza...

Placer indecible de venganza... visión terrorífica de ínfimos muñecos humanos..

Reducción quimérica de toda la humanidad... Seres diminutos con pasiones gigantescas...

LIONEL BARRYMORE
MAUREEN O'SULLIVAN
FRANK LAWTON
Director:
TOD BROWNING
Un Film
METRO-GOLDWYN-MAYER

I. G. VILADOT - CONTROL OBER -

'DEVIL DOLL' ON FILM PROGRAM

Starring Lionel Barrymore, "The Devil Doll" is billed for Thursday and Friday. The story tells of a scientist, gone mad in his effort to discover a means of shrinking the atom. He conceives the theory that if all living creatures might be reduced to one-sixth of their natural size the world food supply would be adequate for all.

A banker, convicted unjustly of a crime, escapes from prison and acquires the mad scientist's uncanny secret. Barrymore portrays the wronged banker who slinks into Paris, disguised as a woman operating a doll shop. Other in the cast are Maureen O'Sullivan, Frank Lawton, Robert Greig, Grace Ford and Lucy Beaumont.

"Earthworm Tractors," Joe E. Brown's new comedy will be on the mount screen Saturday. Playing opposite the big-mouthed comedian are June Travis and Carol Hughes.

Things to Come

Released U.S. September 14, 1936

A glimpse of the world in which your great-great-grandfather will live can be seen in "Things to Come," H. G. Wells' amazing production of the future currently showing at the United Artists Theater.

This breath-taking Alexander Korda production shows the annihilation of the present civilization by the next world war and the reconstruction of the world by a group of scientists.

In this marvelous Utopia of 2036, according to Mr. Wells, life will be lived almost entirely in wonderful, spotless underground cities, flooded with artificial sunlight and ventilated by air conditioning apparatus. Houses will be made entirely of glass, and clothing, furniture and architecture will reach the ultimate in beauty, simplicity and utility.

Mammoth machines will do man's work, life will be leisurely and culture will flower. Science will expand its scope and young people will seek adventure as passengers in a gigantic projectile shot from a space gun to the moon.

The magnificent sets for "Things To Come" were designed by Vincent Korda, with the aid of Frank Wells, son of the author, and Arthur Bliss created their imposing musical background. "Things To Come" is a London Films production.

America's favorite comedian, W. C. Fields, in "Poppy," with Rochelle Hudson is the companion feature with "Things to Come."

The Shape of Things to Come

ORPHEUM BILLS WELLS' FANTASY, 'THINGS TO COME'

H. G. Wells Amazing Story Of Future Events Presented In Picture Now at Ellanay

"Things to Come," Describes Breakdown of Civilization Through Next War, Return To Primitive Living

H. G. WELLS' amazing forecast of the future, "Things to Come," is now at the Ellanay.

The widely-discussed film, which was produced by Alexander Korda, predicts the staggering developments in our world in the next century and its magnitude challenges anything ever attempted in Hollywood.

Opening in the year 1940, "Things to Come" describes the breakdown of our present civilization through the next war, and a return to primitive living.

Out of this hopeless state grows a marvelous new subterranean world—a sane, practical and very livable Utopia.

According to Mr. Wells, the life of the 21st Century will be lived underground almost entirely. The cities will be built in the sides of mountains, lighted by artificial sunlight and ventilated by conditioned air.

The houses will be glass, but windowless, furnishings and clothing will reach a high point of beauty and simplicity, the two-hour day will be a fact and humans will be propelled to the moon from a giant space gun.

Raymond Massey, Ralph Richardson, Sir Cedric Hardwicke, Pearl Argyle, Margaretta Scott and Patricia Hilliard head a cast of 20,000 in this truly stupendous production, which the noted William Cameron Menzies directed.

"Things to Come" is a London film, released through United Artists. The remarkable photography was obtained by Georges Perinal, the trick photography is by Harry Zech and the special effects were achieved by Ned Mann.

Vincent Korda designed the sets, with the aid of Frank Wells, son of the author, and Arthur Bliss is responsible for the musical background.

THE MARVELS OF TOMORROW BEFORE YOUR EYES TODAY!
'You can see the things you'll never live to do!' An amazing picture that will make you gasp with wonder ... thrill with excitement!

Startling Forecast for the Future

H. G. WELLS' THINGS TO COME

An ALEXANDER KORDA Production with Raymond Massey · Ralph Richardson · Sir Cedric Hardwicke · Pearl Argyle and a cast of 20,000 Directed by Wm. Cameron Menzies

"Vincent Lopez Band Act"
"Fox News" of the World

NOW PLAYING
Prices: 15-25-40c

ELLANAY

For those of you who cannot visit the Texas Centennial—you may see it on our screen.

WELLS' UTOPIA IS LIVABLE IN KORDA CINEMA

To Show Thursday And Friday; "Hearts Divided" Is Slated Today Through Tuesday

SURPRISE booking of H. G. Wells' "Things to Come," carded for road show presentation on Thursday and Friday, is highlight of the Paramount calendar.

LAST TIMES TODAY
"TWO AGAINST THE WORLD"
with Humphrey Bogart and Beverly Roberts

FRIDAY and SATURDAY
2 SUPER HITS 2
Feature No. 1
THE MARVELS OF TOMORROW BEFORE YOUR EYES TODAY!
You can see the things you'll never live to do! An amazing picture that will make you gasp with wonder ... thrill with excitement!

Startling Forecast for the Future

H. G. WELLS' THINGS TO COME

An ALEXANDER KORDA Production with Raymond Massey · Ralph Richardson · Sir Cedric Hardwicke · Pearl Argyle and a cast of 20,000 Directed by Wm. Cameron Menzies

A London Film released thru United Artists

ORPHEUM
WILL LOVE BE FORGOTTEN 100 YEARS FROM NOW?
H. G. WELLS
THINGS TO COME
On Same Program
"BUNKER BEAN"

H.G. WELLS' MIRACLE SHOW!

SEE— 1000 PASSENGER AIR LINERS!

SEE— ROCKET SHIP TO THE MOON!

SEE— THE BIRTH OF SUPERMAN!

AN ALEXANDER KORDA SPECTACLE
THINGS TO COME
WITH
RAYMOND MASSEY
RALPH RICHARDSON
SIR CEDRIC HARDWICKE
MARGARETTA SCOTT
AND A CAST OF 20,000
A FILM CLASSICS INC. RELEASE
GOOD PICTURES LIKE GOOD BOOKS NEVER GROW OLD

ROAD SHOW PRODUCTION OF 'THINGS TO COME'

Strand THEATRE

TONIGHT, 7:30 P.M.

SATURDAY—2 Shows, 7 & 9 P.M.
The most startling revelation of the
World of a 100 years from now ever
pictured.

"THINGS TO COME"

SEE: Nations destroy each other!
SEE! The Air-Men re-conquer the
world!
SEE: The giant space gun that
shoots rockets to the moon with humans as passengers—1001 other
marvels!

— also —

Comedy—Novelty—News

Friday show begins 7:30 P.M.—
"Things To Come" on the screen
about 8:30 P.M.
Saturday "Things To Come" will
come on screen about 7:40 and 9:40
P. M. "Law of The Wild" Serial
with above program Friday only.
BANK NITE SAT., 9 P.M.

Raymond MASSEY Margaretta SCOTT
Ralph RICHARDSON Cedric HARDWICKE
John CLEMENTS

MINERVA FILM

NEL 2000 GUERRA O PACE?
(VITA FUTURA)
Regia di
WILLIAN CAMERON MENZIES

'Things to Come' Marvel Film, Is At New Baxter

The trouble with adjectives like
"colossal" and "stupendous" is that
they seem strangely futile when a
reviewer attempts to apply them
to a picture like "Things to Come,"
Alexander Korda's production of
H. C. Wells' amazing predictions
of the developments slated for this
old world in the next century,
showing at the New Baxter theater today and Monday.

For "Things to Come" is without
question, the biggest cinema un-
dertaking it has been this reviewer's privilege to witness. There has
never been anything to approach it
in size, originality or variety and
it merges at once a screen masterpiece and the ultimate in entertainment.

213

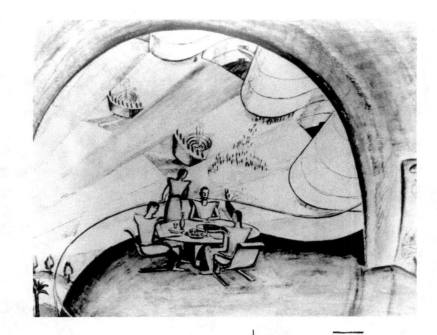

Another member of Britain's literary hierarchy, H. G. Wells, has agreed to write a story specially for the British screen. His scenario will cast a premonitory eye at the future of the world. Although Mr. Wells's book, "The Shape of Things to Come," provided the dramatic inspiration, his cinema narrative will be entirely new. The film will be produced by Alexander Korda, who directed "The Private Life of Henry VIII." With his usual thoroughness, Mr. Wells is making a study of cinema technique. Every now and then he slips into the studio of London Film Productions to watch "Symphony in Purple," which is in production with Douglas Fairbanks Jr. and Elizabeth Bergner. This week Mr. Wells is represented authorially in the local cinema with "The Invisible Man," which is at the Roxy.

"THINGS TO COME" Players: Raymond Massey, Margaretta Scott, Ralph Richardson. Based on H. G. Wells' startling novel. The story outlines the collapse of civilization after another Great War, initiated without notice by thousands of planes bombing defenseless cities. The whole world is impoverished, machines rust and collapse and cannot be replaced; a primitive society evolves in which men live in the ruins of once splendid towns and petty dictators exercise tribal authority. Plague stalks the earth. Order is restored by a band of aviators who, in giant planes, bomb the dictators into submission by a "gas of peace" which causes unconsciousness and no worse. Peace is established on the basis of world rule and mankind sets out on an age of progress founded on science.

"It seems, at first glance, daringly original. Original it is. It is daring only by contrast with Hollywood's timid preference for doing insofar as possible, only what has been done before. 'Things to Come' is therefore magnificent entertainment and a tribute to the sound showmanship that has made Producer Korda the kingpin in England's booming cinema industry . . . It differs from all predecessors in its class by demanding a cerebral rather than an emotional response."—Time. "A: Outstanding; Y: Thrilling; C: Mature."—Christian Century.

CURRENT BILL OFFERS STUDY IN CONTRASTS

Future Envisioned in Wells' Story, 'Things to Come,' as Age of Fantastic Marvels

It probably isn't by design that the seemingly pigmy events of to-day's newsreel follow close upon H. G. Wells' "Things to Come" on the Orpheum screen. But the record of current scientific and more everyday affairs does offer startling contrast to a vision of the world 100 years hence as Wells sees it.

The spectator has had a glimpse of strangely garbed inhabitants of glass houses in underground cities, of airmen reconquering the world, of new fashions in warfare and many other incidents.

"Things to Come," dual billed with Harry Leon Wilson's "Bunker Bean," will be shown until Friday night.

With a great deal of so-called continental froth, considerable sophistication and some downright hilarity, "One Rainy Afternoon," starring Francis Lederer, Ida Lupino, Hugh Herbert and Roland Young will be flanked by "Border Flight," a thrilling story of the heroes of the Border Patrol, featuring Frances Farmer, John Howard, Roscoe Karns and Grant Withers. The new bill starts Saturday.

"One Rainy Afternoon" is said to be perfectly suited to the talent of Lederer, Miss Lupino and Hugh Herbert. The plot revolves around a faux pas committed in a theater. Lederer kisses the wrong girl—the daughter of a prominent man. The fun begins there and is maintained throughout the picture.

H.G. WELLS' Things to come

A LONDON FILM PRODUCTION   DIRECTED BY WILLIAM CAMERON MENZIES.   PRODUCED BY ALEXANDER KORDA.   DISTRIBUTED BY

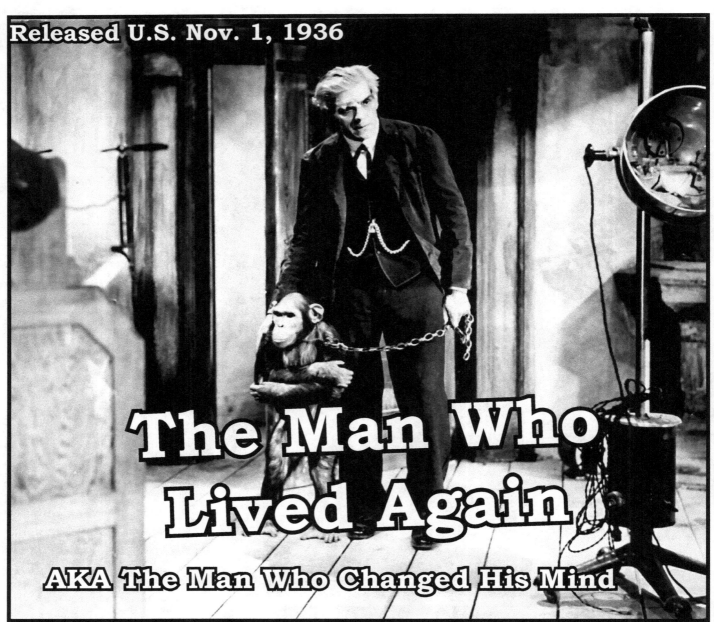

The Man Who Lived Again

AKA The Man Who Changed His Mind

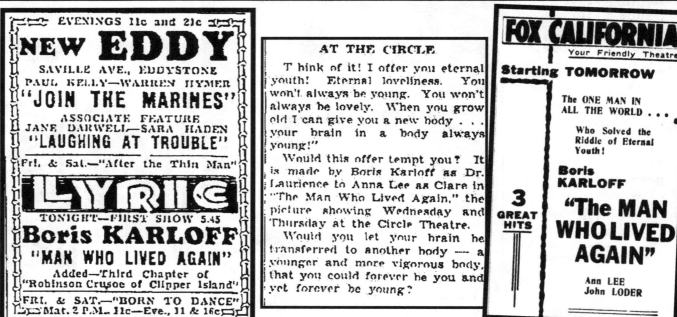

AT THE CIRCLE

Think of it! I offer you eternal youth! Eternal loveliness. You won't always be young. You won't always be lovely. When you grow old I can give you a new body . . . your brain in a body always young!"

Would this offer tempt you? It is made by Boris Karloff as Dr. Laurience to Anna Lee as Clare in "The Man Who Lived Again," the picture showing Wednesday and Thursday at the Circle Theatre.

Would you let your brain be transferred to another body — a younger and more vigorous body, that you could forever be you and yet forever be young?

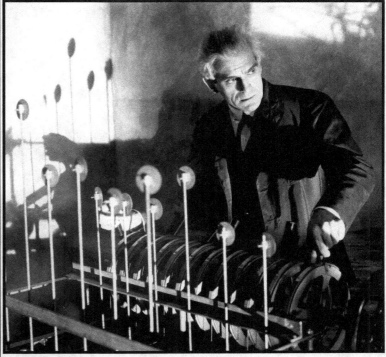

Boris
KARLOFF
in
THE MAN WHO
LIVED AGAIN

with

ANNA LEE
JOHN LODER
FRANK CELLIER
LYNN HARDING

A GB Production

Directed by
ROBERT STEVENSON

BORIS KARLOFF · *THE MAN WHO LIVED AGAIN*

A GB Production

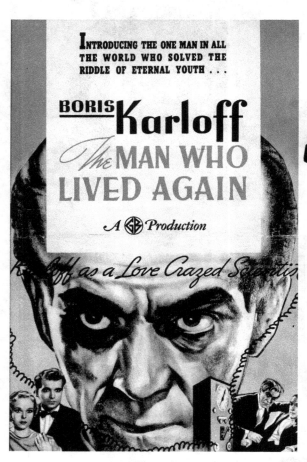

BRITISH FILMS ARE WELCOMED

Ohio Exhibitors Promise To Show Foreign Product.

COLUMBUS (AP) — Independent theater owners of Ohio informed the national sales representative of a British studio last week that they would welcome British films when they reached a par with those produced by Hollywood.

George W. Weeks of New York, sales manager for Gaumont-British productions, told the convention he felt America's prejudices against foreign-made pictures was receding.

"Studios are going up all around London," he said, "and heavy financial promotion is going on at present all over the British empire."

Weeks asserted that British movies were improving steadily, and he felt they offered the American product real competition.

"We are ready to invade the American market in an even bigger way than previously," he said.

In general discussion, the exhibitors, representing more than 300 independent Ohio picture houses, indicated that quality of the product would be their only criterion for judging British or American films.

British-Gaumont films are released by United Artists and occasionally are shown here at the Ohio and Plaza.

1937

The 13th Chair
Sh! The Ocotpus
Flash Gordon's Trip to Mars
The Missing Guest
Mars Attacks the World

The 13th Chair

Released May 7, 1937

Who doesn't know the legend of the thirteenth chair at a dinner? "The 13th Chair" is the Thursday picture at the Beltonian. Mystery prevails in the opening lines of this story and continues throughout. Metro-Goldwyn-Meyer is scoring a hit by bringing well known stars of the immediate past together in stories that require high acting ability. In addition to Dame May Whitty, new English sensation, this picture brings Madge Evans, Lewis Stone, Elissa Landi, Janet Beecher and Ralph Forbes among others. As a stage play, "The 13th Chair" ran 40 weeks on Broadway.

DUAL CHARACTER

Elissa Landi is a dual personality. She is an authoress and screen actress. She only uses her ability as an actress in The 13th Chair, however. This film, with Ralph Forbes in the male lead, closes today at the Strand theater. James

**'THE 13TH CHAIR' AT CALUMET TOMORROW
ON HUGE THRILL-PACKED PROGRAM**

Sh! The Octopus

Released September 12, 1937

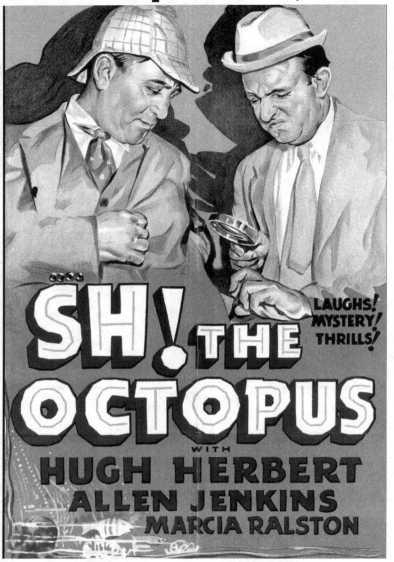

Two of screenland's best comedians, Hugh Herbert and Allen Jenkins are teamed in the Sigma film "Sh-The Octopus" a hilarious mystery comedy. This time they seem to outdo themselves as the world's dumbest detectives. Marcia Ralston and John Eldridge are in the supporting roles.

SH!
THE OCTOPUS
Hugh HERBERT
ALLEN JENKINS
MARCIA RALSTON
PRESENTED BY WARNER BROS

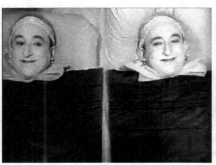

UNCLE CARL SPEAKS AS HE PLEASES

By THOMAS M. PRYOR

OFFICIALLY Carl Laemmle went into retirement in April, 1936, when he stepped down from the presidency of Universal Pictures after thirty years as a leading figure in the motion-picture industry. He was 69 at the time and a millionaire who wanted to learn how to play poker. We don't know whether he has yet mastered the game, but we do know that Mr. Laemmle has not completely divorced himself from the picture business, nor has he any intention of doing so.

At present he owns the distribution rights to the French film "Mayerling" in California, Oregon and Washington; has an interest in a theatre in Switzerland and is weighing the possibilities of re-entering the production field. The latter move will depend on how a screen play which writers now are working on shapes up. And until the script has been completed Mr. Laemmle intends to keep his plans to himself. However, he did say, with a note of finality, that the picture won't cost a million dollars.

* * *

Another indication of Uncle Carl's —as Hollywood affectionately calls Mr. Laemmle—unflagging interest in the movies is that he went shopping for pictures on his recent trip to France. He left here with the idea of buying American distribution rights to any picture or pictures which in his estimation compared favorably with "Mayerling." But he returned last week empty-handed, for the present crop of foreign pictures—the ones he saw, at least—failed to impress him.

Make no mistake about it, Uncle Carl still has his hand on the pulse of the industry. Hollywood's entertainment stock dropped in the public's estimation this year simply because of bad pictures, he says. "Everywhere I go and everybody I have spoken to during the last year has complained about the same thing—bad pictures," he said. The fact that this has been an off season for producers does not necessarily mean that the Hollywood production system has gone haywire, he continued, likening the present situation of the producers to that of the farmer who has a good crop one year and a bad one the next season.

Mr. Laemmle fails to comprehend why Hollywood is so solidly opposed to the pending Neely Anti-Block Booking Bill, for he believes that it will prove to be of benefit to the producers in the long run. "It is a good thing for the industry," he said, "because it will force producers to make only good pictures. After all, the producer should not expect the exhibitor and the public to pay for his bad pictures just the same as for the good ones. The exhibitor should have the privilege of buying pictures one at a time,

Jack Haley in "Alexander's Ragtime Band," playing its fifth week at the Roxy.

passing up those he doesn't like. The producer then will use whatever ability he possesses to make good ones."

Another advantage, according to Mr. Laemmle, is that exhibitors would have to pay higher rental fees. This the exhibitors would not mind, he believes, because the theatre operator—showing only the best pictures obtainable—would more than make up the added cost by increased box-office receipts. Theatre attendance would increase materially, says Mr. Laemmle, if the public honestly felt that it was getting its money's worth in quality.

Uncle Carl, who feels that his fellow-producers will resent his talking this way, also agrees in principle with the Department of Justice, which recently took steps to separate the production end from the exhibition field. "Producers should stick to making pictures," he stated. "If they also operate theatres the independent exhibitor is bound to suffer, because of preference shown the company-owned houses. Yes, it will be a wonderful thing if producers stop owning theatres."

And that was as far as Uncle Carl got in his conversation with us the other evening, for the doorbell rang and other more personal guests took over.

* * *

NEWSREEL THEATRE: A new 550-seat Newsreel Theatre will be opened within a week or so at Broadway and Seventy-second Street. The theatre is part of a taxpayer building erected on the site formerly occupied by the old St. Andrew Hotel. It will be operated by Newsreel Theatres, Inc., which also runs the Embassy Newsreel Theatre on Seventh Avenue near Forty-seventh Street. Like the Embassy, the Seventy-second Street theatre will devote its entire program to newsreels and occasional shorts.

1938

Flash Gordon's Trip to Mars
The Missing Guest
Mars Attacks the World

Flash Gordon's Trip to Mars

15-Chapter Serial, First Chapter Released U.S. March 21, 1938

Flash Gordon's Trip To Mars (Gaiety):

The first three episodes of Universal's serial, "Flash Gordon's Trip to Mars," based on the famous newspaper strip, "Flash Gordon," comes to the Gaiety Theatre to-morrow bringing with it a whirlwind of excitement.

The story revolves around Flash Gordon, an earthman who with his friends, goes to Mars in a rocket ship to destroy a gigantic lamp, which is sucking nitrogen from the earth's atmosphere, causing terrible sandstorms and fires.

Once on Mars, Flash a gaunt let of adventures, inc. ng capture by fierce clay people and battles with men who can walk through fire unharmed.

The roles of Flash Gordon and his sweetheart, Dale Arden, are enacted by Buster Crabbe and Jean Rogers. They played the same roles in the Flash Gordon serial which was released in 1936.

New surprises await those who see "Flash Gordon's Trip to Mars." There are light beams on which people walk and vacuum-tube subways.

The picture was produced by Barney Sarecky and co-directed by Ford Beebe and Robert Hill.

The first three episodes (1) New Worlds to Conquer; (2) The Living Dead; (3) Queen of Magic will be presented at the Gaiety Theatre to-morrow; and at the Movies Theatre on Wednesday. Along with the serial at the Movies on Wednesday, will be shewn "Public Wedding", a full length feature production with Jane Wyman.

YOUR FAVORITE NEWSPAPER ADVENTURE HERO ON THE SCREEN AGAIN!

The New UNIVERSAL presents

"FLASH GORDON'S TRIP TO MARS"

with

LARRY *Buster* CRABBE as "FLASH GORDON"

JEAN ROGERS as "DALE ARDEN"
CHAS. MIDDLETON as "EMPEROR MING"
FRANK SHANNON as "DR. ZARKOV"
BEATRICE ROBERTS as "QUEEN AZURA"
RICHARD ALEXANDER as "PRINCE BARIN"
MONTAGUE SHAW as "CLAY KING"

Original Story and Screen Play by
WYNDHAM GITTENS • NORMAN S. HALL
RAY TRAMPE • HERBERT DALMAS

FROM ALEX RAYMOND'S ASTONISHING
NEWSPAPER STRIP

OWNED AND COPYRIGHTED BY KING FEATURES INC. 2-7-38
DIRECTED BY FORD BEEBE AND ROBERT HILL

15 STARTLING CHAPTERS OF FURTHER ADVENTURES ON A NEW PLANET!

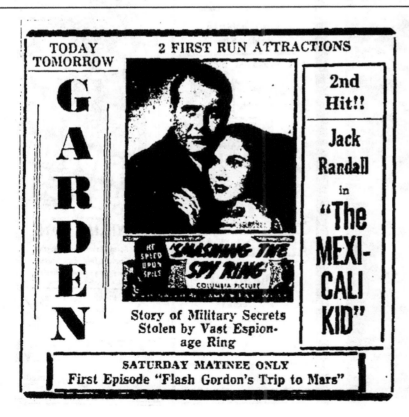

Chapter 8 · THE BLACK SAPPHIRE OF KALU

FLASH GORDON'S *TRIP-TO-MARS*
...LARRY "BUSTER" CRABBE as "Flash Gordon"
A UNIVERSAL PICTURE

A ADD BEAST AT BAY
CHAPTER NO 14
OF THE NEW UNIVERSAL PICTURE
FLASH GORDON'S TRIP TO MARS
LARRY "Buster" CRABBE as FLASH GORDON

JEAN ROGERS as "DALE ARDEN"
CHARLES MIDDLETON as EMPEROR MING
FRANK SHANNON as DR. ZARKOV
BEATRICE ROBERTS as QUEEN AZURA
RICHARD ALEXANDER as PRINCE BARIN
MONTAGUE SHAW as "CLAY KING"

Original Story & Screen Play by
WYNDHAM GITTENS · NORMAN S. HALL · RAY TRAMPE · HERBERT DALMAS
Directed by FORDE BEEBE & ROBERT HILL

From ALEX RAYMOND'S Astonishing NEWSPAPER STRIP Owned and Copyrighted by King Features

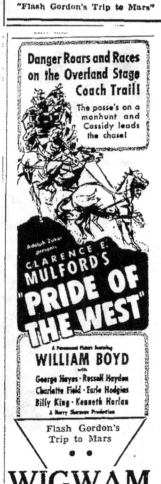

Chapter 9 · SYMBOL OF DEATH

FLASH GORDON'S **TRIP·TO·MARS**
...LARRY "BUSTER" CRABBE as "Flash Gordon"
A UNIVERSAL PICTURE

YOUR FAVORITE NEWSPAPER ADVENTURE HERO
ON THE SCREEN AGAIN!

NEW WORLDS TO CONQUER

CHAPTER No 1

OF THE New UNIVERSAL PICTURE

FLASH GORDON'S TRIP TO MARS

WITH LARRY "Buster" CRABBE as "FLASH GORDON"

JEAN ROGERS as "DALE ARDEN"
CHAS. MIDDLETON as EMPEROR MING
FRANK SHANNON as DR. ZARKOV
BEATRICE ROBERTS as QUEEN AZURA
RICHARD ALEXANDER as PRINCE BARIN
MONTAGUE SHAW as "CLAY KING"

Original Story and Screen Play by
WYNDHAM GITTENS · NORMAN S. HALL
RAY TRAMPE · HERBERT DALMAS

FROM ALEX RAYMOND'S ASTONISHING NEWSPAPER STRIP   OWNED BY KING FEATURES, INC.

Chapter 12 MING THE MERCILESS

YOUR FAVORITE NEWSPAPER
ADVENTURE HERO ON
THE SCREEN AGAIN!

"FLASH GORDON'S TRIP TO MARS"
LARRY "Buster" CRABBE as
"FLASH GORDON"

The Missing Guest

Released U.S. August 12, 1938

Ghostly! Giggly! Grand!

THE MISSING GUEST

with PAUL KELLY
CONSTANCE MOORE
WILLIAM LUNDIGAN

Screenplay by Charles Martin and Paul Perez · A NEW UNIVERSAL PICTURE · Directed by John Rawlins
Based on a story by Erich Philippi · Associate Producer: Barney A. Sarecky

Mysterious slayings and disappearances in an eerie "ghost house" that brings thrills, chills and surprises, alternate with outbursts of hilarious comedy in "The Missing Guest", starring Paul Kelly and Constance Moore coming to the Grand Theatre Tuesday and Wednesday.

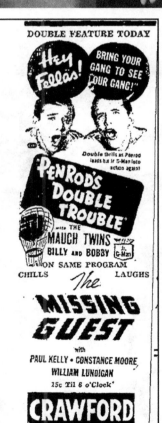

Ghostly! Giggly! Grand!

THE MISSING GUEST

with PAUL KELLY
CONSTANCE MOORE
WILLIAM LUNDIGAN

Screenplay by Charles Martin and Paul Perez
Based on a story by Erich Philippi
• A NEW UNIVERSAL PICTURE •
Directed by John Rawlins
Associate Producer: Barney A. Sarecky

Sparkling with hilarious scenes of comedy set against the spooky background of a mysterious ghost house, and featuring Paul Kelly, William Lundigan, Constance Moore, Edward Stanley, Selmer Jackson, Patrick J. Kelly, Harlan Briggs and other well known players, Universal's latest production, "The Missing Guest," comes to the Ritz Theatre Thursday to Saturday.

The plot deals with the efforts of a fresh and reckless young reporter to solve the mystery of the notorious Blue Room. As a result, ghosts and giggles, thrills, chills and surprises vie for supremacy during the production.

Produced by Barney Sarecky and directed by John Rawlins, "The Missing Guest" is the "new kind" of screen comedy-mystery production. It was written by Charles Martin and Paul Perez.

The *Unseen* Hand..

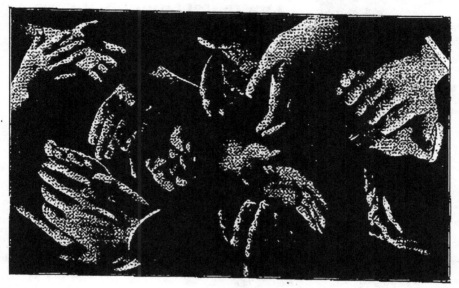

Send an expedition to Africa to film this glorious novel in its authentic locale!

Locate a little English boy to depict the heart-stirring story of a beloved Dickens character!

Search the world for the one man who knows better than all others how people lived in Elizabethan days — what they wore, what they ate, the manner of their dress and their talk!

Reconstruct an historic palace — re-create an historic battle — build a volcano! Erect a city and set it aflame! Loose a flood that will wash whole villages away!

It is *you* who order these things — and they are done. And whether you applaud with your hands or your heart at the conclusion of a motion picture, your approval echoes in the lives of unseen thousands who have collaborated in its making.

It is for your entertainment that an army of the world's greatest talents is ever on the march, forging ahead to open new vistas for your delight — adding brilliant new recruits from all the arts every day in the year.

Spare nothing, says Hollywood, to make the motion picture theatre the happy haven it is, the place to which millions may confidently come for freedom from boredom and care... for suspense that makes the pulse beat faster... for romance that warms the heart... for hearty laughter and eye-filling beauty.

The unseen hands applaud — and we who make motion pictures hear the echo. It guides us, inspires us, challenges us to fresh endeavors to make the movies better and better.

Now — on the eve of the Golden Jubilee of motion pictures — there is ready for you a remarkable array of new productions — the finest, we feel, that have ever been presented in a single season. On them we have lavished all our skill, all our experience, all our resources.

Here are pictures to charm and to thrill — pictures to amaze and amuse — pictures destined to weave their magic about the hearts and the minds of millions of people — to lighten their labor and brighten their lives, to lift them out of the drab, workaday world into a new world of wonder — timeless and boundless.

See them — give yourself up to their spell — relax and let them work their magic. They are a tonic for your mind and your heart — *they are good for what ails you.*

Watch for these new season's pictures at your favorite theatre!

Mars Attacks the World

Released November 7, 1938

SCREEN NEWS HERE AND IN HOLLYWOOD

Universal to Release 'Mars Attacks World' in Effort to Capitalize on Broadcast

NEW PICTURE AT CRITERION

'Girls' School,' With Nan Grey, Anne Shirley and Ralph Bellamy Opens Today

Special to THE NEW YORK TIMES.

HOLLYWOOD, Calif., Nov. 1.—Universal today announced immediate release of an already filmed picture, "Mars Attacks the World," in an effort to capitalize on the Orson Welles radio broadcast. The film, which is a recut edition of their serial "Flash Gordon's Trip to Mars," distributed last Spring, was scheduled for January release, but has been moved up. The cast includes Larry Crabbe, Jean Rogers, Charles Middleton, Frank Shannon and Beatrice Roberts. Ford Beebe and Robert Hill directed from a screenplay by Ray Trampe, Norman S. Hall and Wyndham Gittens based on Alex Raymond's newspaper cartoon strip, "Flash Gordon."

Paramount has purchased "Moon Over Burma," an unpublished novel by Wilson Collison, author of "Red Dust," as a co-starring vehicle for George Raft, Dorothy Lamour and Fred MacMurray. The story is laid in Mandalay and Rangoon and will go into production early next Spring.

At the Rialto

MARS ATTACKS THE WORLD, story and screen play by Ray Trampe, Norman S. Hall and Wyndham Gittens, based on Alex Raymond's newspaper cartoon strip "Flash Gordon," syndicated by King Features, Inc.; directed by King Beebe and Robert Hill; produced by Barney A. Sarecky for Universal.

Flash Gordon	Larry "Buster" Crabbe
Dale Arden	Jean Rogers
Emperor Ming	Charles Middleton
Dr. Zarkov	Frank Shannon
Queen Azura	Beatrice Roberts
Happy	Donald Kerr
The Clay King	Montague Shaw
Prince Barin	Richard Alexander
Tarnak	Wheeler Oakman
Pilot Captain	Kane Richmond
Airdrome Captain	Kenneth Duncan

It's terrible, folks! Your correspondent has just dropped by his office long enough to shout this warning, and then he's heading for the tall timber. For Universal Pictures, on some wild, inconceivable impulse, has just released a new picture called "Mars Attacks the World" and it's wreaking havoc at the Rialto Theatre. Such stark, relentless realism you never saw—with a heroic gentleman named Flash Gordon climbing into a rocketplane with some equally intrepid companions and whizzing off to Mars for the purpose of combat. (Of course, the title should have been reversed, but let's not quibble at this dark moment.) And those appalling death-ray guns and nitron beams and atomic disintegrators—enough to scare the life out of a fellow! They shouldn't do such things.

But maybe your correspondent is inclined to be slightly skittish, for the rest of the patrons at the Rialto seemed strangely apathetic to this terrible thing that transpired. And one was even heard to remark that he had seen it all before, over an extended period of time, as a serial called "Flash Gordon's Trip to Mars," and that this was just a scissors-and-paste job because of——

But your trembling correspondent didn't wait for the explanation. He thought there was no time to waste. So he rushed, pale and shattered, from the theatre shouting, "Keep away! Keep away! It's terrible!" B. C.

THE MAGUS FILM GROUP PRESENTS

MARS ATTACKS THE WORLD & PLANET OUTLAWS

PUBLICITY

CREDITS

Filmcraft presents

"MARS ATTACKS THE WORLD"

With Larry "Buster" Crabbe, Jean Rogers, Charles Middleton, Frank Shannon, Beatrice Roberts, Donald Kerr.

Story and screen play by......Ray Trampe, Norman S. Hall and Wyndham Gittens.

Based on Alex Raymond's newspaper strip "Flash Gordon," syndicated by King Features, Inc.

Directed by ......Ford Beebe and Robert Hill

Associate Producer
......Barney A. Sarecky

Running Time 66 Minutes

CAST

Flash Gordon Larry "Buster Grabbe*
Dale Arden ....Jean Rogers
Emperor Ming ..Charles Middleton
Dr. Zarkov ......Frank Shannon
Queen Azura ...Beatrice Roberts
Happy ....Donald Kerr
The Clay King ...Montague Shaw
Prince Barin .Richard Alexander
Turnak ....Wheeler Oakman
Pilot Captain ...Kane Richmond
Airdrome Captain Kenneth Duncan

FILM SHOWS MARS INVADING WORLD

Filmcraft's new picture "Mars Attacks The World," a film based on a light-ray attack on the world by Martian warriors, such as recently excited the imagination of all America, will appear on the screen at the............. Theatre for a ....day run.

This Barney Sarecky production features Buster Crabbe as the hero whose favorite pastime is getting in and out of danger; Jean Rogers as his lovely leading lady; Frank Shannon in the role of a brilliant scientist and Beatrice Roberts as a cruel, though beautiful, villainness.

The story has to do with a sinister force from Mars which is drawing nitrogen from the earth's atmosphere, dealing death and destruction to its inhabitants. In desparation, a scientist accompanied by friends, starts off in a rocket ship for the purpose of locating and destroying the source of the Martian attack on the earth.

At this point is displayed some remarkable camera magic. To all appearances these men leave the world far behind them. They are attracted by the same force which is sucking the world's nitrogen and apparently hurtle towards Mars, the planet from which this menace is emanating.

One of the wierdest scenes of the picture is when the earthmen on Mars wander into a cavern and suddenly see the clay walls take shape in the form of clay men.

Buster Crabbe battles for life on a strange planet in Filmland's "Mars Attacks The World."

1 COL. SCENE MAT No. 1A

Donald Kerr, Buster Crabbe, Richard Alexander and Frank Shannon in a scene from Filmcraft's thrilling adventure film, "Mars Attacks The World."

2 COL. SCENE MAT No. 2A

MARTIAN ATTACK ON WORLD IN FILM

Unprecedented timeliness of its program schedule enables the ......

Theatre to release its latest feature picture "Mars Attacks The World," based on a story similar to that which has just captured the imagination of the country.

The picture went into production more than a year ago and has been in assembly ever since. Heading the cast is Larry "Buster" Crabbe, with Jean Rogers, Charles Middleton, Frank Shannon and Beatrice Roberts in support. The story was written by Ray Trampe, Norman S. Hall and Wyndham Gittens based on Alex Raymond's newspaper feature, "Flash Gordon" now being serialized in scores of American newspapers.

An elaboration of the serial, the film, "Mars Attacks the World," depicts an attempt by Martians, inhabitants of our sister planet, to destroy the earth by means of a nitron ray and other ultra-scientific means of destruction. The weird methods of warfare of the Martians as they ply their attack, form a thrilling series of scenes which, however, are led to a reassuring climax brought about by the opposing forces of the World headed by a young Earth scientist and his colleagues. They outwit the interplanetary destroyers at their own game.

Frank Shannon Buster Crabbe and Jean Rogers in Filmcraft's "Mars Attacks The World."

2 COL. SCENE MAT No. 2B

SYNOPSIS

(Not for Publication)

Queen Azura of Mars (Beatrice Roberts) and Emperor Ming (Charles Middleton) formerly of the planet Mongo, attempt to destroy the earth by means of a nitron lamp. Flash Gordon (Larry "Buster" Crabbe), Dr. Zarkov (Frank Shannon), Dale Arden (Jean Rogers) with Happy Hapgood (Donald Kerr) a reporter, accompanying them as a stowaway, fly to Mars in a Rocket Ship to save civilization. Forced down by Martians, they hide in a cave where they encounter the Clay People, living under the spell of Queen Azura's baleful magic. Flash and Zarkov leave Dale and Happy with the Clay People. They set out to capture Azura, free the Clay people from her spell and destroy the nitron lamp. Instead they are caught by Azura and Ming. Dale and Happy reach the captive Zarkov and Flash. All four escape from the Queen and the Emperor, accompanied by Prince Barin (Richard Alexander) and Azura and start back to the cave to force her to restore the Clay People to human flesh and blood. Ming gets away from them. He orders his airplanes to bomb the earth folk. The bombs kill Azura. Dying, she gives Flash her white sapphire. By using it he restores the Clay People to humanity. Gathering a band of followers, Flash invades Ming's palace, just as one of the Emperor's subordinates kills the half-crazed monarch. Flash and his friends return to the earth and receive the acclaim of the mankind they have saved.

BEAUTY STARS IN WAR FILM

Being an adventure film heroine is a picnic for Jean Rogers, but is would be a panic for a less courageous girl.

The pretty screen actress is seen opposite Buster Crabbe in Filmcraft's "Mars Attacks The World," a film drama of inter-planetary war, based on the same mythical Martian aggression which recently captured the imagination of all America, and coming to the ......

Theatre on ....

Jean is considered the gamest trouper in Hollywood's most hazardous profession. In her four years as a film heroine Miss Rogers has leaped from burning airplanes, she has featured in automobile crackups and she has been mauled and pushed around by screen heavies. She has jumped from high buildings, she has fallen from galloping horses, and she has been thrown down steep banks. She has never used a "stand-in."

Asked if her thrilling screen experiences had given her any fear complex, Miss Rogers replied in the negative.

Jean Rogers Simply Dotes On Dangers

Being an adventure film heroine is a picnic for Jean Rogers, but it would be a panic for a less courageous girl. The pretty screen actress seen opposite Buster Crabbe in Filmcraft's gripping drama,"Mars Attacks The World," now showing at the...... Theatre, is considered the gamest trouper in Hollywood's most hazardous profession. In her four years as a film heroine Miss Rogers has leaped from burning airplanes, has featured in automobile crackups and she has been mauled and pushed around by screen heavies. She has jumped from high buildings, she has fallen from galloping horses, and she has been thrown down steep banks. She has never used a double or "stand-in."

Asked if her thrilling screen experiences had given her any fear complex, Miss Rogers said during the filming of "Mars Attacks The World."

"Just the opposite. My nerves have become practically shock proof. It isn't that I'm brave. I'm simply immune to the things which used to frighten me when I first entered pictures."

In spite of her present daring, Miss Rogers came to Hollywood as a beauty contest winner, not as a champion athlete. In "Mars Attacks The World" she plays an American girl who accompanies Buster Crabbe to Mars when hostile forces there threaten to destroy the earth.

INTERPLANETARY WAR IS DEPICTED

Electric guns, light ray pistols and rocket ships zooming from planet to planet may soon become a real and practical as radio and airplanes are today.

That is the opinion of Buster Crabbe, former Olympic champion and star of Filmcraft's "Mars Attacks The World," spectacular drama based on the Martian war machines which recently captured the nation's imagination, and coming to .... Theatre on .... For six weeks Crabbe, Jean Rogers, his leading lady and other members of the cast, acted on gigantic Martian sets. Not a single prop, building or costume resembled anything in their lives as present day Americans, but they soon became accustomed to the outlandish gadgets with which they were surrounded.

"After the first few days of shooting," said Crabbe to interviewers, "it felt perfectly natural to walk on light beams. Taking a whirl in our steel rocket ship became as commonplace as taking a taxi."

MARTIAN VILLAIN IS REALLY HUMAN!

Here is an actor who wouldn't be a hero if he could . . . he makes more money being a villain!

This mercenary actor is Charles Middleton, veteran character man, who proudly bears the title of "best hated man on the screen." For years he has betrayed friends, and kidnaped beautiful girls in films and has found that crime decidedly *does pay*. Middleton has the meanest and cruelest role of his career in Filmcraft's "Mars Attacks The World" a film dramatization of a Martian bombardment of the earth similar to that which recently electrified the imagination of America. It comes to the .... Theatre on .... with Buster Crabbe and Jean Rogers in the leading parts. Middleton plays Ming the Merciless, Emperor of Mars, who thirsts to conquer the universe.

Frankly, Middleton admits that he wouldn't care to trade jobs with handsome screen heroes and make love to beautiful movie stars. Although he never wins the girl at the final fade-out, his villainy nets more jobs than he can handle.

"I believe my mean roles on the screen have a definite influence for good among those who see my pictures," he declares. "It is a warning for folks not to be the kind of man I play in the film. Their hatred for these characters prevent them from doing the outrageous tricks that I do on the screen."

In "Mars Attacks The World" Middleton out-does himself in atrocious behavior by bombarding the earth with a barrage of destructive rays. To save the human race, Buster Crabbe, Jean Rogers and Frank Shannon as a daring scientist make a counter attack on Mars by rocket ship.

Buster Crabbe, hero of Filmcraft's "Mars Attacks The World," fights off his foes with his electric ray gun.

1 COL. SCENE MAT No. 1B

VANISHING STARS ARE HIS SPECIALTY

Making people appear and disappear on the screen is a cinch for genial Jerry Ash, master magician of Hollywood studios . . . he used to do it right on the stage.

Jerry, who created the startling illusion scenes of Filmcraft's "Mars Attacks The World" now at the .... Theatre with Buster Crabbe and Jean Rogers featured, once worked for the great Chinese conjurer, Ching Ling Foo. Operating in full view of the audience, he learned how to make elephants vanish and fountains rise from the heads of Chinese stooges. After that turning human faces into clay masks and making movie actors walk on beams of light with a whole studio technical staff to help him build the illusion, was pretty much of a vacation for Ash.

Display Lines

Now — the year's big-thrill feature production. Sixty minutes of the most amazing adventures you ever witnessed! The astounding feature spectacle of strange world adventures!

The most amazing spectacle of the century! A giant rocket ship hurtling through space on a 500-mile-a-minute trip to the planet Mars!

Roar through space aboard a giant rocket ship! Shoot through the stratosphere at 500 mile-a-minute speed! Land on the mystery planet Mars! You'll gasp at weird adventures, uncanny men and amazing battles!

More sensational! More startling! More spectacular thrills than ever before captured by motion picture cameras!

Nothing like it before! Nothing to equal it ever again!

Unforgetable sights and adventures! One youth wielding mechanical marvels—mighty inventions of the world—against weird, destructive creations of menacing super-planets!

Red-blooded youth against monsters of science!

Clashing with fiendish forces on strange planets! Unbelievable! Awe-inspiring! Sensational! An adventure-seeking youth zooms into unfathomable space . . . shielding the World from dreadful doom! . . . In deadly battle with demon creatures of weird sky regions!

Man's wildest dream now comes true! Invading the neighbor planets of the Universe!

See! See! See!

The famous rocket ship hurtle through the stratosphere at bullet speed on its thrilling trip to Mars!
Queer, spectacular, mechanical and electrical inventions!
Escape through the ring of fire!
The amazing stratosled and the nitron loaded plane crash in mid-air!
The radio-active light ray gun!
Feats of super-human strength and daring that will take your breath away!
The disintegrating ray!
The mysterious nitron destructive ray!
The terrific battle to save the world from destruction!
The kingdom of the Clay Men!
The rocket ship plunge headlong to doom!
The magical powers of the black and white sapphires!
The vacuum tube subway!
Weird palaces, laboratories, torture chambers, whole cities that stagger the imagination!

SELL SPECTACULAR AND THRILLING ADVENTURE ON FRONT DISPLAY

"MARS ATTACKS THE WORLD" is definitely an exploitation picture and should be sold thrillingly and spectacularly in your lobby and out front. The front display shown above can be executed with posters, stills, cut-outs and a little ingenuity on the part of your house artist.

(1 and 2) The giant rocket ship and titles, for use atop marquee, are cut-outs from the poster. Brace well with wires and struts and also use wires to attach title to tail of rocket ship. Cloth trailing from tail of ship will give speed effect. Well spot-lighted, this will be an attractive piece day and night.

(3 and 4) The dramatic strange-world stills are great for panels on both sides of front interspersed with "thrill" and "see" lines.

(5) Use cut-out head, from either the posters or lobbies on either end of the marquee.

(6) A shadow-box still display with action stills on rotating belt passing peep-hole in box. Green and red lighting within will give it an eerie effect.

(7) A rocket ship shadow box, explained in lower right hand corner of this page.

(8) Your house artist can fake these satellite cut-outs or use small rocket ship cut-outs, from the one- and three-sheets, above and around box-office.

(9 and 10) Dress your ushers and ballyhoo man in "Man of Mars" costume, as explained to the left, below.

"MARS ATTACKS THE WORLD" BRINGS WILD ADVENTURES OF FUTURE TO SCREEN WITH BREATHLESS REALISM

Weird Air-Thrills-Future Planet-Wars

(Advance)

Filmcraft's picture, "Mars Attacks The World," a film of amazing adventure among the planets, will roar across the screen at the Theatre......for a......day run.

This Barney Sarecky production features Buster Crabbe as the hero whose favorite pastime is getting in and out of danger; Jean Rogers as his lovely leading lady; Frank Shannon in the role of a brilliant scientist and Beatrice Roberts as a cruel, though beautiful, villainess.

The story has to do with a sinister force from Mars which is drawing nitrogen from the earth's atmosphere, dealing death and destruction to its inhabitants. In desperation, a scientist accompanied by friends, starts off in a rocket ship for the purpose of locating and destroying the source of the annihilation.

At this point is displayed some remarkable camera magic. To all appearances these men leave the world far behind them. They are attracted by the same force which is sucking the world's nitrogen and apparently hurtle toward Mars, the planet from which this menace is emanating.

One of the weirdest scenes of the picture is when the earthmen on Mars wander into a cavern and suddenly see the clay walls take shape in the form of clay men.

Film Villainy Proves Highly Profitable

Here is an actor who wouldn't be a hero if he could . . . . he makes more money being a villain!

This mercenary actor is Charles Middleton, veteran character man who proudly bears the title of "best hated man on the screen." For years he has betrayed friends, and kidnaped beautiful girls in films and has found that crime decidedly *does* pay. Middleton has the meanest and crookedest role of his career in Filmcraft's "Mars Attacks The World" which comes to the........Theatre on....... with Buster Crabbe and Jean Rogers in the leading parts. He plays Emperor Ming the Merciless who thirsts to conquer the whole universe.

Frankly, Middleton admits that he wouldn't care to trade jobs with handsome screen heroes and make love to beautiful movie stars. Although he never wins the girl at the final fadeout, his villainy brings him more jobs than he can handle.

"I believe my mean roles on the screen have a definite influence for good among those who see my pictures," he declares. "It is a warning for folks not to be the kind of man I play in the film. Their hatred for the character prevents them from doing the outrageous tricks that I do on the screen."

Battle Of Worlds In Amazing Drama

(Review)

A thrilling new note in adventure yarns was sounded yesterday when Filmcraft's "Mars Attacks The World" opened at the...... Theatre. This is by far the best picture of its kind yet to appear on the cinematic horizon.

The story has to do with a mysterious force from Mars which is causing world ruin by drawing nitrogen from its atmosphere. Frank Shannon as a brilliant scientist sets out in his rocket ship to destroy this menace, accompanied by Buster Crabbe, his adventurer-assistant, and Jean Rogers his fiancee, along with a stowaway newspaper man. Traveling far out into space, they are suddenly pulled to Mars by the same force which is depleting the earth's nitrogen. Here the earth people encounter a series of exciting adventures which builds to an amazing climax.

Buster Crabbe, a former Olympic swimming champion, rounds out a flawless performance as the central character. Other good portrayals in this picture which was directed by Ford Beebe and Robert Hill are turned in by Jean Rogers as the lovely heroine, Frank Shannon as Dr. Zarkov, Charles Middleton as Ming the Merciless and Beatrice Roberts in the role of Queen Azura.

PLANET-TO-PLANET COMMUTING SOON A FACT, SAYS FILM STAR

Electric guns, light ray pistols and rocket ships zooming from planet to planet may soon become as real and practical as radio and airplanes are today.

That is the opinion of Buster Crabbe, former Olympic champion and star of "Mars Attacks The World" spectacular drama of adventure in interplanetary space which comes to the.....Theatre on.....For six weeks Crabbe, Jean Rogers, his leading lady and the other members of the cast, acted on gigantic sets representing Martian cities. Not a single prop, building or costume resembled anything in their lives so present-day Americans, but they soon became accustomed to the outlandish gadgets with which they were surrounded.

"After the first few days of shooting," said Crabbe to interviewers, "it felt perfectly natural to walk on light beams. Taking a whirl in our steel rocket ship became as commonplace as taking a taxi. After all, while strange to us today, all these trick devices in "Mars Attacks The World" are based on real scientific principles and may well become everyday realities in our lifetime."

A former student at the University of Hawaii and a graduate of the University of California at Los Angeles, as well as a champion athlete, Crabbe is an avid student of modern scientific experiment. His special hobby is electro-dynamics. It was his combination of mental and physical prowess that gained him the lead.

Jean Rogers and Buster Crabbe in a dramatic scene from Filmcraft's thriller "Mars Attacks The World."
1 COL. SCENE MAT No. 1C

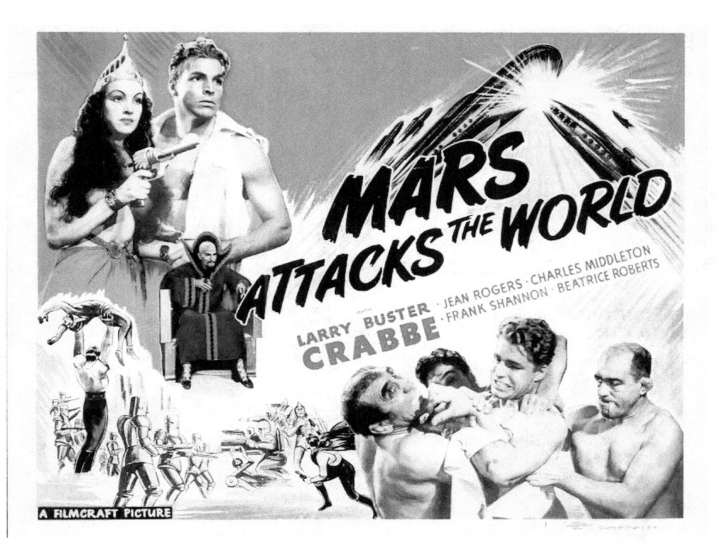

Martian Attack On World in Film

Unprecedented timeliness of its program schedule enables the State Theater to release its latest feature picture, "Mars Attacks The World," starting next Sunday, based on a story similar to that which has just captured the imagination of the country.

The picture went into production more than a year ago and has been in assembly ever since. Heading the cast is Larry "Buster" Crabbe, with Jean Rogers, Charles Middleton, Frank Shannon and Beatrice Roberts in support.

An elaboration of the serial, the film, "Mars Attacks the World," depicts an attempt by Martians, inhabitants of our sister planet, to destroy the earth by means of a nitron ray and other ultra-scientific means of destruction. The weird methods of warfare of the Martians as they ply their attack, form a thrilling series of scenes which, however, are led to a reassuring climax brought about by the opposing forces of the World headed by a young Earth scientist and his colleagues. They outwit the interplanetary destroyers at their own game.

Also on today's agenda is the première of "Mars Attacks the World" (strictly a motion picture) at the Rialto. This is a recut edition of Universal's serial, "Flash Gordon's Trip to Mars," which has been rushed out on the heels of a recent psychic phenomenon. In the cast are Larry "Buster" Crabbe and Jean Rogers.

NEGLECT OF CHILDREN LAID TO FILM HOUSES

Moss Suspends Licenses of Five in City-Wide Drive

A city-wide campaign has been started by the Department of Licenses to enforce regulations concerning children in motion-picture theatres, it was disclosed yesterday by Commissioner Paul Moss. Five Harlem theatres have had their licenses suspended temporarily and the owners of five others have been ordered to appear before the Commissioner today.

The licenses were suspended where theaters were found to have permitted children to sit among adults and adults to sit in sections reserved for children, and where such sections had no matrons visible. The owners of the five theaters, appearing before Mr. Moss yesterday at his office, 105 Walker Street, were warned that if the offenses were repeated their licenses would be canceled, putting them out of business permanently.

Mr. Moss began the campaign Friday afternoon, when he made a hasty inspection tour of Harlem theatres with two of his deputy commissioners and fourteen squads of policemen. After hearing testimony at the East 104th Street police station, he suspended the five theatres' licenses and ordered the owners of five others to appear before him to explain minor violations.

The suspensions were to be effective until the theatre owners saw the Commissioner yesterday, but he permitted the theatres to reopen at 6 P. M. on Saturday. They were the Eagle Theatre, Third Avenue between 102d and 103d Streets; Harlem Grand Theatre, 119 East 125th Street; Jewel Theatre, 11 West 116th Street; New Progress Theatre, 1,892 Third Avenue, and Stadium Theatre, 2,176 Third Avenue.

THE SCREEN CALENDAR

ASTOR—Gone With the Wind: Vivien Leigh, Clark Gable.*
BELMONT—Skeleton on Horseback: Hugo Haas, Z. Stepanek.
CAMEO—Life on the Hortobagy.*
CAPITOL—Gone With the Wind.*
CENTER—Pinocchio, opens Wednesday night.
CINECITTA—Love in Old Naples: Emma Grammatica.*
5TH AVE.—Ultimatum: Erich von Stroheim.
55TH ST.—Entente Cordiale: Victor Francen.*
GLOBE—The Lone Wolf Strikes: Warren William.
HOLLYWOOD—The Blue Bird: Shirley Temple.*
LITTLE CARNEGIE—Louise: Grace Moore.
LOEW'S CRITERION—Judge Hardy and Son: Mickey Rooney;* Wed., Congo Maisie: Ann Sothern, John Carroll.
MUSIC HALL—The Shop Around the Corner: James Stewart;* Thurs., The Swiss Family Robinson: Thomas Mitchell.
PARAMOUNT—Remember the Night: Barbara Stanwyck;* Wed., Geronimo: Preston Foster, Ellen Drew.
RIALTO—Green Hell: Douglas Fairbanks Jr., Joan Bennett.*
RIVOLI—The Grapes of Wrath: Henry Fonda, Jane Darwell.*
ROXY—Little Old New York: Alice Faye, Richard Greene.
STRAND—The Fighting 69th: James Cagney, Pat O'Brien.*
WORLD—Harvest: Fernandel.*

REVIVALS AND SECOND RUNS

APOLLO—Crainquebille and Payment Deferred.
ASCOT—Wuthering Heights: Merle Oberon.*
8TH ST.—Everything Happens at Night; Tues. and Wed., The Housekeeper's Daughter; Thurs., through Sat., Four Wives.
GRAMERCY PARK—Ninotchka; Thurs. and Fri., Invitation to Happiness and Zaza; Sat., Another Thin Man and Night of Nights.
LOEW'S STATE—The Great Victor Herbert: Walter Connolly.
NORMANDIE—Zaza; Mon. and Tues., Fire Over England; Wed. and Thurs., Goodbye, Mr. Chips.
PALACE—Swanee River and Married and in Love.
PIX—Shanghai and Mysterious Mr. Moto on Devil's Island; Mon. through Thurs., Souls at Sea and Easy Living; Fri., History Is Made at Night and True Confession.
PLAZA—Another Thin Man; Tues. through Thurs., The Housekeeper's Daughter.
68TH ST.—Dark Victory; Tues. through Thurs., The Women; Fri. through Sun., The Wizard of Oz.
SUTTON—Goodbye, Mr. Chips and Dancing Co-Ed; Tues. and Wed., I Was a Spy and Craig's Wife; Thurs. and Fri., The End of a Day and Yes, My Darling Daughter.
THALIA—The Informer; Thurs., Tevya: Maurice Schwartz.
TRANS-LUX, Lexington Ave. at 52d St.—The Private Lives of Elizabeth and Essex; Tues. through Fri., Ninotchka.
TRANS-LUX, Madison Ave. at 85th St.—We Are Not Alone; Tues. through Fri., Ninotchka.
*Holdover.

1939

The Phantom Creeps
Buck Rogers
The Gorilla
On Borrowed Time
The Man Who Could Not Hang
The Wizard of OZ
Cat and the Canary
Torture Ship
Return of Dr. X
The Devil's Daughter

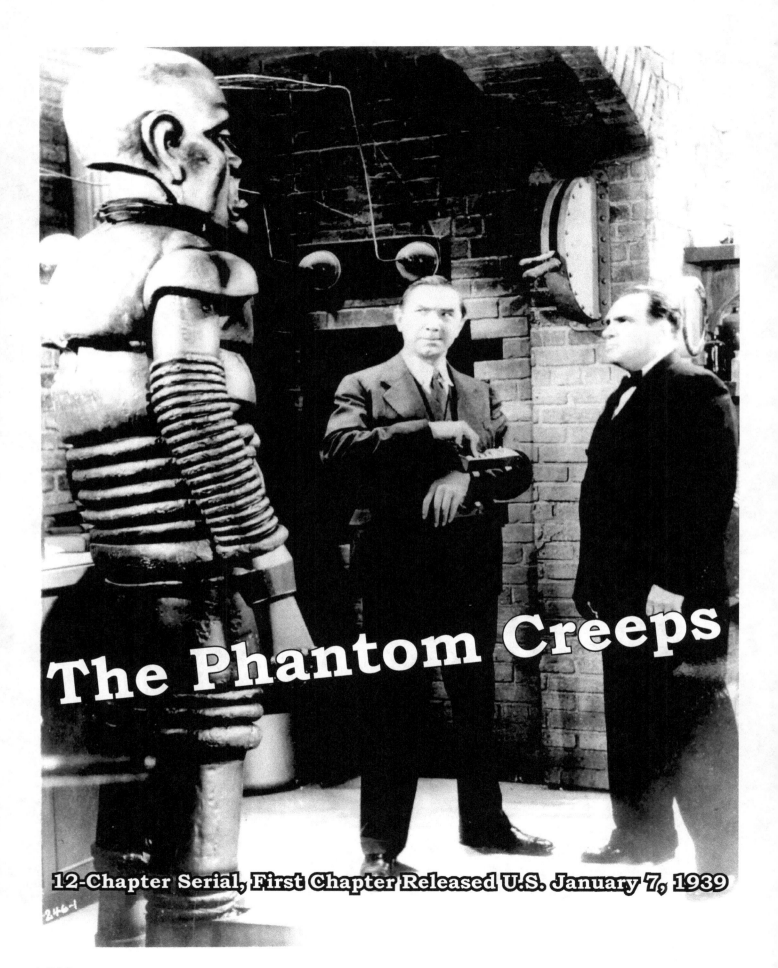

The Phantom Creeps

12-Chapter Serial, First Chapter Released U.S. January 7, 1939

POSTERS

Chapter 4 — "INVISIBLE TERROR"

BELA LUGOSI in THE PHANTOM CREEPS

A NEW UNIVERSAL PICTURE

BELA LUGOSI
THE PHANTOM CREEPS

12 SPINE-SHIVERING ACTION CHAPTERS

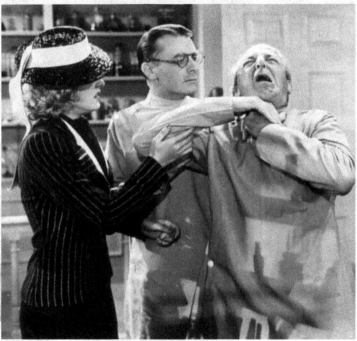

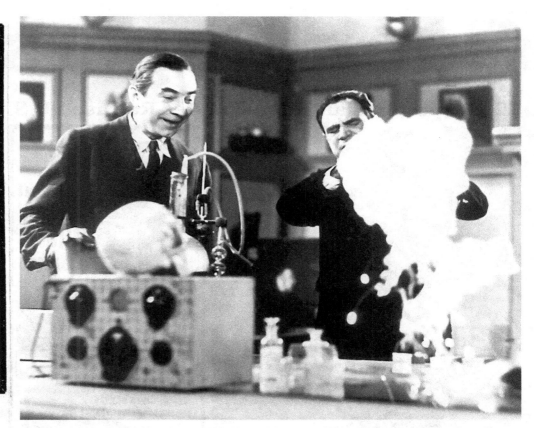

THE "GLAMOUR" boys do not get all the breaks. Bela Lugosi, just returned from a London picture assignment, took more than 15 minutes to make his way from the train at the Los Angeles station to where Mrs. Lugosi and one-year-old Bela, Jr., were waiting for him. A crowd of his picture fans swamped the famous character actor, now playing the star role in Universal's "The Phantom Creeps."

TWO new recruits have just been added to the ranks of the crazy film doctors. You'll see one of them in "Dr. Cyclops," now being filmed in Technicolor, and the other in "The Phantom Creeps," a 12-chapter serial film which has just been completed.

Dr. Cyclops is really Dr. Thorkel, but he's called Dr. Cyclops because he has only one eye like the mythical monsters of that name. He entices five people into a jungle spot in the Andes and shrinks them to one-fifth of their size.

This means that all their surroundings appear five times as big as they really are—so that a cat becomes as big as a tiger and tries to eat them, and when they stray into a clump of prickly pear they have a deuce of a time trying to get out.

The crank in "The Phantom Creeps" is Dr. Zorka, played by Bela Lugosi. Dr. Zorka goes mad in conducting experiments which result in these far-reaching inventions: a "devisualiser" belt, which makes him invisible at will, a robot 8ft tall, which he guides by remote control, and a powerful ray which can induce suspended animation in whole armies. He sets out to use these scientific weapons to make himself ruler of the world.

Dr. Zorka finishes up by being chased in his plane by a swarm of army planes and being shot down into the ocean with all his dangerous equipment. Dr. Cyclops is cast down a deep mine into oblivion.

These violent ends seem final enough—but there's no telling!

Buck Rogers

12-Chapter Serial, First Chapter Released U.S. April 11, 1939

BUCK ROGERS

LARRY CRABBE

with

Constance MOORE · Jackie MORAN · Wheeler OAKMAN · Philson AHN · Henry BRANDON · Jack MULHALL

THE NEW UNIVERSAL Presents

12 AMAZING THRILL-THRONGED CHAPTERS

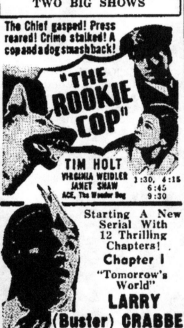
PIX and SHUFFLES
BY CHARLIE ELLIS

One of my secret agents, a thin, grizzled, wiry old man who keeps a cold twinkle in his eyes when he talks, laid down the paper and said: "I wonder what's going to happen to Alley Oop in the funny strip?"

We casually remarked that we hadn't the slightest idea, but that we thought Dr. Wonmug's time machine was a rather impractical bit of pseudo-science.

"On the contrary," said the little gentleman, allowing his feet to slip silently off my desk and down to the floor, "it is most practical and is a reality."

Offended at my snort, he pulled his chair closer and pointed a finger at me.

"It is neither impractical nor impossible, because I have been the subject of an experiment with a time machine and know its possibilities."

We were still not impressed, albeit a bit amazed at such a statement from one whom we had come to rely upon as the soul of veracity.

"Sure," he said, tapping my knee with a brown, bony forefinger, "a scientist whose name I am not at liberty to divulge sent me into the year 2027 and I met that much-talked-of hero, Buck Rogers."

Our face must have borne a look of animated scorn, because he grew more sincere in his attempt to convince.

"It was in 1927," he continued, "and I was sent 100 years ahead of my time. I met Buck Rogers and his fiancee, Wilma Dooring and Killer Kane and Dr. Huer; all the bunch that Phil Nowlin and Lt. Dick Calkins put into their stories and their adventure strip in the newspapers.

"And let me tell you something else—Buck Rogers isn't anything like the Buck Rogers they've put into the movies now."

We recalled that the fifth chapter of the Universal serial, "Buck Rogers," is showing currently at the Majestic.

"No sir," said the old man, filching a cigarette from my desk supply, "not anything like it or like Buster Crabbe.

"And those rocket ships they have in the movie are absolute misconceptions of the ships Buck Rogers really uses.

"The real rocet shipks send a spurt of intense blue flame behind the exhaust ports, but they don't drop a shower of sparks and smoke such as those in the picture.

"WAR OF THE PLANETS"

Chapter 12
BUCK ROGERS

with
LARRY CRABBE

Constance MOORE · Jackie MORAN
Henry BRANDON · Wheeler OAKMAN
Philson AHN · Jack MULHALL

A NEW UNIVERSAL PICTURE

Screen play by NORMAN HALL and RAY TRAMPE · Original Cartoon Strip by Dick Calkins and Phil Nowlan
Directed by FORD BEEBE and SAUL GOODKIND · Associate Producer: BARNEY SARECKY

Our face must have borne a look of animated scorn, because he grew more sincere in his attempt to convince.

"It was in 1927," he continued, "and I was sent 100 years ahead of my time. I met Buck Rogers and his fiancee, Wilma Dooring and Killer Kane and Dr. Huer; all the bunch that Phil Nowlin and Lt. Dick Calkins put into their stories and their adventure strip in the newspapers.

"And let me tell you something else—Buck Rogers isn't anything like the Buck Rogers they've put into the movies now."

We recalled that the fifth chapter of the Universal serial, "Buck Rogers," is showing currently at the Majestic.

"No sir," said the old man, filching a cigarette from my desk supply, "not anything like it or like Buster Crabbe.

"And those rocket ships they have in the movie are absolute misconceptions of the ships Buck Rogers really uses.

"The real rocet shipks send a spurt of intense blue flame behind the exhaust ports, but they don't drop a shower of sparks and smoke such as those in the picture.

"If the kids of this generation are shown things like the rocket ships in the serial, they'll grow up to have the wrong impression about the future. The kids who see that show should know right off that those tubs indicate no advancement in aeronautical streamlining or design. They're phonies."

He went on: "The same thing goes for all those other elaborate futuristic machines and pieces of equipment. They look too phony for the youngsters to believe in them, and they can't realize that such things will actually exist in

---

"BODIES WITHOUT MINDS"

Chapter 9
BUCK ROGERS with LARRY CRABBE

"THE PHANTOM PLANE"

Chapter 5
BUCK ROGERS
with LARRY CRABBE

Constance MOORE · Jackie MORAN · Henry BRANDON
Wheeler OAKMAN · Philson AHN · Jack MULHALL

Screen play by NORMAN HALL and RAY TRAMPE · Original Cartoon Strip by Dick Calkins and Phil Nowlan
Directed by FORD BEEBE and SAUL GOODKIND · Associate Producer: BARNEY SARECKY

Saturday, October 14

"Colorado Sunset," in which Gene Autry the top star of musical westerns, Smiley Burnette, his comical blundering pal, and pretty June Story appear together as a trio for the fourth time, is an exciting story using the cattle country of Colorado for a background. Gene and the Texas Troubadors, played by the Texas Rangers, hillbilly singing experts, buy a cattle ranch. Smiley, acting as purchasing agent, buys a dairy ranch instead and the boys find themselves in the midst of a milk price war until Gene, having been elected sheriff, brings fair play and fair prices. Larry Crabbe, Robert Barrat and Barbara Pepper are in the supporting cast. Also on Saturday, is the beginning of another twelve weeks of thrilling adventure, "Buck Rogers" taken from the original cartoon strip. Preserved in a state of suspended animation for 500 years by the "Nirvano" gas in the gondola of their dirigible wrecked in artic ice wastes, Buck Rogers and Buddy are rescued by scientists in the year 2500 to find the world under despotic rule of Killer Kane and his super-gangsters. Taken to the secret Hidden City, Buck and Buddy agree to join scientist Dr. Huer and his friends in a war to wipe out Killer Kane.

* * * * * *

BLAIR

THURSDAY - FRIDAY

This Coupon admits one person FREE with one paid adult admission Thurs. - Fri., Oct. 12-13

— Added Special —
NEWS IN PICTURES

HUMAN · HILARIOUS ROMANCE!

STOP LOOK and LOVE

With Jean Rogers - William Fawley

—SATURDAY—
— FROM THE ORIGINAL CARTOON STRIP —

Space ships exploded by giant ray machines!

Mountains crumbled by disintegrating machines!

FEATURE PICTURE

AUTRY'S GREATEST PICTURE
Here's Gene again, your Public Cowboy No. 1, in the most exciting, most tuneful, most amusing film he has ever made.

Gene AUTRY
Smiley Burnette
COLORADO SUNSET
JUNE STOREY · BARBARA PEPPER
LARRY Buster CRABBE · ROBERT BARRAT
PATSY MONTANA and CBS KMBC
TEXAS RANGERS

See him battle human robots ...blast amazing obstacles...foil fantastic foes!

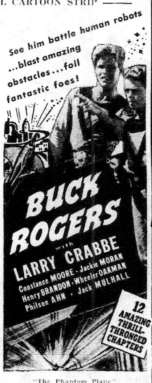

BUCK ROGERS
with
LARRY CRABBE
Constance MOORE · Jackie Moran
Henry BRANDON · Wheeler OAKMAN
Philson AHN · Jack MULHALL

12 AMAZING THRILL-THRONGED CHAPTERS

"The Phantom Plane"
"War on the Planets"
"Bodies Without Minds"
"Tragedy on Saturn"
"Tomorrow's World"

"BODIES WITHOUT MINDS"
Chapter 9

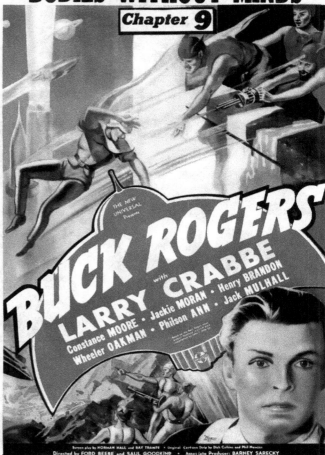

THE NEW UNIVERSAL Presents
BUCK ROGERS
with
LARRY CRABBE
Constance MOORE · Jackie MORAN · Henry BRANDON
Wheeler OAKMAN · Philson AHN · Jack MULHALL

Screen play by NORMAN HALL and RAY TRAMPE · Original Cartoon Strip by Dick Calkins and Phil Nowlan
Directed by FORD BEEBE and SAUL GOODKIND · Associate Producer: BARNEY SARECKY

"THE ENEMY'S STRONGHOLD"

Chapter **3**
BUCK ROGERS with **LARRY CRABBE**
A NEW UNIVERSAL PICTURE

WINTERGARDEN EARLS COURT

"WHERE THERE IS ALWAYS A BETTER SHOW."

MATINEE TODAY 1.45 P.M.   TONIGHT 7.15 P.M.
AND AT WINTERGARDEN MONDAY AND TUESDAY

AN ENTRANCING DRAMATIC ROMANCE!

Here Come the Brides...
GAY!
GLORIOUS!
GORGEOUS!
GRAND!

THE "FOUR DAUGHTERS"
Priscilla Lane
Rosemary Lane
Lola Lane · Gale Page

Four Wives
with Claude Rains
JEFFREY LYNN · EDDIE ALBERT
May Robson
Frank McHugh
Dick Foran
Henry O'Neill
JOHN GARFIELD
A WARNER BROS. Picture

NEVER A DULL MOMENT
...in its hilarious, screamlined fun!

UNITED ARTISTS

HAL ROACH presents
STAN LAUREL · OLIVER HARDY
in
A CHUMP AT OXFORD
FOR GENERAL EXHIBITION

"BULLDOZING THE BULL"
(Popeye Cartoon)
AUSTRALIAN and BRITISH NEWS.

At the Matinee in Addition, Episode 2 of "BUCK ROGERS," entitled "TRAGEDY ON SATURN."

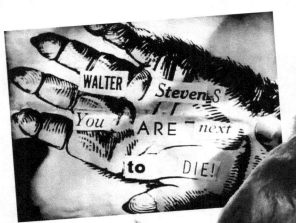

The Gorilla

**Released U.S.
May 26, 1939**

RITZ BROTHERS SUED FOR $150,000 BY FOX

Damages Asked for Failure to Work in 'The Gorilla'

Special to THE NEW YORK TIMES.

HOLLYWOOD, Calif., Jan. 31.—Twentieth Century-Fox this afternoon filed suit in the Los Angeles Superior Court for $150,000 damages against the Ritz brothers as a result of the comedians' failure to appear yesterday to begin work in "The Gorilla." Suspension of the brothers was announced last night, with the statement that the studio would hold them responsible for financial loss suffered by the company because of their sudden withdrawal from the picture.

The studio's claim includes the cost of preparing the scenario of "The Gorilla" and salaries of Alan Dwan, the director, and the supporting cast—Anita Louise, Patsy Kelly, Bela Lugosi and Edward Norris.

It is understood that the Ritzes withdrew because of their dissatisfaction with the vehicle. The studio's decision some weeks ago to make their pictures on restricted budgets is believed to have influenced their action. Lou Erwin, their manager, said that the matter has been put in the hands of attorneys.

Milton Black, their lawyer, declared that no similar case, in which a studio has sued a recalcitrant player for damages, had, to his knowledge, ever reached a verdict. In 1934 Fox penalized Spencer Tracy $40,000 for failure to report for a picture. The sum was deducted from his salary, and no court action was taken.

258

Ritz Brothers Face Large Damage Suit

HOLLYWOOD, Feb. 1. (AP)—A $150,000 price tag was pinned today on the Ritz brothers' temperament.

Twentieth Century-Fox studio asked this sum in a damage suit which alleged the brothers refused to act in "The Gorilla" last Monday.

The picture was called off, although $150,000 had been spent on its preparation, because no other comedians were available to fill the roles to which the Ritzes objected, the suit stated.

On Borrowed Time

Released U.S. June 7, 1939

STRONG CAST SET IN MOVIE

'On Borrowed Time' Stars Barrymore

In the screen presentation of last year's sensational Broadway stage success, "On Borrowed Time", Lionel Barrymore, in the featured role, is supported by a strong cast of screen players including, Sir Cedric Hardwicke, Beulah Bondi, Una Merkel and Bobs Watson.

As a picture "On Borrowed Time" is one of the most daring stories ever filmed. It is thought-provoking, inspiring and full of heart-warming humor and affection. Briefly, it is the story of an old grandfather who is afraid to die lest his grandson whom he adores fall into the hands of a scheming and unscrupulous aunt. Barrymore, as the grandfather, gives what will probably be hailed as one of the finest contributions he has ever made to the art of motion pictures.

"On Borrowed Time" is booked for showing Tuesday and Wednesday at the Capitol Theatre in Brownsville and at the Arcadia Theatre in Harlingen, Tuesday, Wednesday and Thursday.

1939
U.S.A.
FANTASTIQUE

L'ÉTRANGE SURSIS
ON BORROWED TIME

RÉALISATEUR
Harold S. Bucquet

THEATRE MANAGEMENT ANNOUNCES INSTALLATION OF A MODERN FRIGIDAIRE AIR-CONDITIONING UNIT

Manager E. F. Brady announces the completed installation of a modern Frigidaire air-conditioning system at the Rivoli Theatre in San Benito.

The planning and installation of the new equipment, during the past few weeks, has been under the direct supervision of C. E. Holmes, chief refrigeration engineer of Interstate Theatres, and will be in operation Sunday.

Mr. Holmes stated that the air-conditioning equipment installed in the Rivoli Theatre is of the very latest type, is capable of producing 47 tons of refrigeration and will discharge thirty thousand cubic feet of cool filtered air per minute.

This results in a complete change of air throughout the entire theatre every six minutes.

"The house temperature," said Mr. Holmes, "will range from seventy-five to seventy-eight degrees with a fifty per cent relative humidity and at no time will there be any drafts felt in the theatre."

Temperatures will be automatically controlled thus eliminating any guess work as to the patrons' comfort. All air entering the theatre passes through spun steel filters which completely rids it of all dust and impurities.

The Rivoli's air-conditioning system is the fourth refrigeration plant to be installed in Valley Theatres by the Interstate Circuit. Other installations include the Arcadia Theatre in Harlingen; the Palace Theatre in McAllen; and the Capitol Theatre in Brownsville.

262

Lionel Barrymore In "On Borrowed Time" At The Logan

Death Introduced as a Kindly Old Person in "On Borrowed Time" Film

In a motion picture which introduces death as a kindly gentleman in the person of Mr. Brink, Hollywood has produced a simple and beautiful fantasy in "On Borrowed Time" at the Cecil theater, through Thursday. Based on the Broadway success which was a dramatization of Lawrence Edward Watkin's novel of the same name, the plot concerns the efforts of an old man to stay alive to protect his grandson, Pud.

Lionel Barrymore, playing the role of Gramps, gives more than his customary excellent performance to this part which he has declared his best in the motion pictures. In complete sympathy with Gramps is Bobs Watson in the role of Pud, the orphaned grandchild, whose performance is a scintillating revelation.

An unusually outstanding cast supports the two with Sir Cedric Hardwicke playing the role of Mr. Brink; Beulah Bondi, Granny; Una Merkel, Marcia Giles; Nat Pendleton, Mr. Grimes; Henry Travers, Dr. Evans; Grant Mitchell, Mr. Pilbeam; Eily Malyon, Miss Demetria Riffle.

A Spell Is Cast . . .

When Mr. Brink comes after Gramps, the old man refuses to go with him and when he comes back a second time after he has taken Granny, Gramps is still not ready to go because he cannot bear to leave Pud behind to Demetria, his aunt. Through a piece of childish magic, a spell has been cast on the golden russet apple tree in the back yard of the Northrup home, so that anyone who climbs the tree must stay there until Gramps lets him down.

Gramps manages to get Mr. Brink up the tree and death ceases, except for those who touch the tree. He further manages to outwit Aunt Demetria, the doctor and the sheriff, but Mr. Brink finally is able to get Pud up the tree on a dare and the child topples over to the ground, fatally injured, but unable to die, until Gramps lets Mr. Brink down from the tree.

The spiritual and thought-provoking qualities of "On Borrowed Time" are important, and just as important is the happy blending of humor of which gives the audience many chuckles. For character, situation and interest of plot, "On Borrowed Time" is most satisfactory.

. . .

Death Plays Leading Role: "On Borrowed Time" Gentle, Tender Picture

By LON JONES

Hollywood invariably veers away from the subject of death in movies because it is a touchy subject to most people and in the past has proved to be non-box office. But Metro Goldwyn Mayer broke away from tradition and superstition and produced "On Borrowed Time," which as a play, was an outstanding Broadway hit.

"On Borrowed Time" deals with an old man who fights fiercely against death so that he might live long enough to rear his dead son's little boy. I think the last picture that had death as its central theme was that fine picture "Death Takes a Holiday," which still draws huge crowds when revived periodically at Hollywood's famous Filmarte Theatre, home of revivals.

"On Borrowed Time" is so beautifully handled by the cast and director that you do not think of death as the grim spectre it should be. Death, or "Mr. Brink," as the shadowy figure is known as in the screen play, is brought so tenderly into the lives of a homely, simple family in a small town that there is nothing very grim about the picture or terrifying and the director, Harold Bucquet, is to be congratulated on having achieved an artistic success.

NOT SLANTED AT BOX OFFICE

What appeals to me about this picture is the fact that it is not definitely slanted at the box office. The producers must have known that in spite of a strong cast the subject of death was not popular movie fare, yet they went ahead and made it at a big cost.

The director has treated death in such a manner that it is not only beautiful but sometimes seems awfully comforting, and it leaves little or no sting.

Briefly, the story of "On Borrowed Time" deals with an old man who tries desperately to hang on to life in order to guide his little grandson over the usual pitfalls.

"DEATH TAKES HOLIDAY"

Mr. Brink, played by Sir Cedric Hardwicke, calls the old man (Lionel Barrymore) but he turns a deaf ear. He sentences Mr. Brink to remain in an apple tree and while Brink is death is thus imprisoned "death takes a holiday." No one can die not even those to whom death would be a relief.

I will not tell you the rest of the story because it might spoil it for you.

This apple tree sequence did not appeal to me. It was unbelievable and I think some other means of imprisoning death should have been found.

BARRYMORE'S GREATEST ROLE

Lionel Barrymore, that grand old trouper of the screen has gone down a little into his part, not the magnificence but that of an old man who fights death with all his art. I think this is best about Lionel's greatest role and I think all fans should doff their hats to him because he made it under the most trying conditions and perhaps with much more reality than the play would intended for Lionel has been a very sick man for some time now. Arthritis has made a cripple of him and he played his role in a wheel chair.

There is no doubt that this grand old actor was fighting pain as well as real death during the entire filming of the picture. Lionel just refused to stop working. If he has to die he says he wants to die in harness.

"On Borrowed Time" Rates With Best of Season, Stuart; Hardy Family, Nebraska; 2 At Varsity

On Borrowed Time

STUART: Started Wednesday. Stars Lionel Barrymore, features Bobs Watson. Directed by Harold S. Bucquet; Screenplay, Alice D. G. Miller, Frank O'Neill and Claudine West; from the novel by the same name, by Lawrence Edward Watkin.

Gramps .... Lionel Barrymore
Brink .... Sir Cedric Hardwicke
Nellie .... Beulah Bondi
Marcia .... Una Merkel
Pud .... Bobs Watson
Grimes .... Nat Pendleton
Evans .... Henry Travers
Pilbeam .... Grant Mitchell
Demetria .... Eily Malyon
Sheriff .... James Burke
Minister .... Charles Waldron
Wentworth .... Ian Wolfe
Lowry .... Philip Terry

For those who haven't been thinking about dying, and those who have been worrying about it, "On Borrowed Time" lends a simple, inviting, calm theory on the Great Mystery. Besides that, it's one of the season's really big pictures, done in a homely, but strikingly effective manner, which will sink home on all who see it.

Aside from the theory being presented, it capitalizes on the great affection of an orphaned grandson (Bobs Watson) for his grandad (Lionel Barrymore), and vice versa. Watson's desire to emulate anything the crusty old man does, go him one better lying, cussing, even to imitating his mannerisms, is one of the most

faithful patternings of juvenile reaction ever drawn on the screen. Beulah Bondi is nearly everybody's grandmother, o; she is Bobs'.

There have been other films made regarding death—"Outward Bound" and "Death Takes a Holiday," being the most notable versions—but they were nowhere nearly as simply put, or as attractively presented for mass understanding. In "On Borrowed Time," death comes in the person of a man called Mr. Brink (Sir Cedric Hardwicke), and when he calls, very few deny him. Around the fact that Barrymore won't give up without a battle, and a previous good deed which allowed him any wish he wanted, this story is framed.

This picture will do its bit to haul little kids out of the nightmare stage, give the worried a bit of rest, and make those who haven't been thinking about "the day" start thinking.

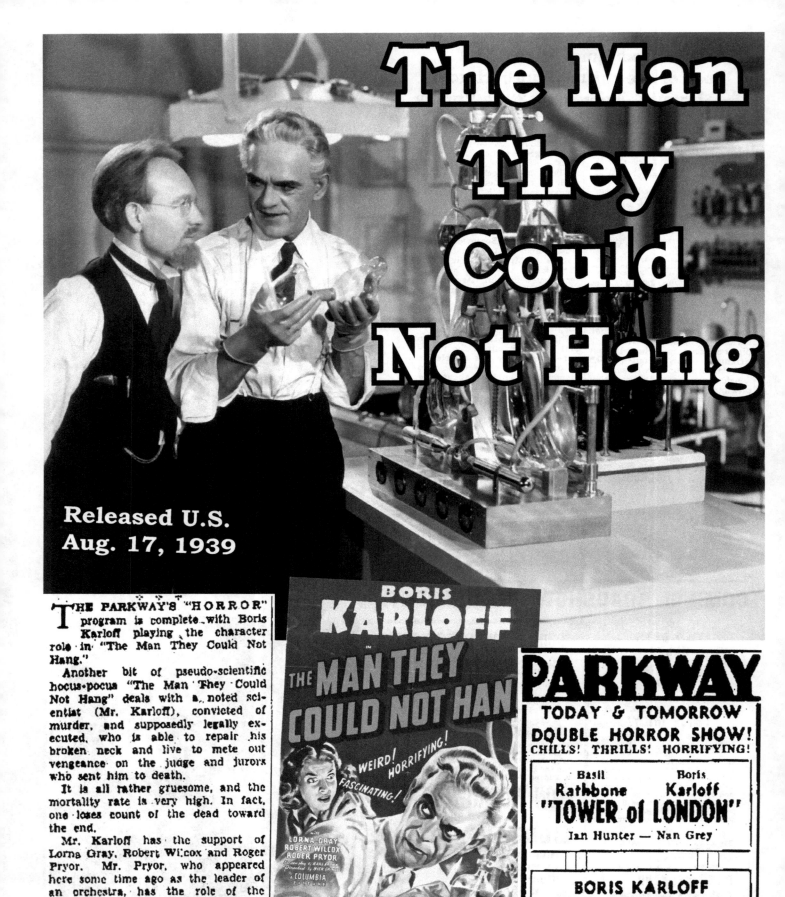

The Man They Could Not Hang

Released U.S.
Aug. 17, 1939

THE PARKWAY'S "HORROR" program is complete with Boris Karloff playing the character role in "The Man They Could Not Hang."

Another bit of pseudo-scientific hocus-pocus "The Man They Could Not Hang" deals with a noted scientist (Mr. Karloff), convicted of murder, and supposedly legally executed, who is able to repair his broken neck and live to mete out vengeance on the judge and jurors who sent him to death.

It is all rather gruesome, and the mortality rate is very high. In fact, one loses count of the dead toward the end.

Mr. Karloff has the support of Lorna Gray, Robert Wilcox and Roger Pryor. Mr. Pryor, who appeared here some time ago as the leader of an orchestra, has the role of the prosecuting attorney. He's definitely not a dramatic actor, as Columbia's horror-thriller proves. Mr. Karloff is in his element in the photoplay.

Boris Karloff In Honor Film

Boris Karloff stars in the weird and fascinating horror-film, "The Man They Could Not Hang." due at the Grand on Fri., Sat.. Oct. 20-21. Central figure is a crazed scientist who returns from the dead to leave a bloody trail of vengeance across the lives of those who had him executed. Lorna Gray, Robert Wilcox and Roger Pryor are featured and others in the cast include Ann Doran, Charles Trowbridge, Byron Foulger and Don Beddoe. Nick Grinde directed from a screenplay by Karl Brown.

Boris Karloff Cast In Thrilling Drama

Master portrayer of sinister-type roles on the screen Boris Karloff is seen in his latest thriller, "The Man They Could Not Hang." at the Rialto Theatre in Harlingen Sunday Only.

AT IOWA THEATRE

Boris Karloff, the king of horror dares you to see his latest film, "The Man They Could Not Hang" which is showing at the Iowa theatre tonight as a special bargain feature. He thrills, excites, and terrifies as a doctor turned demon, in the greatest role of his career. A new Happy Hour unit of selected shorts are added.

267

The Wizard of OZ

Released U.S. August 25, 1939

The MEASURING STICK

GILBERT I GARRETSON

We don't make a practice in the Measuring Stick of advertising any particular brand or product, but when such a product as the Wizard of Oz comes along, we feel that we are only doing our duty in calling attention to our readers to the wonderful exhibition which George Spence is going to show at the Tivoli Sunday, Monday and Tuesday.

We don't know how many parents have the same problem we do, but our children have heard the story from their mother so many times that they know it by heart. Several days ago Mr. Spence put up a sign board on Guadalupe Street featuring the picture. Now, every night there is a howl unless we drive out here and stop and interpret the meaning of each picture. Furthermore, they are counting the hours until they can do and see the picture. To miss it would be one of the tragedies of childhood and of course we are not going to let that tragedy happen.

✣ ✣ ✣ ✣ ✣

THE WONDER SHOW! OF SHOWS•

GIANT CAST! 7 SMASH TUNES!

TECHNICOLOR HIT!

JUDY GARLAND
(The Merry Musical Maid!)

FRANK MORGAN
(He's a Whiz of a Wiz!)

RAY BOLGER
(He's a Jitterbug Straw Man!)

BERT LAHR
(Uproarious Comedian!)

JACK HALEY
(See Why He Can't Go Out In The Rain!)

SUNDAY MONDAY TUESDAY
Nov. 12-13-14

AMES DAILY TRIBUNE, AMES, IOWA   SATURDAY, SEPTEMBER 2, 1939

PAGE EIGHT

"Wizard Of Oz" Opens "New Ames" In Blaze Of Color Wed. & Thur.

TRANSPORTING YOU TO THE MAGIC LAND OF OZ

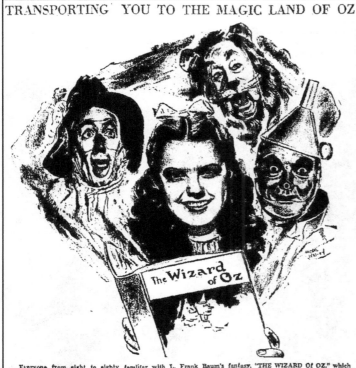

The Wizard of Oz

Everyone from eight to eighty familiar with L. Frank Baum's fantasy, "THE WIZARD OF OZ," which has gone down into history as the most famous legend of make-believe ever written. Now "The Wizard of Oz" comes to the screen starting Sunday at the Tivoli Theatre in a magnificent presentation of Technicolor, songs and dances, camera wizardy and spectacle. Above, you'll recognize Judy Garland as little Dorothy whom a cyclone transports to the magic land of Oz, Ray Bolger as the Scarecrow, Bert Lahr as the Cowardly Lion and Jack Haley as the Tin Woodman.

Une éblouissante fantaisie en couleurs!

LE MAGICIEN D'OZ

JUDY GARLAND · FRANK MORGAN · RAY BOLGER
BERT LAHR · JACK HALEY · BILLIE BURKE
MARGARET HAMILTON · CHARLEY GRAPEWIN
ET LES MUNCHKINS
Réalisation de VICTOR FLEMING

ORPHEUM NOW

Meet The Wizard!

A Metro Goldwyn Mayer Pictures

COME TO THE EMERALD CITY . . . MINGLE WITH THE FUNNY little Munchkins . . . see the trees that talk . . . and the monkeys that fly . . . watch the Scarecrow . . . the lion . . . and the Tin Woodman . . . live the wonders of the glorious hit all Phoenix has taken to its heart! Bring the whole family to enjoy it!

BERT LAHR
JACK HALEY
Billie · Margaret · Charley
BURKE · HAMILTON · GRAPEWIN
AND THE MUNCHKINS

JUDY GARLAND
FRANK MORGAN
RAY BOLGER

The WIZARD of Oz

IN TECHNICOLOR

STARTS FRIDAY
BING CROSBY—"THE STAR MAKER"
His New Paramount Song Filled Musical
WITH WALTER DAMROSCH

C.I.A.

Judy
GARLAND
Frank
MORGAN

in

TECHNICOLOR

il MAGO di OZ

PRODOTTO DA MERVYN LE ROY   Regia: VICTOR FLEMING

METRO-ROMA

CENTRE

THE AMAZING   Starts TODAY

TECHNICOLOR HIT

Wizard of Oz

STARTS

TODAY

and TOMORROW

at

11:00 A. M.

COME EARLY AND JOIN
THE HAPPY CROWDS

SUN. MON. TUES, Oct. 29, 30, 31
Mat. Sunday at 3—Adm. 10-26c

2 HOURS

of magic enter-
tainment un-
matched since
"Snow White"!
PHOTOGRAPHED IN
TECHNICOLOR

The WIZARD OF OZ

with
Judy GARLAND
Frank MORGAN
Ray BOLGER
Bert LAHR
Jack HALEY

A Metro-Goldwyn-Mayer PICTURE

Directed by VICTOR FLEMING
Produced by MERVYN LeROY
A Metro-Goldwyn-Mayer Picture

Note: Account no increase in
prices all children not in arms
must have a 10c ticket.

METRO-GOLDWYN-MAYER'S TECHNICOLOR TRIUMPH!

WE'RE OFF TO SEE THE WIZARD..
THE WONDERFUL..

WIZARD OF OZ

with
Judy GARLAND • **Frank MORGAN**
Ray BOLGER, Bert LAHR, Jack HALEY
Billie Burke, Margaret Hamilton
Charley Grapewin and the Munchkins
Directed by Victor Fleming   Produced by Mervyn Le Roy

FOR GENERAL EXHIBITION

BIGGEST SENSATION SINCE "SNOW WHITE"

Metro-Goldwyn-Mayer PICTURE

DON'T MISS
THE WIZARD OF
OZ
AT LOEW'S PALACE

CINÉMONDE

Childhood's Exciting Classic Of Adventure Pictured In Technicolor Here

HERE ARE THREE DRAMATIC scenes from the technicolor version of "The Wizard Of Oz," showing at The Fox theatre. At left, Kansas' Dorothy rushes into the Wizard's private office where Dorothy dances with the Scarecrow and the Tin Woodman and the Cowardly Lion joins them in song. But when they leave for the Haunted Forest, the Witch's Winged Monkeys carry off Dorothy to her castle. Despite a fight, the Scarecrow, Woodman and Lion are captured too and are held in a high tower of the Witch's castle.

272

Technicolor Classic "The Wizard of Oz" At The Logan
"Bachelor Mother" Starring Ginger Rogers At The Roxy
Jack Cooper At The Paramount In "Streets Of New York"

'Wizard of Oz' Famed Fantasy of Syracusan,
Makes Comeback to Thrill Millions of Children

L. Frank Baum in 1910   Beloved Characters in Film Revival   Baum Residence in Hollywood

HOLLYWOOD REVIVES INTEREST IN OZ. L. Frank Baum, left, author of "The Wizard of Oz," is shown in a picture taken in 1908 at the height of his popularity. In center are famous Oz characters, in M G M new technicolor: Judy Garland as Dorothy, Frank Morgan, the Wizard, Ray Bolger, the Scarecrow, Jack Haley, the Tin Woodman and Bert Lahr, the Cowardly Lion. Oz, at right, is Mrs. Baum's home in Hollywood. It was built by her husband in 1911.

Critics Pick 'The Wizard Of Oz' As Screen's Finest Production

Critics say Metro-Goldwyn-Mayer's "The Wizard of Oz" will be singled out by everyone who sees it as the highest result the screen has reached to date, no matter from what angle it is judged.

"The Wizard of Oz" continues its engagement at the Orpheum, where there is no abatement in the interest or enthusiasm it has aroused. Audiences are carried away by its beauty, its technique, its charm, its music, its magnificence, and its sheer entertainment.

Frank Baum's "Wizard of Oz" comes to life—bringing to vivid reality the land of dreams that has thrilled children and grownups for some 40 years. And it comes to life so thoroughly and completely, it is immediately accepted as a fantasy come true—everything you have associated with the Land of Oz is in the picture—its fabulous beauty—its charming if strange inhabitants—the funny tin man, the cowardly lion, the eccentric scarecrow—Glinda the Good—and the evil witch—the happy little munchkins—and trees that sing and dance—there is so much to "The Wizard of Oz" a reviewer could write a volume and then not be sure he has not overlooked some of its wonders.

Surpasses Them All

The nearest approach Hollywood technique has made to that employed in "The Wizard of Oz" was "Snow White" which swept through the entire world on the wings of the greatest acclaim perhaps ever given a motion picture. But it was only an approach. Previewers agree "The Wizard of Oz" is so far superior in beauty, effects, illusion, and magnitude to the Disney classic, it can be compared with absolutely nothing that has preceded it. Its technique cannot be adequately described in any cold type review, any more than can be

adequately in conversation — no matter how complete the raid on adjectives and superlatives.

But for that very same reason it will not be forgotten by anyone who sees it.

Mervyn Leroy, producer, and Victor Fleming, director, may well take bows for bringing to the screen what will be more thoroughly relished, this reviewer predicts, than any picture of a fantastic nature ever produced. Fantastic is used here only as a category tag—for 'The Wizard of Oz' is fantasy humanized with an appeal no one will escape.

Judy Garland makes a perfect "Dorothy" to establish herself as indeed a young artiste of unquestioned genius. Frank Morgan adds more laurels to his screen fame as the delightful humbug—the Wizard. Three top flight comics and dancers depict the Scarecrow, the Wooden Tin Man and the Cowardly Lion—in Ray Bolger, Jack Haley and Bert Lahr. Billie Burke is perfect as "Glinda the Good" and Margaret Hamilton is equally as effective as the wicked witch. One could go on indefinitely singling out perfect contributions to the entertainment in "The Wizard of Oz"—not forgetting "Toto" the dog.

Music Is Superb

Musically "The Wizard of Oz" is a treat. Kept in modern tempo

"The Wizard of Oz" at Iowa Starting Sunday

Ever since first news came that Metro-Goldwyn-Mayer was planning to film "The Wizard of Oz," screengoers have been wondering why it took Hollywood 39 years to discover that this L. Frank Baum story, published in 1900, is excellent motion picture material.

The answer will be found at the Iowa theatre where "The Wizard of Oz" will play Sunday, Monday and Tuesday. It is difficult to see how this story could possibly have been made without all of the perfection in color, sound, music, casting and amazing effects of 1939.

"The Wizard of Oz" is an all-family picture. It will delight adults. The picture has all of the charm of Baum's delightful book which millions have read. But the story has an adult-appeal in plot, cleverness in lines and situations, lilting songs which will delight all from 3 to 103, lyrics which will amuse the youngsters and bring chuckles to the grown-ups.

In addition, it has some of the most amazing color scenes the screen has ever had. If you can figure out how some of those tricks are done, you're a magician.

Judy Garland gives one of the screen's greatest child performances of all time as Dorothy. Frank Morgan, as the Wizard, was never funnier while his scene where he grants the heart-felt wishes of the principals has a heart tug and a philosophy which will never be forgotten.

CURTAIN CALLS: OZ BOOKS WRITTEN IN HOLLYWOOD

L. Frank Baum's Works Produced Before City Became Center of Movies

By WOOD SOANES

Today the long-awaited film version of L. Frank Baum's "The Wizard of Oz" comes into Oakland, proof, if nothing more, of what an amazing man Baum was.

His widow lives in a gray frame house, a block removed from the center of Hollywood's business district, a cottage built in 1911 and one that will not be sold in her lifetime because of the memories it contains.

She can sit in the same chair

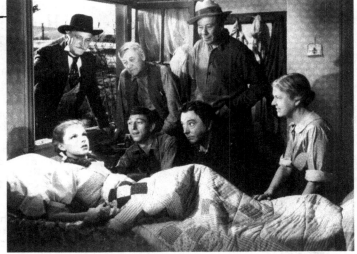

"The Wizard of Oz" Billed at Cecil Early September

Famous Production Has Cast of 9,200; Judy Garland Stars

The management of the Cecil theater announced Wednesday that one of Hollywood's newest screen productions has been booked in the near future at that playhouse. That production is "The Wizard of Oz," greatest best-seller of modern fiction written by L. Frank Baum, and is booked at the Cecil the early part of September.

A cast of 9,200 was used with such headliners of the screen as Judy Garland, Frank Morgan, Ray Bolger, Bert Lahr, Jack Haley and Billie Burke, and last but not least, is Toto, the wonder dog.

Produced by the Metro-Goldwyn-Mayer all the resources of the film company were used. Thirty-two sound stages, 65 specially built sets, and two years in the making represent the amount of work in making this picture.

The musical score demanded a symphony orchestra of 120 pieces, and a chorus of over 300 voices.

And to leave nothing unturned much expense was added when "Wizard of Oz" was filmed in glorious technicolor, which brings forth all the naturalness of the characters and surroundings.

To Pick Youngsters For Ride in Carriage Of the 'Wizard of Oz'

Five youngsters from Salamanca and vicinity will be chosen to ride in the same carriage used in the production of the "Wizard of Oz" when that movie comes to the Andrews theatre here.

The winners will be chosen in a contest announced today by Carl R. Dickerson, local theatre manager.

The five contest winners not only will have a ride in the Wizard of Oz carriage—drawn by the two famous ..... Wizard and Oz used in the movie production—they also will be furnished Wizard of Oz costumes to wear during the ride, Mr. Dickerson said.

The special costumes have been made by Hollywood designers. he continued, and will represent five famous Wizard of Oz characters, including a Dorothy, the Scarecrow, the Tin Woodman and the Wizard himself.

The boys and girls who come closest to the right measurements to fit the costumes will be the winners, Mr. Dickerson explained. Entrants must clip the contest coupon from the Salamanca Republican-Press today, fill in their measurements and leave the coupon at the box office of the theatre—or mail it to the theatre—before 6 p. m. Friday. Winners will be announced in Saturday's edition of the Press.

"Wizard of Oz" Contest Entry Blank

Name ....

Street Address ....

Age .... Yrs. Height .... Ft. .... In.

Color of Eyes .... Hair .... Weight .... lbs.

All entries must be delivered or post marked not later than 6 P. M. Friday, Sept. 8th.

All entrants must use a contest blank clipped from this newspaper. Results and winner's names will be published in the Saturday edition of this newspaper.

Classics In Weird Adventure Brought To Screen For Fair

Three Million Dollar Production Of "Wizard of Oz" Heads Movie List

By The Movie Editor

A prize in every package is the movie maestro's guarantee Hutchinson fair goers—and from the line-up, it is evident there w be no gyping at the box office. It is another super-colossal week.

Carrying on its 10th anniversary "better pictures" policy, t Fox management has booked four stellar attractions which are "mu sees" in approximately the order named: "The Wizard of Oz," "T Man in the Iron Mask," "Beau Geste" and "Angels Wash The Faces." Here's the dope:

"The Wizard Of Oz"

Fox—Cast: Judy Garland, Frank Morgan, Ray Bolger, Bert Lahr, Jack Haley, Billie Burke, Margaret Hamilton, Charley Grapewin, Pat Walshe, Clara Blandick, Toto the Singer midgets.

This $3,000,000 production is the season's rainbow lollipop of entertainment — a super-super that seems almost worth the money spent on it.

You'll have to be pretty old and crotchety not to like it, and if you're feeling that way it might just might make you feel ten years younger. When Dorothy, the Kansas kid, finds herself whisked by that cyclone to a never-never land of gorgeous color and incredible happenings called Oz, you'll miss a lot of fun if you don't go along with her, whole-heartedly and with joyous spirit.

Beautiful Color

The color camera never caught more gorgeous sets than those of Munchkinland and Oz with its Emerald City where the Wizard lived; and no camera ever focused on a more engaging set of characters than Garland's Dorothy, Bolger's Scarecrow, Haley's Tin Woodman, Lahr's Cowardly Lion —each inquest of a favor from Morgan's Wizard.

As this quartet follows a rollicking routine down the Yellow Brick Road to the Emerald City. beset by the menace of Margaret Hamilton's scary, green-faced Witch with her bag of dirty tricks, there is whimsy and humor. adventure and suspense, and a generous load of song and dance.

As Good As Disney

The technical effects here—the cyclone, the materialization of the good witch Glinda (Burke) from a bubble, the fiery vanishings of the bad witch and her ultimate "liquidation,"—are done practically as convincingly as Disney could do them. Most Disney-ish of all: the talking, moving apple trees. Also Disney-ish: the Singer Midgets as the Munchkins.

will grow, slowly choking hi to death.

That mask, as you'll doubtle guess, winds up on the king's ov head, with Philippe free to r France justly and marry Ma Theresa. (After the picture en presumably, Philippe goes predecessor one better in prof gacy and leaves his kingdom t hind the eight-ball, but that neither here nor there.)

Taken straight or tongue-i cheek, "The Man in the Ir Mask" is high-class fun.

"Beau Geste"

Strand—Cast: Gary Cooper, Ray Milla Robert Preston, Brian Donlevy, Su

277

Sweeney Todd: The Demon Barber of Fleet Street

Released U.S. September 29, 1939

THE **DEMON BARBER** OF **FLEET STREET**

SELECT ATTRACTIONS, INC. *Presents*

THE **DEMON BARBER** OF **FLEET STREET**

SELECT ATTRACTIONS INC. *Presents*

EUROPE'S **DOUBLE THRILL HORROR SHOW!**

SELECT ATTRACTIONS, Inc. *Presents*

Edgar Wallace's

The **RETURN** of the **FROG**

with GORDON HARKER · UNA O'CONNOR
RENE RAY · HARTLEY POWER

and

The **DEMON BARBER** of **FLEET STREET**

with **TOD SLAUGHTER**
EUROPE'S **HORROR** MAN

279

SELECT ATTRACTIONS, INC.
Presents

THE DEMON BARBER OF FLEET STREET

WITH

TOD SLAUGHTER
EUROPE'S HORROR MAN

Midnight 'Horror' Show Planned For Victory Fans

Excitement is guaranteed in the hair-raising, thrill-horror show scheduled for a special showing Saturday at midnight at the Victory theater, with not only one single chilling feature, but a pair offered. These two full length excitement creating productions are "The Return of the Frog" and "The Demon Barber of Fleet Street."

"The Return of the Frog" is based on one of Edgar Wallace's greatest books, "The India Rubber Man," and prominent in its cast are Gordon Harker, Una O'Connor, Rene Ray and Hartley Power. The second scare show, "The Demon Barber of Fleet Street," stars the man who threatens to outshine Lugosi and Karloff, the sinister, death-dealing Tod Slaughter.

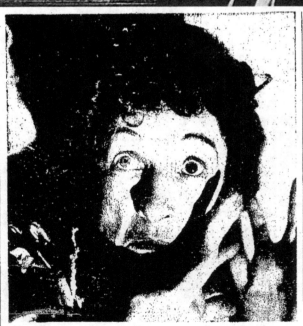

AT THE RKO KEITH'S

Horror! Una O'Connor registers it with spine-chilling emphasis in this scene from "The Return of the Frog" and, in doing so, reflects the atmosphere that will prevail at the RKO Keith theatre beginning tomorrow with the opening of the "twin horror show." "The Demon Barber of Fleet Street" will assist "The Frog" in keeping the RKO Keith patrons tense every second.

LAST TIMES TODAY! GRUESOME! HORROR SHOW!
"RETURN of the FROG" & "DEMON BARBER OF FLEET ST."

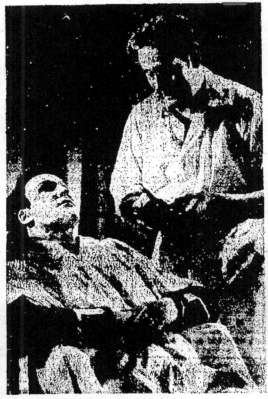

IN HORROR DRAMA

All lathered up and ready for...death! Bruce Seton sits
in Tod Slaughter's barber chair and dares "The Demon
Barber of Fleet Street" to do his bloodiest. "The Demon
Barber of Fleet Street" opens Thursday at the RKO Keith
theatre, together with "The Return of the Frog" to make
an all-horror show.

At The Theaters

Tonight

Fitchburg—"Golden Boy" and
"Smashing the Money Ring."

Strand—"Juarez" and "In Old
Caliente."

Universal—"The Return of the
Frog" and "The Demon Barber of
Fleet Street."

Shea's—"Television Spy" and "Sa-
botage."

Cumings—"Pacific Liner" and
"The Divorce of Lady X.'"

TWIN THRILLERS TO START PLAZA WEEK

"Return of the Frog," and "The
Demon Barber of Fleet Street"
Have First Run.

Coming to the screen of the Plaza
Theater for four days starting
Sunday are a pair of twin-thrillers,
or a double horror-show, titled "The
Return of the Frog," and "The
Demon Barber of Fleet Street."
"The Return of the Frog," is a
screen version of one of Edgar
Wallace's most mystifying novels,
"The India Rubber Man," and it
brings to the screen, in the role of
Scotland Yard Inspector Elk, one
of filmland's most famed detectives,
Gordon Harker. Seen in the supporting cast are Una O'Connor, who
portrays the part of the police-
defying Mum Oaks. Pert Rene Ray,
plays the part of Mum's impudent
niece, Lila, and Hartley Power, who
injects a gangster-like quality into
his part of Sanford, an American
detective bent on learning some of
Scotland Yard's most treasured
secrets in crime-detection.

In "The Demon of Fleet Street,"
the title role falls into the hands of
Tod Slaughter, whose name is aptly
chosen, for he is one of the most
diabolical of all screen murder-
maniacs. Eve Lister, a pretty
brunette actress, is the outstanding
member of Slaughter's supporting
cast.

The Cat and the Canary

Released U.S. Nov. 10, 1939

COMING SUNDAY
PAULETTE GODDARD - BOB HOPE in
"CAT AND THE CANARY"

1939
U.S.A.
COMÉDIE

LE MYSTÈRE DE LA MAISON NORMAN
THE CAT AND THE CANARY

RÉALISATEUR
Elliott Nugent

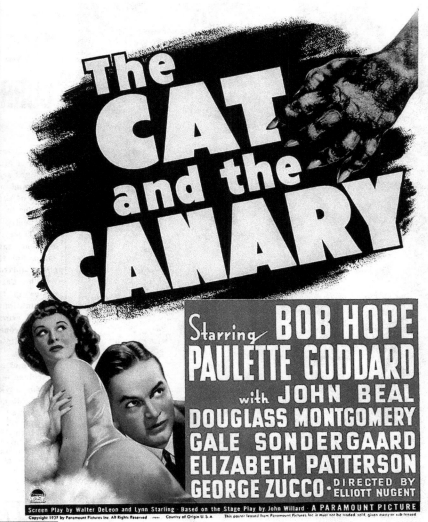

The CAT and the CANARY

Starring BOB HOPE
PAULETTE GODDARD
with JOHN BEAL
DOUGLASS MONTGOMERY
GALE SONDERGAARD
ELIZABETH PATTERSON
GEORGE ZUCCO
DIRECTED BY ELLIOTT NUGENT

Screen Play by Walter DeLeon and Lynn Starling · Based on the Stage Play by John Willard · A PARAMOUNT PICTURE

Copyright 1939 by Paramount Pictures Inc. All Rights Reserved ····· Country of Origin U.S.A.   This poster leased from Paramount Pictures Inc. it must not be traded, sold, given away or sub-leased

FAMED MYSTERY PLAY IS FILMED

BASED ON the famous stage play of the same title, which has both terrified and amused Broadway playgoers for hundreds of performances, "The Cat and the Canary" is adapted to the screen with Paulette Goddard and Bob Hope in co-starring roles.

The picturization of "The Cat and the Canary" is a rare combination of fine acting on the part of every member of the cast, and of consummate handling of sundry sliding panels, secret passageways, fearsome, clutching hands and of all the devices ever conceived—plus some new ones—for striking terror.

Before the entrance of "The Cat" into the picture, Hope, Miss Goddard, and four others of the feature cast—it includes Douglas Montgomery, John Beal, Gale Sondergaard, Elizabeth Patterson and George Zucco—proceed to a deserted mansion in the Louisiana bayous to hear a reading of the will of the deceased owner.

"The Cat and the Canary" is scheduled for showing Tuesday and Wednesday at both the Capitol Theatre, in Brownsville, and the Palace Theatre, in McAllen, and at the Rivoli Theatre, in San Benito, Friday and Saturday.

283

EN FASANSFULL NATT

[THE CAT AND THE CANARY]

"THE CAT AND THE CANARY" CURRENT ON SIGMA'S SCREEN

Connoisseurs of that type of motion picture which masterfully combines scary doin's with clever quips and more than a few moments of romance have a distinct treat in store for them at the Sigma theatre where "The Cat and the Canary," starring that preeminent gagster of screen and radio, Bob Hope, and lovely Paulette Goddard, opens Saturday.

"The Cat and the Canary" comes to the screen as a rare combination of fine acting on the part of every member of the cast, and of consummate handling of sundry sliding panels, secret passageways, fearsome, clutching hands and of all the devices ever conceived — plus some new ones — for striking terror. And, of course, it goes beyond that, presenting as the menace a thing called "The Cat."

Before the entrance of "The Cat" into the picture, Hope, Miss Goddard, and four others of the feature cast—it includes Douglass Montgomery, John Beal, Gale Sondergaard, Elizabeth Patterson and George Zucco — proceed to a deserted mansion in the Louisiana bayous to hear a reading of the will of the deceased owner. Present, too, are the deceased's housekeeper and a lawyer.

Miss Goddard, named as the heiress, is terrified to learn that a second heir will be named if she is insane or dead in a month's time. Then "The Cat" appears, introduced, to use a polite term, by a keeper from a nearby insane asylum who describes "The Cat" as a murderous maniac broken loose, and wandering around the bayous.

The identity of "The Cat" will amaze moviegoers, and it should be virtually impossible to identify before it admits who it is.

Credit for the excellent direction belongs to Elliott Nugent, and every member of the cast — from Hope and Miss Goddard down to the smallest role rates a bow for intelligent grasp of how to play mystery-comedy in the manner which creates just the proper mood of fearfulness and fun.

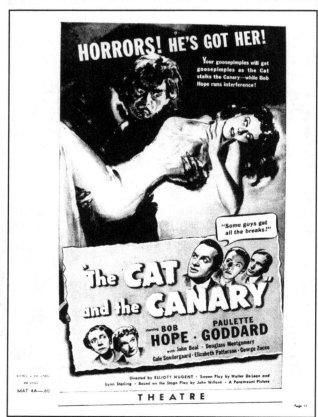

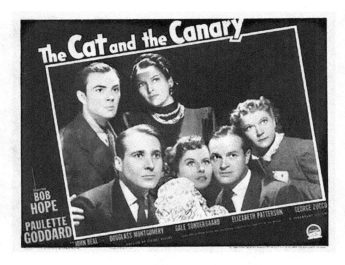

BOB HOPE
PAULETTE GODDARD

SCALERA FILM

il fantasma
di mezzanotte

REGIA DI
ELLIOTT NUGENT

TWO MAJOR HITS !!!!!

TWO DESPERATE
KIDS AGAINST
THE BIG GUY OF
THE BIG HOUSE!

Your goosepimples will
have goosepimples as
the Cat stalks the Canary
—while Bob Hope runs
interference!

VICTOR
McLAGLEN
JACKIE
COOPER
THE
BIG GUY
WITH
ONA MUNSON
PEGGY MORAN
EDWARD BROPHY

"THE CAT
and the
CANARY"

A Paramount Picture starring
BOB HOPE
PAULETTE GODDARD
with John Beal · Douglass Montgomery
Gale Sondergaard · Elizabeth Patterson
George Zucco · Directed by Elliott Nugent

The Cat and the Canary

BOB
HOPE
PAULETTE
GODDARD
with JOHN BEAL · DOUGLASS MONTGOMERY · GALE SONDERGAARD · ELIZABETH PATTERSON · GEORGE ZUCCO

MAKE EVERY KID A WALKING BALLY FOR YOUR SHOW WITH MASK GIVEAWAY OF "THE CAT"

GIVE AWAY these masks of the "Cat" to the kids who will have fun wearing them. Here's a workable gag that you can use either for your regular campaign or as a "spook show" souvenir, and that will fill the town with walking ads for "The Cat and the Canary."

The mask in the illustration shows a reduced reproduction of the actual mask, to show you how to combine it with credits and instructions for use. But the mask itself is actually life-size, ten inches wide.

You can print it up in green ink on one-ply cardboard, or any satisfactory stock available at a local print-shop, and distribute flat to the kids who will know how to get it in working order. Incorporate this stunt in your campaign either as a theatre give-away, or use it in conjunction with with a local advertiser who will sustain costs of printing to include it in his herald.

Illustration shows mask in reduced size. Art in full ten-inch width on

MAT 5EA—.75

MEET "THE CAT"! MOST TERRIFYING KILLER THE SCREEN HAS EVER UNMASKED!

Beware! THE CAT

SEE THIS monster of menace and find out what it's like to be really frightened! Watch Hollywood's craziest comedian stalk the one-man crime-wave and you won't know whether to laugh or scream! Don't miss it!

Instructions for wearing the cat mask
Trim the mask outline with sharp scissors. Punch holes at temple and use cord or elastic band for fastening about head. Punch holes indicated in eye pupils. Perforate the nose of the mask about the dotted line and mask will conform to your face.

(BILLING AND THEATRE)

RADIO... spot announcements...

50 WORDS

ANNOUNCER: Tingling terror in the year's big thrill hit — "The Cat and the Canary!" An eerie whine in an old macabre mansion and "The Cat" running amok! Bob Hope and Paulette Goddard co-star for the first time. Don't miss its chills and chuckles, on .... at the .... Theatre.

75 WORDS

ANNOUNCER: Who is "THE CAT?" Its movements soundless. Its approach unnoticeable. Its vengeance swift! Who will feel its hairy grasp next? Who among six startled heirs to a madman's fortune, stranded on the foggy Louisiana bayous? Even your goose pimples will have goose pimples as Bob Hope and Paulette Goddard shudder and chuckle their way through the thrill hit of the year — "The Cat and the Canary" opening on .... at the .... Theatre. See it!

100 WORDS

ANNOUNCER: An eerie whine in a macabre old mansion on foggy Louisiana bayous . . . . a monstrous, marauding thing — "THE CAT" — running amok among six startled heirs to a madman's fortune! It's havoc-streaked horror . . . mind-teasing mystery . . . runaway romance. It's "The Cat and the Canary." opening .... at the .... Theatre. There's Bob Hope hoping a gag's as good as a gun to get ghosts on the go, and Paulette Goddard huddling in his arms! It's a chill-and-chuckle chase with a fortune at stake and a monster at large! It's on every must-see, must-thrill, must-laugh list!

FREE SCRIPT

BOB EDWARDS' HOLLYWOOD CHATTER COLUMN OF THE AIR, a fifteen-minute script of gossip and information about "The Cat and the Canary," its background and players, is available to all theatres and radio stations writing in for it at no cost whatsoever. It is written so that separate items can be "lifted" from it and planted in other radio programs or movie columns in the newspapers. For your copy of this free script, write to:

•

PRESS BOOK EDITOR
PARAMOUNT PICTURES INC.
1501 Broadway   New York City

Page 7

Torture Ship

Released U.S. October 28, 1939

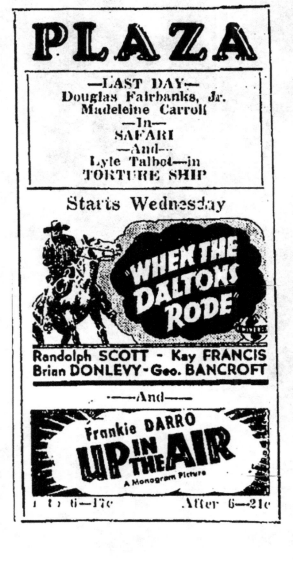

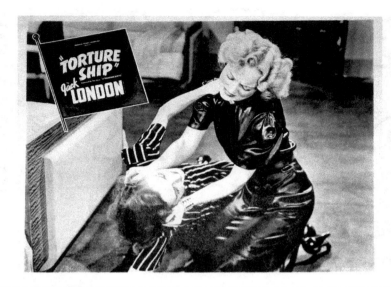

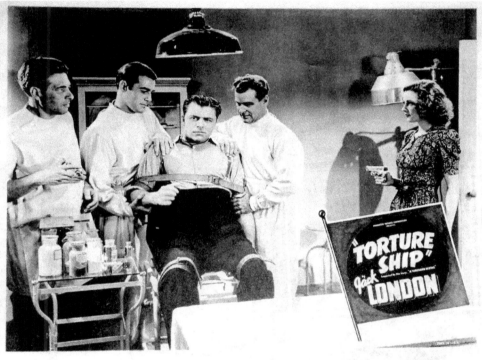

* * *

"Torture Ship."

The three Mesquiteers are back in town again and this time will be seen in "The Kansas Terrors." These three thrill-hunters are played by Bob Livingston, Raymond Hatton and Duncan Renaldo. The co-feature at the Park theater for Friday and Saturday will be "Torture Ship." suggested by the story "A Thousand Deaths" by Jack London. This picture tells the story of a medical researcher who embarks on a bizarre sea voyage with eight desperate criminals, all of whom he believes he can cure of their criminality.

* * *

The Return of Dr. X

**Released U.S.
Dec. 2, 1939**

OHiO

Tomorrow Nite
Is The Nite
—SCREEN—
Humphrey Bogart
in "Return of Dr. X"
and May Robson
in 'Granny Get
Your Gun'

WAYNE MORRIS
ROSEMARY LANE
HUMPHREY BOGART
DENNIS MORGAN
THE RETURN OF
DOCTOR X

JOHN LITEL · LYA LYS · Directed by VINCENT SHERMAN
Presented by WARNER BROS.

RIALTO

Friday-Saturday   January 12-13
Wayne Morris
Rosemary Lane
Humphrey Bogart
in
"The Return of Dr. X"

'The Devil's Daughter'

Released U.S. Dec. 12, 1939

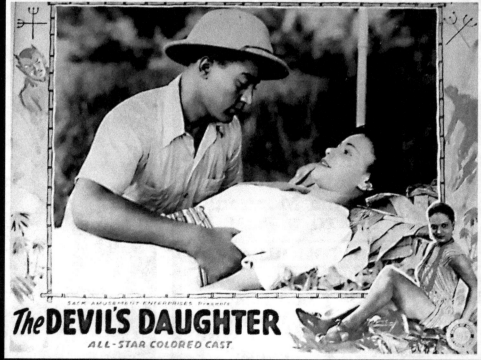

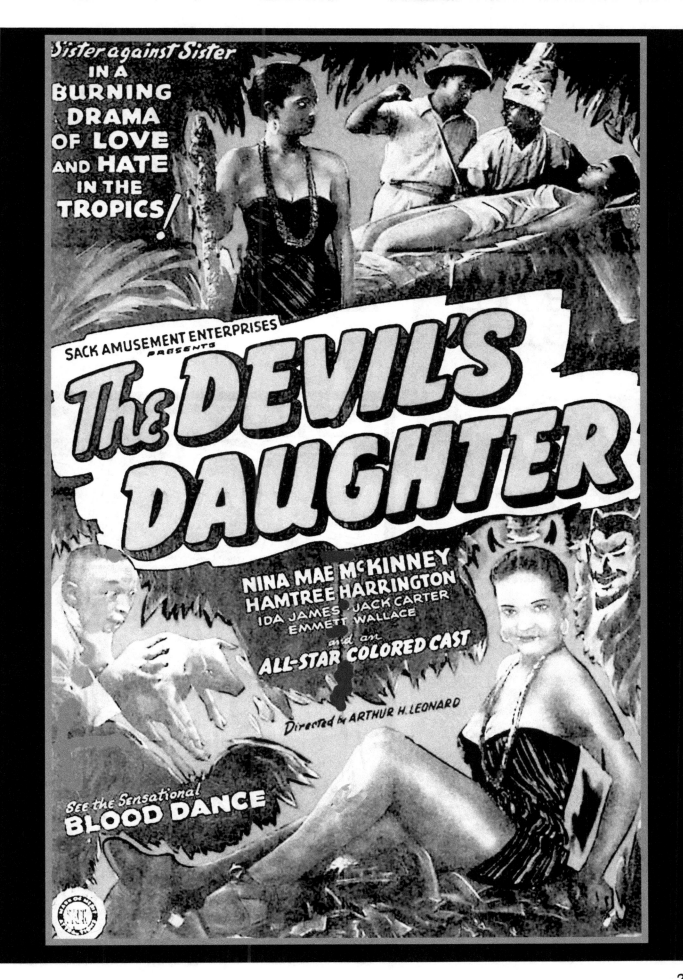

3 Col. Scene Mat 31

EXPLOITATION

COMEDIAN FEARS ROASTED PORK

Roast pork may be a delicacy to many people; but to Hamtree Harrington, popular Harlem comedian, it's a warning—a warning that his soul is in danger and that he may be roasted for purgatory.

In "The Devil's Daughter," new all-Negro motion picture which will be shown at the .... Theater ....

[remainder of column illegible]

ACTUAL LOCALES IN NEW PICTURE

Satisfied with only the "real thing," Director Arthur H. Leonard insisted on actual locations for "The Devil's Daughter," new all-Negro motion picture which will be shown at the .... Theater .... and consequently the entire cast, as well as a complete technical crew, was flown from Hollywood to Kingston, Jamaica, locale of the story.

Consequently, every scene in "The Devil's Daughter" is authentic, having been filmed on actual location of the spot mentioned in the story.

TROPICAL LOVE IN NEW PICTURE

A West Indian man—said to be the most romantic of all sexes—bears down upon the tropical love-making in "The Devil's Daughter," new all-Negro motion picture which will be shown at the .... Theater for .... days beginning ....

With the story taking place in Jamaica, an entire Hollywood cast and technical crew were flown down to the West Indies for the production of "The Devil's Daughter," which stars the popular Nina Mae McKinney.

[remainder of column illegible]

FORBIDDEN BY LAW FOR YEARS....
BUT *NOW* YOU CAN SEE IT!! THE
BLOOD DANCE
SEX-ATIONAL DANCE OF THE DAMNED!
FOR ADULT EYES ONLY!
FEATURED IN THE
SENSATIONAL ALL-NEGRO DRAMA
"The Devil's Daughter"
WITH
NINA MAE McKINNEY
HAMTREE HARRINGTON
and BIG COLORED CAST

3 Col. Ad Mat 42

TRAILER

De luxe 460-foot trailer—showing the most sensational scenes from the picture, including the "Blood Dance"—is available on "The Devil's Daughter." This trailer—a genuine seat-seller—can be booked from your nearest Book exchange.

PICTURE SOLVES VITAL PROBLEM

Suppose your sister was jealous of you because the man she loved cared for you instead of her.

And suppose your sister was the leader of a bush-woods cult, which performed mystic rites, and suppose this sister decided to sacrifice you on a burning altar.

What would you do?

For the answer to this problem, see "The Devil's Daughter," new all-Negro motion picture, which will be shown at the .... Theater for .... days beginning ....

The cast supporting Nina Mae McKinney in "The Devil's Daughter" includes Hamtree Harrington, ace comedian, Jack Carter and Ida James.

1 Col. Ad Mat 41

2 Col. Ad Mat 31

You can research old movies for yourself at

NY Times: Times Machine at www.nytimes.com
Newspaper Archives at newspaperarchives.com
Variety at Variety.com

They do charge a yearly fee, although the NY Times Machine is free to subscribers.

for models and model kits some of the largest vendors are:
Monsters in Motion at https://www.monstersinmotion.com
Rocketfin Hobbies at http://www.rocketfin.com
Sideshow at https://www.sideshowtoy.com
ebay.com
amazon.com

Rare and B- (and Z-) movie titles
Alpha/Oldies at http://www.oldies.com or phone 1-800-336-4627
Sinister Cinema at http://www.sinistercinema.com or phone 1-541-773-6860

For a catalog of Midnight Marquee titles visit our website at www.midmar.com or send $2 for a catalog Midnight Marquee Press, Inc. 9721 Baltimore, MD 21234 410-665-1198